CREDIT, CURRENCIES AND CULTURE

African Financial Institutions in Historical Perspective

Edited by

Endre Stiansen and Jane I. Guyer

NORDISKA AFRIKAINSTITUTET 1999

Indexing terms

Financial institutions
Money management
Credit
Currencies
Islamic banking
Economic history
Africa

Front cover: Reproduction of commercial document from Timbuktu.
Courtesy of Stephanie Diakité.

ISBN 91-7106-442-7

Printed in Sweden by Elanders Gotab, Stockholm 1999

Contents

Preface

Most of the papers in this collection were first presented as a seminar series, "Financial Institutions in Africa: Historical and Contemporary Perspectives," at the Program of African Studies, Northwestern University in Evanston, Illinois, during the winter of 1996.[1] Endre Stiansen was in residence as a visiting scholar; Jane Guyer was Director of the Program and had recently published a book on currencies and value in West Africa.[2] Together with John Hunwick, professor in the Department of History, we combined our interests in an attempt to do justice to the historical depth and cultural variety of money-management institutions in Africa. Africa's economies became more pervasively commercialized during the four centuries of the slave and inter-regional commodity trades from the end of the fifteenth to the end of the nineteenth centuries, and during the sixty years or so of colonial rule. Institutions were developed for managing currency transactions such as valuation, conversion, storage, security, forecasting, trust, and profit. The forms of those institutions were diverse and fluid owing to the cultural variety of Africa and the contingencies of a turbulent history. But certain salient themes are evident: the nexus of Muslim frameworks for commerce, both past and present; emergent indigenous ideas and practices in the great centers of population, such as Dahomey and Yorùbáland, and in the complex borderlands between them; and the imposition of colonial blueprints. Although we address all these issues, we would like to stress that the essays presented here are not meant to be an overview of the entire subject of African financial institutions. They are intended to present case studies, to describe the institutional structures through which money has been managed in Africa, to address the long-term challenges posed by monetary change, and to suggest lines for further research and debate.

When organizing the seminar, we were fortunate to be able to draw on the financial support of the Program in International Cooperation in Africa, funded by the John D. and Catherine T. MacArthur Foundation. We are also grateful to our copy editor, Dr. Allen Streicker of the Northwestern University Archives, and to Ms. Sonja Johansson, of the Nordic Africa Institute's publication department, who gave the manuscript its present form.

---

[1] Jan Hogendorn's paper was written especially for this collection, and Endre Stiansen's contribution is different from that presented at the seminar.

[2] Jane I. Guyer, ed., *Money Matters: Instability, Values and Social Payments in the Modern History of West African Communities* (Portsmouth, New Hampshire, 1995).

Transliteration and Spelling of Non-English Words

When transcribing Arabic words we have in general followed the system used in Hans Wehr's *Dictionary*, but have made some concessions to reflect local pronunciation, in particular with regard to proper names and place names. When transcribing Yorùbá words, we follow standard practice in noting tonal and vowel diacritics.

Endre Stiansen and Jane I. Guyer
Uppsala and Evanston

Introduction

Endre Stiansen and Jane I. Guyer

Africa's commercial history has been illuminated by decades of work on regional market systems, indigenous currencies, the slave trade and colonial economic history. Specialized studies of both West and East Africa have demonstrated how trade constituted a fundamental feature of the social fabric,[1] and Hogendorn and Johnson's pioneering work on the massive imports of cowry currency in the era of the slave trade must by itself dispel any simple evolutionary concept of Africa's monetary history.[2] And yet, in the 1990s, a new development effort devoted to provision of credit to ordinary producers and households is building up steam,[3] in such a way as to imply that micro-level financial management did not exist. What social and economic processes, it is worth asking, have resulted in this misconception of a lack of financial institutions, such that at the end of the twentieth century, after hundreds of years of commerce and a century of development of formal-sector money management, international aid is used to develop them as if from scratch? This question evokes several others: whether there is any continuity between past and present with respect to indigenous modes of monetary management; what cultural codes of honor and disrepute have justified credit and debt over decades or even centuries, and have sanctioned contracts and guided careers of enrichment; how colonial policies shaped the institutions to which ordinary people had recourse; and where case material can be found to provide a solid and coherent evidentiary basis to address these and other related questions?

---

[1] See A.G. Hopkins, *An Introduction to the Economic History of West Africa* (London, 1973); Philip D. Curtin, *Economic Change in Precolonial Africa: Senegambia in the Era of the Slave Trade* (Madison, 1975); Edward A. Alpers, *Ivory and Slaves: Changing Patterns of International Trade in East Central Africa to the Later Nineteenth Century* (Berkeley, California, 1975); and Ralph A. Austen, *African Economic History: Internal Development and External Dependency* (London, 1987).

[2] Jan Hogendorn and Marion Johnson, *The Shell Money of the Slave Trade* (Cambridge, 1986).

[3] We have in mind the NGO-led movement to introduce Grameen-style banks in diverse communities throughout the continent. For one example, see Michael Kevane, "Qualitative Impact Study of Credit With Education in Burkina Faso," Freedom from Hunger Research Paper No. 3, Davis, Ca, 1996.

Financial institutions have certainly been alluded to in the historical and anthropological literature,[4] and one that has been particularly important in Africa, namely, labor-pawning, has been comprehensively reviewed in relation to economic growth in the nineteenth century, and its historical demise has been traced in the twentieth.[5] But the record is still far from clear on the social differentiation of wealth and need that is bridged by credit and debt. Moreover, certain phases of monetary circulation are known better than others. In the case of labor pawning, the conditions of repayment have been described in more detail than the circumstances of wealth and the advancing of credit. Conversely, for the colonial Provident Societies described by Mann and Guyer in this volume, the sources are much stronger for understanding the structure of credit than for analyzing loan repayment. In all cases, the ideal frameworks are better described than are the actual workings of transactions, especially as productive and commercial conditions fluctuated over time. How much could be postponed, and for how long? How was the death of the debtor dealt with? When currency values changed, were debts renegotiated? How were records witnessed and memory preserved? All of this suggests the need for further detailed historical work on several aspect of the institutions themselves: cultural or religious sanctions on financial transactions, key social organizations through which moral authority was exercised, the routine or intermittent recourse people had to borrowing, lending and building up assets, and all the many ways in which monetary management figured in society and culture more broadly.

Particularly at issue in Africa are the long-term regulatory frameworks for money management that in the West developed at the intersection of the banking industry and the state, and therefore in national and international arenas.[6] Africa's commercial civilizations arose through long-distance trade,

---

[4] A good survey of the historical experience and the literature on West Africa is Gareth Austin, "Indigenous Credit Institutions in West Africa, c. 1750-c. 1960," in *Local Suppliers of Credit in the Third World, 1750–1960*, ed. Gareth Austin and Kaoru Sugihara (Basingstoke, 1993), 93–159. Unfortunately, there are no similar surveys for other parts of Africa.

[5] Toyin Falola and Paul E. Lovejoy, eds., *Pawnship in Africa: Debt Bondage in Historical Perspective* (Boulder, Colorado, 1994).

[6] Studies of early national banking are Eric Kerridge, *Trade & Banking in Early Modern England* (Manchester, 1988), and the Center for Medieval and Renaissance Studies (University of California, Los Angeles), *The Dawn of Modern Banking* (New Haven, 1979). The growth of international banking is described in K.E. Born, *International Banking in the 19th and 20th Centuries* (Leamington Spa, 1983), and Geoffrey Jones, *British Multinational Banking 1830–1990* (Oxford, 1993). Broad surveys of banking in Africa can be found in Giordano Dell'Amore, *Banking Systems in Africa* (Milan, 1971); J.K. Onoh, *Money and Banking in Africa* (London, 1982); Ann Seidman, *Money, Banking and Public Finance in Africa* (London, 1986); Paul A. Popiel, *Financial Systems in Sub-Saharan Africa* (Washington, D. C., 1994), and Martin Brownbridge and Charles Harvey, *Banking in Africa: Botswana, Ethiopia, Ghana, Kenya, Nigeria, Uganda, Zambia, Malawi, Tanzania, Zim-*

which then underwrote state development in some places and instigated broader popular engagement with markets and money almost everywhere on the continent.[7] In most areas money management escaped comprehensive state control; trade networks and local production depended on other modes of valuation and sanctioning.[8] Even today money circulates largely through transactions that are not taxed, nor do most people depend on the services of the formal banking sector. But this does *not* mean that no financial services have been (or are) available at all. What is striking is the volume of commerce and production that has been possible without the full panoply of credit, insurance, futures markets, stock companies, limited liability, and other legal and financial services that make up the formal sector of modern economies.

The African present is so turbulent as to offer an uncertain context for establishing the historical repertoire of financial practices that developed for centuries at a tangent to the state and formal-sector financial institutions. The particular advantage of a historical perspective in the study of money management is that it allows us to identify those beliefs, practices, organizational frameworks and regulatory functions that apparently have remained in place over long periods. Longevity is not only an indicator of success in financial affairs. In a context where risk is not statistically calculated, as it was not even in the West until two hundred years ago, repeated experience is a component of sustainability since it permits prediction and fosters confidence among those in a position to exploit opportunities. Whether or not they still exist or are realistically accessible to people, institutions that served sturdily over time afford important insights into the interface of official authorities, religio-legal frameworks of trade diasporas, and the more diffuse authority of commonly endorsed practices.

The fact, however, that most of the institutions we study precede formal-sector banking in Africa does not mean that the latter is completely irrelevant to their history. The European and Muslim presence in African financial transactions goes back several centuries, so it may well be that formal financial practices were taken as examples and benchmarks as well as contrasts or

---

babwe, The Gambia (Oxford, 1998). While these studies have different emphases, they share two characteristics, i.e., lack of historical perspective and a disregard for the informal sector. For an assessment of the importance of the judicial framework and the role of the state, Douglass C. North's *Institutions, Institutional Change and Economic Performance* (Cambridge, 1990) is indispensable.

[7] General histories are John Iliffe, *Africans: The History of a Continent* (Cambridge, 1995), and P. Curtin, S. Feierman, L. Thompson and J. Vansina, *African History: From the Earliest Times to Independence*, 2nd. ed. (New York, 1995).

[8] Not even the state bureaucracy of the classical "model" of administered trade, Dahomey in the pre-colonial era, was able to control the most important aspect of money management: the supply of currencies; see Robin Law, "Royal Monopoly and Private Enterprise in the Atlantic Slave Trade: the Case of Dahomey," *Journal of African History* 18, no. 4 (1977):555–77, and Law's contribution to this volume.

counterpoints in the development of locally endorsed institutions. The state and international financial institutions continue to be one of the highly innovative sectors of western economic life, encouraging constant refinements in statistical techniques that allow risk to be calculable, and in legal developments that allow terms and time-frames of transactions to be fixable by law. The financial history of Africa relates to these developments but is not encompassed by them. It lies in both international and continental arenas, in state and non-state institutions, in their interactions over time, and in the experience of different economic agents in changing market situations.

Formal and Informal Financial Institutions in African History

The history of banks themselves covers only a part of the entire domain we would include under the rubric of financial institutions, since they are a late development and deal only intermittently and indirectly with large areas of national economies. One of the persistent images of modern banking in Africa has been of banks and cooperatives carrying a heavy burden of bad debts.[9] Default has been quite frequent, not least owing to the difficulty of mediating between the sheer unpredictability of economic and personal life in Africa and the precise time-frames of capital accounting. But the ordinary vicissitudes of life for bank customers give only part of the explanation for the checkered history of banking. Among other factors, weak internal controls and inadequate supervision by government authorities stand out as particularly important. The contrast between colonial banks and indigenous banks is instructive.[10] While the colonial banks benefited from centuries of experience and exact procedures for all transactions, the indigenous banks could not build on the same traditions and the threat of legal action was not enough to prevent fraud and embezzlement.[11] Consequently colonial banks prospered while indige-

---

[9] Modern banking, however, was introduced around the middle of the nineteenth century, but did not really thriveuntil the colonial period. For a study of an early bank, see Ghislaine Lydon, "Les péripéties d'une institution financière: la banque du Sénégal, 1844–1901," (paper presented at the Commemoration du Centenaire de la Creation de l'Afrique Occidentale Française [A.O.F.], Dakar, June 1995), Direction des Archives du Sénégal, 1995, 475–91.

[10] Colonial banks can be defined as banks owned and operated by Europeans (often such banks were only branches of banks headquartered in Europe), while indigenous banks were owned and operated by Africans.

[11] A brief survey of the establishment of indigenous banks in West Africa can be found in Austin, "Indigenous Credit," 135–6. For more detailed studies, see Chibuike Uche, "Indigenous Banks in Colonial Nigeria" (paper presented at the conference on Financial Institutions in the Political Economy, June 1998, Rosendal [Norway]); Eric Davis, *Challenging Colonialism: Bank Misr and Egyptian Industrialization, 1920–1941* (Princeton, New Jersey, 1983); A.G. Hopkins, "Economic Aspects of Political Movements in Nigeria and the Gold Coast 1918–1939," *Journal of African History* 7, no. 1 (1966):133–52; Ian Duffield, "The Business Activities of Duse Mohammed Ali: An Example of the Economic Dimen-

nous banks suffered waves of failures, more often due to malfeasance by officials than to default by debtors. Colonial restrictions on African access to credit were powerful. After independence, relaxation of discriminatory practices did not benefit all citizens alike but favored owners, managers and large depositors. Extending well into the present day, limitations and loopholes in regulations have brought intermittent bank scandals and crashes, and the parallel development of systemic corruption and weakening of state power have seriously undermined national banking systems.

At the same time, the historical record suggests that other financial institutions—in the sense of conventions, rules and norms—have served entrepreneurs and communities without state supervision or regulation. The autonomy of the commercial sector in pre-colonial states sometimes had spatial expression, as when the main commercial emporia of the savannah states were located some distance away from the political capitals.[12] Instead of seeking recourse from the state to enforce contracts, merchants and others relied on institutions such as the extended family, kinship groups, religious fraternities and codes of honor.[13] The culture of communities may have reduced high transaction costs by providing conduits for information, spaces for sanctions and incentives, and by facilitating transfer of money over long distances. Long-term commitments entailed a moral authoritarian matrix, rather than a legal contractual matrix, as a basis for trust.

In the legal and economic transformation that followed in the wake of colonial conquests such non-state institutions remained the bedrock of much commercial activity, owing both to the limited formal financial services that were offered and the difficulty of operating on the basis of finely defined contracts in the fluid African context of price and other instabilities. As experience demonstrates, large-scale business operators can work optimally when they have recourse to both kinds of systems, and therefore have a real interest in the maintenance of what the "modern sector" may consider to be a "traditional" form of moral authority and financial power. The Mourides of Senegal, for example, have built substantial transnational financial structures

---

sion of Pan-Africanism, 1912–1945," *Journal of the Historical Society of Nigeria* 4, no. 4 (1969):571–600.

[12] Darfur, where it was one day's journey from Kobbei to al-Fashir, is a good example; see R.S. O'Fahey, *State and Society in Dār Fūr* (London, 1980).

[13] Abner Cohen's celebrated article, "Cultural Strategies in the Organization of Trading Diasporas," in *The Development of Indigenous Trade and Markets in West Africa*, ed. Claude Meillassoux and Daryll Forde (London, 1971), 266–78, explains the rationale of an autonomous network. Other relevant examples can be found in Avner Greif, "Contract Enforceability and Economic Institutions in Early Trade: The Maghribi Trader's Coalition," *The American Economic Review* 83, no. 3 (1993):525–48. For a comparative perspective, Paul R. Milgrom, Douglass C. North and Barry R. Weingast, "The Role of Institutions in the Revival of Trade: The Law Merchant, Private Judges, and the Champagne Fairs," *Economics and Politics* 2, no. 1 (1990):1–23, may be consulted.

that draw on formal legal organizations for some purposes and religious authority relations for others.[14]

The parallel development of these two kinds of institutional framework has its own history. In the pre-colonial period, there are few cases of Africans away from the coastal zones adopting foreign institutional solutions, and the process of technology transfer may to some extent have gone the other way since European merchants working in the interior became successful by adapting to local ways.[15] The colonial conquests marked a radical change in attitudes. Local means of money management were considered unsuitable or inadequate by colonial administrators who established their own channels for money transfer and currency regulation and encouraged private metropolitan banks to set up branches in the colonial capitals. Demonetization of the old media of exchange was fairly swift and decisive in most key economic sectors, leaving the foreign-owned and -operated banks in control of import and export trade, and serving the needs of expatriates and members of the local bourgeoisie. Some specialist institutions were set up to serve local needs of government for financial conduits into and out of communities: post-office savings banks in British Africa, especially in areas where migrant workers sent remittances home, and Sociétés de Prévoyance in French Africa, which served to avert famine and foster commercial cropping (see Mann and Guyer's contribution to this volume). These banks were not capitalist in the sense of being primarily profit-oriented institutions, but were means to achieve policy objectives like "development," "modernization," "industrialization," and instilling providence in poor rural populations presumed to lack means of income-smoothing and mitigating the risks of changing conditions.

In most French and British colonies the late 1950s saw unprecedented expansion of financial infrastructure for political and economic development.

[14] This field begs for more research, but for important introductions see M. C. Diop and M. Diouf, "Notes sur la reconversion des marabouts dans l'économie urbaine," *Année Afrique 1992–1993*, (Bourdaux, 1993), 323–32; Mouhamed Moustapha Kane, "L'empreinte de l'islam confrérique sur le paysage commercial sénégalais: Islam et Société en Sénégambie," *Islam et Sociétés au Sud du Shara* 8, (1994):17–42; Eva Evers Rosander, "Morality and Money: The Murids of Senegal," *Awrâq: estudios sobre el mundo árabe e islámico contemporáneo* 16, (1995):43–66; and Ottavia Schmidt di Friedberg, "The Mouride Brotherhood: An Alternative to the State?" (paper presented at the Middle East Studies Association thirtieth annual meeting, Providence, Rhode Island, November 1996). The broader issue of religio-political networks, with a Nigerian case study (with trajectories to Senegal), is well covered in Roman Loimeier and Stefan Reichmuth, "Zur Dynamik Religiös-Politischer Netzwerke in Muslimischen Gesellschaften," *Die Welt des Islams* 36, no. 2 (1996):145–85; and R.S. O'Fahey, *Enigmatic Saint: Ahmed Ibn Idris and the Idrisi Tradition* (London, 1990) describes the growth of an international network based on the teachings of one man.

[15] For one example, see Endre Stiansen, "Franz Binder: A European Arab in the Sudan, 1852–1863," in *White Nile Black Blood*, ed. Stephanie Beswick and Jay Spaulding (Lawrenceville, New Jersey, [forthcoming]).

Ambitious development plans injected large amounts of money into African economies, both as capital and as incomes for small-holder production. These and later innovations in capital availability through formal-sector financial institutions have been controversial. Since loans from "special purpose banks" were subsidized (i.e., priced at interest rates that either did not meet real costs or were set below those for commercial loans), the distribution of credit on concessionary terms did not reach target groups ("the poor" or "the exploited rural population"), but benefited merchants and farmers with the right connections.[16] Cheap loans were also distributed by politicians eager to strengthen their power bases and reward supporters, and in general the close link between governments and financial institutions encouraged rent-seeking. The incentive structure of "special purpose banks" also worked against prudent banking practices. Employees were rewarded not so much according to the performance of the loans they signed, but on the basis of the volume of credit they disbursed. Moreover, frequent transfers of bank staff from one job to another encouraged short-sightedness and limited individual accountability; the banks wasted or lost huge amounts but nobody could be held responsible. In brief, that these institutions were called "banks," "societies," and "cooperatives" does not mean that they functioned in the same way as their counterparts in the metropoles, or that they "failed" (when and if they did) for reasons having largely to do with specifically African conditions. By looking at the older forms one can identify some bases for the authority that underlies self-reliance and self-policing in networks and communities below and beyond, but also in relation to, the state.

Indigenous Concepts and Long-Term Dynamics

What are the sources and repertoires of endogenous formations? The record needs examining on questions such as the categories and terminologies of financial transactions, the relations between ideology and social practice in the creation of trust, the mutual implication of honour and punitive damages and the place of authorities other than the secular state in contract enforcement. And ultimately there arises the question that all the papers in this volume address: how do specific institutions work systemically to circulate capital, to generate employment, and to mediate accumulation?

Ideologies and cosmologies provide alternative and coexisting languages for financial dealing beyond the formal sector. The most striking example, to which several chapters in this volume refer (see the contributions of Hunwick,

16 Scholars associated with Ohio State University led the assault on subsidized credit, and their position is set out in Dale W. Adams, Douglas H. Graham and J.D. von Pischke, eds., *Undermining Rural Development with Cheap Credit* (Boulder, 1984); the Ohio School's impact and contribution are critically assessed in David Hulme and Paul Mosley, *Finance Against Poverty*, vol. 1 (London, 1996), 1–11.

Stiansen, and Hogendorn), is Islam and the Arabic commercial vocabulary. Not only are many basic terms of the marketplace used in the Koran, but to trade is in itself to emulate the Prophet, and can therefore be seen as imbued with spiritual value. It follows that a religious credo is used to evaluate commercial practices and to relate them as a system: the earning of interest, the rules regarding inheritance, taxation and other forms of revenue collection, and the detailed provisions covering many aspects of behavior in the market place. Islam provides both a comprehensive set of interlocking concepts and ideas that are mutually meaningful to the community of believers *and* an explicit manual for business conduct. The papers on Muslim thinking address the specifically African workings of a common system of law and practice. They point out three levels at which systematicity should be addressed: the coherence of ideas; their selective application under varying material conditions (see Hunwick's contribution); and the way in which the exigencies and contradictions of financial practice generate their own doctrinal challenges (see Stiansen's contribution). Unlike other cases (as far as we know), the religious authority of Muslim law provided not only guidelines for action, but institutional means of mediating differences of doctrine, in keeping with a body of legal provisions.

Other African cultures have produced their own vocabularies to inscribe a metaphysics and a morality into the language for financial transactions. The Yorùbá are a case in point.[17] Popular sayings resonate with ideas embedded in the indigenous religious culture and give meaning to the vicissitudes of the marketplace. In contrast to the Islamic case, the Yorùbá conceptualization of economic relations did not extend to articulation of a class of distinct business practices, but many ideas had implications for business relations (see Adebayo's contribution). An example was pawning, which also is one of the few clear examples of a popularly accessible financial institution that enhanced the productive capacity of the lender.[18] Up to the 1920s, a person could pawn himself, or a proxy, to a lender in return for a loan; for the duration of the contract period (i.e., until the loan was repaid in full), the pawn's labor output belonged to the lender, and it therefore represented the equivalent of interest.[19] Pawning was clearly differentiated from slavery. There were detailed

---

[17] See Adebayo's contribution to this volume, and Karin Barber, "Money, Self- Realization and the Person in Yorùbá Texts," in *Money Matters: Instability, Values and Social Payments in the Modern History of West African Communities,* ed. Jane Guyer (London, 1995), 205–24.

[18] On pawning, see E. Adeniyi Oroge, "Iwofa: An Historical Survey of the Yoruba Institution of Indenture," *African Economic History* 14 (1985):75–106, Toyin Falola and Paul E. Lovejoy, "Pawnship in Historical Perspective," in Falola and Lovejoy, *Pawnship,* 1–26; and Toyin Falola, "Pawnship in Colonial Southwestern Nigeria," in Falola and Lovejoy, *Pawnship,* 245–66.

[19] Strictly speaking, since the pawn-holder was responsible for the pawn's subsistence, the labor output minus individual subsistence represented interest.

legal practices for making the contract, enacting its rights and obligations, and defining its limits and completion. The major benefit of pawnship was to provide a mechanism for people in need of gaining access to capital, and for people with excess resources to invest their surplus with both security and expectation of a reasonable return. While loans obtained through pawning often were used to meet religious obligations, funeral expenses, and court fines, such credit could also be used for trade or as investment capital. The pawn-holder, for his part, increased his "wealth in people".[20] In an economy where value was generated by labor, the systemic logic of pawnship was impeccable. When slavery was being phased out this was particularly important, and quite possibly the continuation of the system into the present century was related to the need to replace slaves in agriculture and household economies.

The gender dimension adds complexity to the issue of interest, in systems where people's capacities to produce, reproduce, and generate new knowledge constituted wealth. Most pawns may well have been female, and Falola and Lovejoy argue that "pawnship was used to obtain females with marriage to the creditor [i.e. the lender] or a relative of the creditor in mind." Hence, "a convenient, if sometimes painful, strategy of debtors was to place girls in pawn in the hope that they would one day marry the creditor or the relative of the creditor and thereby cancel the debt."[21] Interest was therefore an extremely flexible concept, and debt contracts were not fixed but could be re-negotiated until they were either canceled or transformed into a different form of contract. An implied consequence of the constant negotiations was that default, as an absolute category, did not exist.

The Islamic and Yorùbá cases, moreover, demonstrate how the rubrics that make up a commercial ideology spanning the great changes of political history are sufficiently ambiguous to allow reinterpretation and contradiction. Reinterpretation of economic concepts and ideas within the Yorùbá tradition does not have to take the form of a legal discourse as it does in Islam. This does not, however, preclude a vigorous debate that juxtaposes inherent contradictions and rearranges established hierarchies of meaning. The Yorùbá associational system with regard to occupations, and their continual response to changing markets, have facilitated a kind of populist reworking of common ideas for new conditions (see Adebayo's paper).

Institutions in states such as Dahomey, Sokoto, and in frontier zones, were more vulnerable to change. In his contribution to the present volume, Webb argues that practices and monies on the borderlands of major political-financial systems were considerably more ephemeral than some anthropological writing might imply. He goes so far as to suggest that new money goods (such as cowry shells, *guinée* cloth, and glassware) only remained in monetized cir-

[20] This concept is elaborated in Jane I. Guyer, "Wealth in People and Self-Realization in Equatorial Africa," *Man* 28, no. 2 (1993):243–65.

[21] Falola and Lovejoy, "Pawnship", 11.

cuits for a limited period before being converted to some other use. Merchant relations depended on personal trust, and credit appears to have been practiced mainly through advances of goods, due to the volatility of currency values. As in some of the credit relations of the coastal slave trade (see Law's contribution), each credit-debt transaction was particular and terminated at the end of the trade episode. In brief, there was a system of concepts and practices with respect to credit, but not really a system of money-capital circuits that they mediated.

The financial control of the great state systems was also vulnerable, in this case to any change that undercut the value or capacity of state intervention into what would otherwise have been interpersonal transactions. Systemic circuits in Dahomey passed through the state coffers, which were depleted by people's retreat from commercial life as cowrie inflation set in in the second half of the nineteenth century (again, see Law's contribution). Accumulation and redistribution through tribute were also disrupted by the demonetization of slaves as units in that system (see Hogendorn's contribution). While these nineteenth-century state financial systems were successful in their own terms, it is mainly the popular level of financial-conceptual and institutional-financial development that remains accessible in people's repertoires into the twentieth century. And according to Law, these may be relatively recent in origin, as is the case with the Yorùbá pawning institution of *ìwọ̀fà*.

The expansion of the colonial presence, in the form of European law and Christianity, may have disseminated novel ideas while at the same time imposing rigid and exclusive interpretations of key concepts. As it relates to finance, the notion of the temporal, for instance, has undergone a radical transformation. In earlier times and outside the "Western" formal sector, the temporal frames of credit were always flexible in one way or another, as all the papers show. Time was a fluid concept in credit and debt management. But from the turn of the century the Western understanding of time as a fixed measure was imposed wherever the formal sector met popular institutions. In principle, cooperative membership dues and loan repayments had to be made according to fixed schedules, which opened up new terrain for the possibility of default. [22] The Sociétés de Prévoyance in the French colonies combined features that adjusted contributions, loans, and repayment more closely to the rhythm of rural incomes: annual membership dues, loans and repayment in kind, and varied and flexible functions (see Mann and Guyer's contribution). At the same time, the form itself remained alien, associated as it was with the administration and its shifting purposes rather than with the *prévoyance*—the quality of foresight—needed to make a more secure living in the face of volatile climates and markets.

---

[22] On the transformation of money-management institutions, see Toyin Falola, "'My Friend the Shylock': Money-Lenders and Their Clients in Southwestern Nigeria," *Journal of African History* 34, no. 3 (1993):403–23.

Further Issues

One of the great unanswered questions about Africa's financial history concerns the uses to which pools of monetary wealth have been put. The study of inheritance has been part of kinship studies but much less a part of economic and financial studies. It is not clear how the monetary wealth of Africa has been invested, and how monetary assets, commitments, and debts have been inherited from one generation to the next. As the papers that are focused primarily on trade indicate, varied institutions have arisen that reduce risk and manage transaction costs over the relatively short duration—a few months to several years—from the inception of a deal to its completion. Only tangentially, and only in three of the papers, do we address long-term investment in production. Labor pawning allowed monetary wealth to be invested in a way that augmented production over a period of years. In the era of cocoa expansion farmers also used money to acquire land. Otherwise, the investment of money in the long-term productivity of economic units, especially those of other people, seems not to have been deeply institutionalized up to the twentieth century. People appear to have invested in production, but not predominantly with money. Although master craftsmen, such as blacksmiths, may have become rich during the boom in iron production in the nineteenth century there is little documentation so far on the uses of their money except in social payments such as membership in title societies and marriage.[23]

If the sources on the spending of money have not yet been synthesized, there is also relatively little on how savings worked. In much of West Africa there was an architecture of treasure houses. Often they were also shrines, so that spirits stood on guard and punished thieves. Probably considerably safer was loaning out against a valuable collateral, such as occurred in eastern Nigeria, with the right to enslave delinquent debtors in the nineteenth century and the right to annex land in the twentieth. Several incentives to saving were thereby differently linked to an accumulative dynamic, including display for purposes of status accumulation, social payment that widened effective networks, productive investment that increased returns over time, and loaning out that allowed collateral annexation. Surely the incentive to build up and dispose of monetary resources must have involved complex calculations: between the advantage of ownership and the burden of guardianship, between the lure of great gain and the risk of equal loss (from political requisition, theft in war and devaluation), between the utility of different forms of interest and the cost of collecting, and so on.

Our cases give some indication of how savings have worked, and whether the credit institutions of trade were adapted to the longer-term credit needs of the peaks and troughs of a lifetime, or the requirements of productive ven-

[23] Felicia Ekejiuba, "Currency Instability and Social Payments Among the Igbo of Eastern Nigeria, 1890–1990," in Guyer ed., *Money Matters*, 131–61.

tures. The fact that colonial governments tended to impose forced money savings to cover these needs suggests that they found indigenous institutions either too economically weak to serve new needs or too draconian in their implementation of provisions that were contrary to the aim of displacing old political controls. But the topic of savings and inheritance of monetary assets and liabilities remains one of the under-described aspects of African financial dynamics, even now. As states try to manipulate the customary law of kinship, which governs asset transmission over time, kinship law has to be addressed within the same legal-philosophical framework as contract law. Present-day entrepreneurs draw on and combine the kinds of institutions described in these papers: institutions developed in both the formal and informal sectors, sanctioned both by morality and secular law, mediated by both kinship and contract.[24] Whereas we expect novelty in the combinations, already many of the elements have been developed on the African continent in local transactions or through its long engagement with world commerce. It is with a view to illuminating the politics, economics and culture of the development trajectories of indigenous and long-term institutions, many of which still exist or have left their mark, that we present these case studies.

Bibliography

Adams, Dale W., Douglas H. Graham and J.D. von Pischke, eds. *Undermining Rural Development with Cheap Credit.* Boulder, 1984.

Alpers, Edward A. *Ivory and Slaves: Changing Pattern of International Trade in East Central Africa to the Later Nineteenth Century.* Berkeley, 1975.

Austen, Ralph A. *African Economic History: Internal Development and External Dependency.* London, 1987.

Austin, Gareth. "Indigenous Credit Institutions in West Africa, c. 1750-c. 1960," in *Local Suppliers of Credit in the Third World, 1750–1960,* eds. Gareth Austin and Kaoru Sugihara, 93–159. Basingstoke, 1993.

Barber, Karin. "Money, Self-Realization and the Person in Yorùbá Texts," in *Money Matters: Instability, Values and Social Payments in the Modern History of West African Communities,* ed. Jane Guyer, 205–24. London, 1995.

Born, K.E. *International Banking in the 19th and 20th Centuries.* Leamington Spa, 1983.

Brownbridge, Martin and Charles Harvey. *Banking in Africa: Botswana, Ethiopia, Ghana, Kenya, Nigeria, Uganda, Zambia, Malawi, Tanzania, Zimbabwe, The Gambia.* Oxford, 1998.

Center for Medieval and Renaissance Studies, University of California, Los Angeles. *The Dawn of Modern Banking.* New Haven, 1979.

[24] See Gwendolyn Mikell, "The State, the Courts and 'Value': Caught between Matrilineages in Ghana," in Guyer ed., *Money Matters,* 225–44.

Cohen, Abner. "Cultural Strategies in the Organization of Trading Diasporas," in *The Development of Indigenous Trade and Markets in West Africa*, eds. Claude Meillassoux and Daryll Forde, 266–78. London, 1971.

Curtin, Philip D. *Economic Change in Precolonial Africa: Senegambia in the Era of the Slave Trade*. Madison, 1975.

Curtin, P., S. Feierman, L. Thompson and J. Vansina. *African History: From the Earliest Times to Independence*. 2nd. ed. New York, 1995.

Davis, Eric. *Challenging Colonialism: Bank Misr and Egyptian Industrialization, 1920–1941*. Princeton, 1983.

Dell'Amore, Giordano. *Banking Systems in Africa*. Milan, 1971.

Diop, M.C. and M. Diouf, "Notes sur la reconversion des marabouts dans l'economie urbaine," in *Année Afrique 1992–1993*, 323–32. Bordeaux, 1993.

Duffield, Ian. "The Business Activities of Duse Mohammed Ali: An Example of the Economic Dimension of Pan-Africanism, 1912–1945," *Journal of the Historical Society of Nigeria* 4, No. 4 (1969):571–600.

Ekejiuba, Felicia. "Currency Instability and Social Payments Among the Igbo of Eastern Nigeria, 1890–1990," in *Money Matters: Instability, Values and Social Payments in the Modern History of West African Communities*, ed. Jane Guyer, 131–61. London, 1995.

Evers Rosander, Eva. "Morality and Money: The Murids of Senegal," *Awrâq: estudios sobre el mundo árabe e islámico contemporáneo* 16, (1995):43–66.

Falola, Toyin. "'My Friend the Shylock': Money-Lenders and Their Clients in Southwestern Nigeria," *Journal of African History* 34, no. 3 (1993):403–23.

—. "Pawnship in Colonial Southwestern Nigeria," in *Pawnship in Africa: Debt Bondage in Historical Perspective*, eds. Toyin Falola and Paul E. Lovejoy, 245–66. Boulder, 1994.

Falola, Toyin and Paul E. Lovejoy, eds. *Pawnship in Africa: Debt Bondage in Historical Perspective*. Boulder, 1994.

—. "Pawnship in Historical Perspective," in *Pawnship in Africa: Debt Bondage in Historical Perspective*, eds. Toyin Falola and Paul E. Lovejoy, 1–26. Boulder, 1994

Greif, Avner. "Contract Enforceability and Economic Institutions in early Trade: The Maghribi Trader's Coalition," *The American Economic Review* 83 (1993):525–48.

Guyer, Jane I. "Wealth in People and Self-Realization in Equatorial Africa," *Man* 28, no. 2 (1993):243–65.

—. ed. *Money Matters: Instability, Values and Social Payments in the Modern History of West African Communities*. Portsmouth, New Hampshire, 1995.

Hogendorn, Jan and Marion Johnson. *The Shell Money of the Slave Trade*. Cambridge, 1986.

Hopkins, A.G. *An Introduction to the Economic History of West Africa*. London, 1973.

—. "Economic Aspects of Political Movements in Nigeria and the Gold Coast 1918–1939," *Journal of African History* 7, no. 1, (1966):133–52.

Hulme, David and Paul Mosley. *Finance Against Poverty*. Vol. 1. London, 1996.

Iliffe, John. *Africans: The History of a Continent*. Cambridge, 1995.

Jones, Geoffrey. *British Multinational Banking 1830–1990*. Oxford, 1993.

Kane, Mouhamed Moustapha. "L'empreinte de l'islam confrérique sur le paysage commercial sénégalais: Islam et société en Sénégambie," *Islam et Sociétés au Sud du Shara* 8 (1994):17–42.

Kevane, Michael. 1996. "Qualitative Impact Study of Credit With Education in Burkina Faso." Freedom from Hunger Research Paper No. 3. Davis, Ca, 1996.

Kerridge, Eric. *Trade & Banking in Early Modern England*. Manchester, 1988.

Law, Robin. "Royal Monopoly and Private Enterprise in the Atlantic Slave Trade: the Case of Dahomey," *Journal of African History* 18, no. 4 (1977):555–77.

Loimeier, Roman and Stefan Reichmuth. "Zur Dynamik Religiös-Politischer Netzwerke in Muslimischen Gesellschaften," *Die Welt des Islams* 36, no. 2 (1996):145–85.

Lydon, Ghislaine. "Les péripéties d'une institution financière: la banque du Sénégal, 1844–1901," paper presented at the Commemoration du Centenaire de la Creation de l'Afrique Occidentale Française (A.O.F), Dakar, 16–23 June, 1995 Dakar, Direction des Archives du Sénégal, 1995, 475–91.

Mikell, Gwendolyn. "The State, the Courts and 'Value': Caught between Matrilineages in Ghana," in *Money Matters: Instability, Values and Social Payments in the Modern History of West African Communities*, ed. Jane Guyer, 225–44. London, 1995.

Milgrom, Paul R., Douglass C. North and Barry R. Weingast. "The Role of Institutions in the Revival of Trade: The Law Merchant, Private Judges, and the Champagne Fairs," *Economics and Politics* 2 (1990):1–23.

North, Douglass C. *Institutions, Institutional Change and Economic Performance*. Cambridge, 1990.

O'Fahey, R.S. *State and Society in Dār Fūr*. London, 1980.

—. *Enigmatic Saint: Ahmed Ibn Idris and the Idrisi Tradition*. London, 1990.

Olukoshi, Adebayo. "The Impact of Recent Reform Efforts on the African State," in *Domination or Dialogue? Experiences and Prospects for African Development Cooperation*, eds., Kjell Havnevik and Brian Van Arkadie, 48–70. Uppsala, 1996.

Onoh, J.K. *Money and Banking in Africa*. London, 1982.

Oroge, E. Adeniyi. "Iwofa: An Historical Survey of the Yoruba Institution of Indenture," *African Economic History* 14 (1985):75–106.

Popiel, Paul A. *Financial Systems in Sub-Saharan Africa*. Washington DC, 1994.

Schmidt di Friedberg, Ottavia. "The Mouride Brotherhood: An Alternative to the State?" Paper presented at the Middle East Studies Association's 30th annual meeting, Providence, Rhode Island, 21–24 November 1996.

Seidman, Ann. *Money, Banking and Public Finance in Africa*. London, 1986.

Stiansen, Endre. "Franz Binder: A European Arab in the Sudan, 1852–1863," in *White Nile Black Blood*, eds. Stephanie Beswick and Jay Spaulding. Lawrenceville, New Jersey, 1999.

Uche, Chibuike. "Indigenous Banks in Colonial Nigeria." Paper presented at conference on Financial Institutions in the Political Economy, Rosendal (Norway), 11–14 June 1998.

Finance and Credit in Pre-Colonial Dahomey

Robin Law

The operation of credit in pre-colonial West Africa has not attracted much in the way of detailed study.[1] Such published research as there is concentrates on the extension of credit by European traders, particularly with reference to its widening scale in the nineteenth century.[2] The role of indigenous credit institutions has been even more neglected, especially with regard to the pre-colonial period,[3] though a recently published collection of essays on the practice of "pawnship" represents an important pioneering contribution in this field.[4] The present paper is concerned with credit in Dahomey, the dominant military and commercial power on the section of the West African coast known to Europeans as the "Slave Coast" for most of the eighteenth and nineteenth centuries; it also makes reference to the two states that preceded Dahomey in this region, Allada and Whydah, which were conquered by it in the 1720s.[5]

Pre-colonial Dahomey (and Allada and Whydah before it) had a money economy, employing a currency of cowrie shells (called locally *àkué*). Many commercial transactions, most taxes, and to some extent social payments such as bride wealth were monetized. In particular, exchange in local markets was

---

[1] See, however, Ray A. Kea, *Settlements, Trade and Polities in the Seventeenth-Century Gold Coast* (Baltimore, 1982), 236–47.

[2] C.W. Newbury, "Credit in Early Nineteenth Century West African Trade," *Journal of African History* 13, no. 1 (1972):81–95. For earlier periods, see K.Y. Daaku, *Trade and Politics on the Gold Coast 1600–1720* (Oxford, 1970), 41–44; Kea, *Settlements*, 239–43.

[3] See Gareth Austin, "Indigenous Credit Institutions in West Africa, c.1750– 1960," in *Local Suppliers of Credit in the Third World, 1750–1960*, ed. Gareth Austin and Kaoru Sugihara (Basingstoke, 1993), 93–159.

[4] Toyin Falola and Paul E. Lovejoy, eds., *Pawnship in Africa: Debt Bondage in Historical Perspective* (Boulder, Colorado, 1994).

[5] For the history of these societies, see especially Robin Law, *The Slave Coast of West Africa 1550–1750* (Oxford, 1991); I.A. Akinjogbin, *Dahomey and Its Neighbours 1708–1818* (Cambridge, 1967); C.W. Newbury, *The Western Slave Coast and its Rulers* (Oxford, 1961); Patrick Manning, *Slavery, Colonialism and Economic Growth in Dahomey 1640–1960* (Cambridge, 1982). For the economic organization of pre-colonial Dahomey, see also Karl Polanyi, *Dahomey and the Slave Trade* (Seattle, 1966). Despite many inaccuracies in detail and dubious interpretations, this remains a very useful summary of a great deal of (especially ethnographic) literature.

fully monetized, all transactions being normally for cash.[6] This applied not only to local people but also to Europeans who wanted to purchase in the market. The European factories, for example, found that if they ran out of cowries they could not procure provisions by bartering other commodities, but had to sell goods such as iron bars or even slaves to obtain cowries for use in purchasing food.[7]

Cowries were imported into West Africa, ultimately from the Indian Ocean. They are first attested in the Slave Coast, both as an imported commodity and as a circulating currency, in the seventeenth century, when they were being imported by European traders in exchange for slaves. It is probable that cowries were introduced into the region by Europeans, as local tradition generally asserts. Although cowries had been imported into West Africa across the Sahara from the Islamic world even before the beginnings of European maritime trade, it is unlikely that such overland supplies of cowries ever reached the Dahomey area. Muslim merchants from the West African interior did trade with the Slave Coast, but they penetrated it fairly late and seem to have been attracted there by pre-existing European trade. Muslim merchants are said to have come to Whydah for the first time only in 1704, and they were not then importing cowries but purchasing them, among other commodities, from the Europeans in exchange for slaves.[8] It is conceivable that some alternative form of currency was in use prior to the introduction of cowries,[9] but local tradition does not recall the use of any such earlier currency and generally assumes that earlier trade was conducted by barter (and was consequently limited in scale).[10] The monetization and commercialization of the local economy was therefore a consequence of its involvement in trade with the Europeans, and dated only from the sixteenth century.

This monetization through the cowrie currency tended to promote the expansion of credit.[11] Although credit can of course be given in goods (as was frequently done, as will be seen, in the trade with Europeans), the use of money certainly facilitated its extension, since currency affords both a convenient means of storing wealth from which loans may be made, and a stan-

[6] Polanyi, *Dahomey and the Slave Trade*, 84–5; see also Law, *Slave Coast*, 48–9.

[7] See, e.g., Robin Law, ed., *Further Correspondence of the Royal African Company of England relating to the "Slave Coast", 1681–1699* (African Studies Program, University of Wisconsin-Madison, 1992): John Thorne, Offra, to Cape Coast Castle, 28 January 1683, no. 23, pp. 25–6; Josiah Pearson, Whydah, to Cape Coast Castle, 24 November 1694, no. 80, pp. 58–9.

[8] Jean-Baptiste Labat, *Voyage du Chevalier des Marchais en Guinée, isles voisines et à Cayenne*, 2d ed., (Amsterdam, 1731), 2:218–36.

[9] See Manning, *Slavery, Colonialism and Economic Growth*, 24.

[10] E.g., Maximilien Quénum, *Au pays des Fon*, 3d ed. (Paris, 1983), 133.

[11] See Félix Abiola Iroko, "Les cauris en Afrique Occidentale du Xe au XXe siècle" (thèse de Doctorat d'État, Université de Paris I, 1987), 382–9.

dard of deferred payment. As Jane Guyer (quoting Keynes) has recently observed, "money is a link between the present and the future."[12]

The operation of credit in pre-colonial Dahomey has hitherto attracted little attention in published research, apart from a recent study by this writer of the practice of "pawning" persons or goods as security for loans.[13] The present paper attempts a more rounded consideration of the operation of credit. Inevitably, given the uneven nature of the available documentation, its primary focus is on credit in the European trade, but some reference is also made to the operation of credit and financial institutions in the domestic economy. Moreover, in view of the close interconnections between overseas trade and the domestic economy,[14] it is argued that one may legitimately make inferences from one to the other.

Commercial Credit in the European Trade (1): Extended by Europeans

There are many references to the extension of credit by European traders in the form of goods supplied in advance of the delivery of the slaves (and later, palm produce) for which they were paid. In the earliest period of European trade on the Slave Coast for which any detailed evidence survives—that of the Dutch trade at Allada in the 1640s—credit was already being extended to African suppliers of slaves, and the practice became standard subsequently.[15] When the French began trading at Allada in 1670 they also granted credit, and when some of those with whom they traded failed to clear their debts they had to appeal to the King to enforce payment.[16] The extension of credit was also normal in the European trade at Whydah in the 1690s, as was described by the Dutch trader Willem Bosman. By this time, at least in some cases, this practice did not reflect merely delayed payments, but represented an advance of capital to finance trading ventures into the interior. Bosman explained that "if there happen to be no stock of slaves, the [European] factor must then resolve to run the risque of trusting the inhabitants with goods to the value of one or two hundred slaves; which commodities they send into the inland

[12] Jane I. Guyer, "Introduction," in *Money Matters: Instability, Values and Social Payments in the Modern History of West African Communities*, ed. Jane I. Guyer (Portsmouth, New Hampshire, 1994), 6.

[13] Robin Law, "On Pawning and Enslavement for Debt in the Pre-Colonial Slave Coast," in Falola and Lovejoy, *Pawnship in Africa*, 55–69.

[14] Contrary to the assumptions of Polanyi, *Dahomey and the Slave Trade*; for some critical comments, see Law, *Slave Coast*, 219–20.

[15] Law, *Slave Coast*, 217–18.

[16] [Delbée], "Journal du voyage du Sieur Delbée," in *Relation de ce qui s'est passé dans les Isles et Terre-ferme de l'Amérique pendant la dernière guerre avec l'Angleterre*, ed. J. de Clodoré (Paris, 1671), 2:426.

country, in order to buy with them slaves at all markets, and that sometimes two hundred miles deep in the country."[17]

Bosman's account might seem to imply that this credit was only short-term, debts being cleared at the end of a ship's trading, but other evidence shows that credit was sometimes extended for longer periods: The factory records of the English Royal African Company at Whydah in 1682, for example, list among its assets fifteen slaves "standing out," which had been "acknowledged before the King and assured to be paid off at the arrival of the next Company's ship."[18] Moreover, in practice debts were sometimes left unpaid beyond the agreed term. When the Dutch began trading in Allada (1636), within a few years substantial debts had been accumulated—by 1643 the King alone owed the value of 345 slaves, two chiefs ("nobles") 100 slaves each, and other individual traders up to twenty slaves each.[19] Tensions over these debts led to the temporary suspension of Dutch trade with Allada in 1643–4; although in 1645–6 the Dutch attempted to collect on them they were able to secure only fifty of the outstanding slaves.[20] The English evidently faced similar problems. In 1680 their factory at Offra, the port of Allada, was trying to recover "old debts" owed by the King, and in 1682 the King still owed for thirty slaves, which were then written off in settlement of an unrelated claim.[21] Similar problems continued, and perhaps increased, under later Dahomean rule in the eighteenth and nineteenth centuries. On one occasion in 1777, an English trader went to the capital, Abomey, in an attempt to collect 100 slaves owed to him, but he succeeded in obtaining only fifty; and in 1782 the Director of the English fort at Whydah was owed 120 slaves, 315 "ounces" (i.e., £630) in goods and nearly 600 ounces (£1,200) in cowries (together equivalent to the value of around 600 slaves) by various Dahomean chiefs, besides possibly even greater debts owed by the King.[22]

---

[17] William Bosman, *A New and Accurate Description of the Coast of Guinea* (London, 1705), 363a.

[18] "Receipt for goods in the Whydah factory," 13 October 1682, in Law, *Further Correspondence*, no. 19a, p. 22.

[19] Ernst van den Boogaart and Pieter Emmer, "The Dutch Participation in the Atlantic Slave Trade, 1596–1650," in *The Uncommon Market: Essays in the Economic History of the Atlantic Slave Trade*, eds., Henry A. Gemery and Jan S. Hogendorn, (New York, 1979), 360.

[20] Robin Law, "The Slave Trade in Seventeenth-Century Allada: A Revision," *African Economic History* 22 (1994):67–8.

[21] John Mildmay, Offra, to Royal African Company, 13 October 1680, no. 4, pp. 16–7 in *Correspondence from the Royal African Company's Factories at Offra and Whydah on the Slave Coast of West Africa in the Public Record Office, London, 1678–93*, ed. Robin Law, (Centre of African Studies, University of Edinburgh, 1990); John Thorne, Offra, to Cape Coast Castle, 28 January 1683, no. 23, pp. 25–6, in Law, *Further Correspondence*.

[22] Akinjogbin, *Dahomey and Its Neighbours*, 142, 161.

In the nineteenth century, problems arising from uncleared debts feature in the surviving correspondence of a Brazilian merchant resident at Whydah, José Francisco dos Santos. In 1846, for example, he complained that "you have to give credit to the Blacks here and they pay late or never." In December of that year, dos Santos paid the Yevogan, or Governor of Whydah, cowries for thirty slaves to be supplied by King Gezo; by February of the following year, the bulk of these had been delivered, but five remained outstanding, and these had still not been supplied by April 1847. The situation was no different in the 1860s, when dos Santos had abandoned the slave trade for that in palm oil: he complained in 1865 of Gezo's successor, King Glele, that "He buys and doesn't pay," and still owed him for tobacco from three separate ships.[23] The British trader Swanzey, later in Glele's reign, during the 1870s, advised that "The greatest caution is requisite in giving credit to the natives," because although they would settle small amounts, "once allow them to exceed a certain sum, and they cease to pay anything further." However, it was evidently impossible to refuse credit to the King, who "rarely pays ready cash or produce for his purchases, and he is generally a debtor to my agents of from $200 to $400."[24]

On one occasion such uncleared debts had momentous consequences for Dahomey's internal political history. In the early nineteenth century, King Adandozan is said to have failed to pay debts owed to the Brazilian merchant Francisco Felix de Souza, and when the latter came to Abomey to demand repayment, he was imprisoned by the King—an incident which provoked de Souza's subsequent support for the coup d'état which overthrew Adandozan in favour of his brother Gezo in 1818.[25] In return de Souza was installed as Gezo's agent at Whydah (with the title Chacha), but this position, though initially highly remunerative, had by de Souza's death in 1849 left him deeply in debt—ironically, according to local tradition, because of accumulated debts left unpaid by King Gezo in turn.[26]

From time to time European traders sought to refuse or restrict the granting of credit to African suppliers. When an ambassador from the King of Allada came to France in 1670, the French demanded not only that the King

---

[23] Pierre Verger, *Les afro-américains* (Dakar, 1952), Dos Santos correspondence: Dos Santos, Whydah, to Manoel Luiz Pereira, Bahia: 3 March 1846, no. 28, p. 68; Dos Santos, Whydah, to Guerino Antonio, Bahia, 28 December 1846, no. 43, p. 72; Dos Santos, Whydah, to Francisco Lopez Guimaraes, Bahia, no. 52, pp. 75–6; Dos Santos, Whydah, to Antonio Guerino [*sic*], Bahia, 19 February 1847, no. 59, pp. 78–9; Dos Santos, Whydah, to J. Gbr. Baeta, Bahia, 13 April 1847, 19 January 1865, no. 104, pp. 93–4.

[24] A. Swanzey, "On the Trade in West Africa," *Journal of the Society of Arts* 22 (1874), 481–2.

[25] Akinjogbin, *Dahomey and Its Neighbours*, 198; see also Paul Hazoumé, *Le pacte de sang au Dahomey* (Paris, 1937), 28; Simone de Souza, *La famille de Souza du Bénin-Togo* (Cotonou, 1992), 20.

[26] Hazoumé, *Le pacte de sang*, 109.

should undertake to enforce payment for goods advanced on credit, but also that they should not be obliged to give credit to any of the chiefs ("seigneurs") who were not known to be "good payers."[27] In 1685 a newly appointed Dutch factor at Offra was instructed to "be very careful not to give credit, without some important reasons, to people who are not beyond any doubt able to pay back", since "much damage has been done by this practice."[28] But normally the Europeans' bargaining position was too weak to allow them to withhold credit. In 1681, for example, the English factor at Offra tried to refuse it to the Governor of the town, but the latter's displeasure "forced [him] to comply."[29] And under Dahomean rule, the French factor at Whydah in 1781 explained that he was obliged to supply goods on credit since this was "the only way to maintain their friendship."[30]

One change in the character of European commercial credit which has been noted in the late nineteenth century was a shift from the practice of advancing goods to African suppliers to employing Africans (or Afro-Europeans or Brazilians) as local agents of European firms.[31] This evidently occurred, at least to some degree, in Dahomey, where by 1876 the son of the now deceased José Francisco dos Santos, Jacinto da Costa Santos, was serving as an agent of the British firm of Swanzey. When he became involved in a dispute with the Dahomean authorities, who confiscated the goods in his possession, Swanzey's principal local agent demanded their restitution, on the grounds that Jacinto was "only an agent" and "the goods belonged to the firm which he represented." The Dahomeans, however, were unwilling to recognize the distinction.[32] It was this dispute which provoked the British naval blockade of Whydah in 1876–7.

In addition to straightforward commercial advances, Europeans sometimes extended credit to Dahomey's kings for non-commercial purposes. In 1779, for example, King Kpengla demanded guns and gunpowder on credit, presumably for a projected campaign;[33] again in 1789, for a campaign against Ketu, he "took upon trust all the guns and powder which could be found among the shipping."[34] The debts owed by King Gezo to Francisco de Souza

---

27 "Suite du journal du Sieur Delbée," in de Clodoré, *Relation de ce qui s'est passé*, 2:546–8.

28 Albert van Dantzig, ed., *The Dutch on the Guinea Coast 1674–1742: A Collection of Documents from the General State Archive at The Hague* (Accra, 1978), no. 15, p. 26: Instruction for Willem de la Palma, 8 December 1685.

29 William Cross, Offra, to Royal African Company, February 1681, no. 6, p. 25, in Law, *Correspondence*.

30 Akinjogbin, *Dahomey and Its Neighbours*, 162.

31 Newbury, "Credit in Early Nineteenth Century West African Trade," 86.

32 Édouard Foà, *Le Dahomey* (Paris, 1895), 33.

33 Akinjogbin, *Dahomey and Its Neighbours*, 161.

34 Archibald Dalzel, *The History of Dahomy* (London, 1793), 201.

at the time of the latter's death in 1849 are also said to have been for the purchase of arms, for campaigns against the Mahi to the north.[35] These instances might be thought of as quasi-commercial in character, since the projected campaigns would be expected, if successful, to yield captives, some of whom would be given in payment for the munitions. In 1865, however, King Glele owed dos Santos not only for tobacco from commercial transactions, but also for some thousands of dollars' worth of cowries which he had borrowed in order to redeem prisoners taken in the previous year's defeat at Abeokuta.[36]

Commercial Credit in the European Trade (2): Extended by Africans

One feature of the operation of the Atlantic trade which is often overlooked is that credit was not extended only by Europeans to Africans, but often in the opposite direction as well.[37] An English merchant who traded at Whydah in the early eighteenth century before its conquest by Dahomey in 1727, noted that the Whydah traders were happy to grant him credit "for ten days together" when the state of the sea prevented the landing of goods from his ship—though he found the King of Dahomey's traders after the conquest much less tolerant of such delays.[38] A Danish trader at Whydah in 1784 likewise reports that slaves were purchased in town from traders who subsequently went to the European factory involved to collect their goods, and that sometimes this involved delays in payment when goods could not be landed immediately because of the state of the sea. He observes that "The slave traders here are great capitalists; they may often have a credit from the Europeans to the extent of a thousand or more thalers [equivalent to around seventy slaves]."[39] A British trader in 1803, in fact, made clear that by then, if not earlier, the extension of credit was not only due to the vicissitudes of conditions off Whydah beach, but was a regular feature of the trade: "The black traders seldom receive payment for a slave, from the whites, at the time of delivery," preferring to be paid the full amount due to them "at the winding up of accounts."[40]

These accounts seem to imply that such credit was essentially short-term—being cleared within a few days, or at least at the end of a ship's trading—but other evidence shows that it could be extended by Africans to Europeans over longer periods. In 1697 the Dutchman Bosman, having got his

[35] Hazoumé, *Le pacte de sang*, 109.

[36] Dos Santos, Whydah, to J. Gbr. Baeta, Bahia, 19 January 1865, no. 104, pp. 93–4, in Verger, *Les afro-américains*.

[37] See Austin, "Indigenous Credit Institutions," 131–2.

[38] William Snelgrave, *A New Account of Some Parts of Guinea* (London, 1734), 87–8.

[39] Paul Erdman Isert, *Letters on West Africa and the Slave Trade*, trans. Selena Winsnes (Oxford, 1992), 98.

[40] John M'Leod, *A Voyage to Africa* (London, 1820), 89.

slaves on board his ship but unable to land the goods to pay for them due to a storm lasting for several days, mooted the idea of dispatching the ship without paying for its slaves. He found the King and "other Great Men" of Whydah quite happy to have him promise "that they receive payment at the arrival of other ships" (though in the event the weather improved, and Bosman was able to pay them in the normal way).[41] Similarly, when the British navy in the nineteenth century was active in intercepting illegal slave ships, King Glele in 1863 explained that although he was usually paid before ships took the slaves away, "sometimes he risks them on trust" and so lost out when a slaver was captured.[42]

As with African debts to Europeans, the extension of credit to Europeans by Africans did not always go smoothly. In 1682, for example, when the chief factor of the English Royal African Company was arrested and deported by the local authorities, one of the grievances cited against him was his delay in paying for fifteen slaves supplied him on credit by a local chief. On occasion debts owed by Europeans remained uncleared or accumulated over longer periods. The English factor in 1682, in fact, was suspected of "endeavouring to gett into their debts ... with a designe to goe off" without settling them.[43] The King of Allada claimed in 1722 that he was owed for 100 slaves supplied to the English, and even seized an employee of the English company as a "slave" (i.e., pawn) in an attempt to force payment of the debt.[44]

Such problems arising from default on credit granted to Europeans continued under Dahomean rule. King Kpengla of Dahomey complained in 1786 about non-payment for slaves which he had supplied on credit to an English captain.[45] And in the nineteenth century, although Whydah tradition, as mentioned earlier, claims that Francisco Felix de Souza was ruined by King Gezo's failure to discharge his debts, a contemporary account reports that when de Souza died in 1849 it was, in fact, he who owed $80,000 (equivalent to the value of 1,000 slaves) to King Gezo.[46] Likewise, José Francisco dos Santos, who had complained about the failure of Gezo's successor Glele to pay his debts in the 1860s is said to have left unpaid at his death in the 1870s a

---

[41] Bosman, in Albert Van Dantzig, "English Bosman and Dutch Bosman: A Comparison of Texts—VI," *History in Africa* 7 (1980):284–5. This passage is omitted in the English edition of Bosman's book.

[42] House of Commons, "Despatches from Commodore Wilmot respecting his Visit to the King of Dahomey," *Sessional Papers, 1863*, vol. 53, p. 10.

[43] Andrew Crosbie, Whydah, to Royal African Company, 1 September 1682, no. 16, pp. 16–7, and enclosure in Timothy Armitage, Whydah, 24 October 1682, no. 18a, pp. 18–9 in Law, *Further Correspondence*.

[44] Snelgrave, *New Account*, 8.

[45] Akinjogbin, *Dahomey and Its Neighbours*, 145.

[46] House of Commons, "Correspondence Relating to the Slave Trade 1849–50," *Sessional Papers, 1850*, vol. 55, ii, Vice-Consul Duncan, Whydah, to Viscount Palmerston, 22 November 1849, no. 7, pp. 9–10.

debt owed to the King for forty slaves.[47] A Spanish trader, one Don Juan, who died in the early 1860s, is also reported to have owed $200 to King Glele, in consequence of which, it is said, a house at Whydah belonging to him was seized for the King.[48] When Julião de Souza, the first Chacha's son and fourth successor in the office, was executed by King Glele in 1887, one of the charges against him was that he owed the King $30,100 for slaves supplied to the Portuguese.[49] The convention whereby Europeans were prohibited from leaving Dahomey without the King's permission is explained in one account of the 1860s as intended to prevent them from absconding without settling their debts.[50]

It bears noting that credit was given to Europeans by private Dahomean merchants as well as by the King: the praise-name of Gnahoui, one of the leading merchants of Whydah in the mid-nineteenth century, illustrates his great wealth by the fact that "You lend money [*àkué*, i.e. cowries] to the white man."[51] Also, Africans extended credit to Europeans in non-commercial contexts as well as commercial ones. The English factor at Offra in 1681, for example, finding himself without cowries to defray his local subsistence expenses, borrowed them "off the Blacks," to be repaid at the next ship's arrival; the debt thus incurred was still uncleared in the following year, and the local authorities in consequence forbade the factor from embarking for England.[52]

Commercial Credit in the European Trade (3): Origins

What were the origins of this system of commercial credit in the form of advances of goods? It might seem natural to suppose that the practice of credit was introduced into coastal West Africa by the Europeans. A difficulty with this view, however, is that there is no clear evidence for the extension of credit by Europeans to Africans before the 1640s. The Dutch advances to Allada chiefs and traders in that decade, in fact, constitute the earliest evidence for the practice on a large scale. As regards the Dutch specifically, it is likely that this extension of large-scale credit in Allada was an innovation. On the Gold

[47] Catherine Coquery, "Le blocus de Whydah (1876–1877) et la rivalité franco-anglaise au Dahomey," *Cahiers d'Études Africaines* 2 (1962):375.

[48] Richard Burton, *A Mission to Gelele, King of Dahome,* (London, 1864), 1:83.

[49] Letter of King Glele to King of Portugal, 6 July 1887, in Adrien Djivo, "Le roi Glèlè et les Européens: L'échec du protectorat portugais sur le Danhomè (1885–1887)," *Cahiers du Centre de Recherches Africaines* 8 (1994):279.

[50] Renzo Mandirola and Yves Morel, eds., *Journal de Francesco Borghero, premier missionnaire du Dahomey (1861–1865)* (Paris, 1997), 96.

[51] Casimir Agbo, *Histoire de Ouidah du XVIe au XXe siècle* (Avignon, 1959), 235–6.

[52] John Thorne, Offra, to Cape Coast Castle, 4 December 168, no. 7, pp. 5–6, and Thorne to Cape Coast Castle, 25 March 1682, no. 12, pp. 10–1, in Law, *Further Correspondence.* Likewise on the Gold Coast, employees of English factories sometimes borrowed gold locally in order to pay for their subsistence. Kea, *Settlement*, 236–7.

Coast earlier, de Marees, in the early 1600s, although noting that local interpreters and brokers often tried to obtain goods from the European factors on credit, advised that credit not be given and stated that "big traders buy everything for cash [i.e., gold], and pay immediately."[53] The Dutch and other European traders on the Gold Coast did adopt the practice of extending credit on a large scale, but this is not clearly documented before the second half of the seventeenth century.[54] There is likewise no evidence of the Dutch giving credit in Benin (for the cloth trade) before the later seventeenth century.[55]

Since de Marees makes clear not only that Africans on the Gold Coast were pressing Europeans for credit in the early seventeenth century, but also that credit was already being used in local markets there,[56] the inference is that, here at least, it was the Dutch who were conforming to African practice and expectations rather than vice versa. It is quite possible, of course, that the extension of credit had been introduced earlier into the West African trade by the Portuguese—other evidence indicates that they had initially given credit in Warri, but that the Dutch refused it when they began trading there in the 1640s.[57] But even if this is so, it may be that the idea of credit originated in the domestic economy and was extended from there into the European trade. At any rate, it is striking that the earliest recorded instance of the offering of credit in the West African trade, at Benin in 1553, came from the African rather than the European side. The king of Benin then offered English traders credit until their next voyage, should their goods prove insufficient to pay for a whole cargo of pepper.[58]

Credit in Local Transactions

Although there is far less evidence in regard to the strictly domestic economy, clearly credit was extended in purely intra-African transactions, as well as in the trade with Europeans. The principal evidence for this relates to the practice of enslaving and selling insolvent debtors, referred to in contemporary European sources from the late seventeenth century onwards. Although generally cast in the language of slavery, such references should probably be

---

53 Pieter de Marees, *Description and Historical Account of the Gold Kingdom of Guinea*, trans. Albert Van Dantzig and Adam Jones (Oxford, 1987), 50; but de Marees does refer elsewhere to a boy left on a ship "as a pawn on account of a debt" (41).

54 Kea, *Settlements*, 239–40.

55 A.F.C. Ryder, *Benin and the Europeans 1485–1897* (London, 1969), 130–2. Note, however, an earlier (1652) reference to goods "given in credit in the Rio Benyn and impossible to recover," *West Africa in the Mid-Seventeenth Century: An Anonymous Dutch Manuscript*, ed. Adam Jones (African Studies Association Press, 1995), 149.

56 De Marees, *Description*, 102.

57 Olfert Dapper, *Naukeurige Beschrijvinge der Afrikaensche Gewesten*, 2d ed. (Amsterdam, 1676), 2d pagination, 133.

58 Ryder, *Benin and the Europeans*, 77–8.

interpreted as relating to the pawning of a debtor (or one or more of his household) as security for a debt; in principle, such pawns were distinct from slaves, and were protected from sale into the trans-Atlantic trade, though it is evident that this prohibition was often violated in practice.[59]

The sources do not throw much light on the circumstances under which debts might be contracted, apart from references to people "selling [i.e. pawning] themselves" to get money (cowries) to feed themselves in times of famine,[60] and (in one nineteenth-century account) to people falling into debt through gambling.[61] One nineteenth-century account implies that the credit used to finance military operations included not only advances of arms and ammunition to the king from European traders, but also cash advances to subordinate officers (more probably from local sources) to cover their subsistence expenses. An officer of the royal army of female soldiers ("Amazons") was reported as saying, during a debate at the Dahomean court on where the next major campaign should be launched, "For my part I am in debt for my provisions for last war, I must go again to get money."[62]

It also appears that Dahomean merchants as well as Europeans and Brazilians were called upon to finance the operations of the state. In the second half of the nineteenth century, when the monarchy was experiencing severe financial difficulties, due partly to the fiscal problems posed by the ending of the Atlantic slave trade, Europeans reported recurrent complaints not only of increased taxation, but also irregular (and allegedly arbitrary) financial impositions, directed especially at the wealthy merchants of Whydah. At least one account describes these as taking the form of "forced loans [sous forme d'emprunt forcé]."[63] Such "loans" to the king were, however, often effectively irrecoverable.[64]

Enforcement

The prominent role played by credit implies the existence of (normally) effective mechanisms for the enforcement of debt repayment. In an earlier publication I drew attention to the practice of enforcing repayment by "panyarring," i.e., seizing a person who might be sold to clear the debt, which was practiced in early times, but apparently suppressed under Dahomean rule.[65] One late nineteenth-century account which has since come to my attention does, in fact, explicitly record the abolition of these traditional practices in Dahomey,

---

59 See Law, "On Pawning and Enslavement for Debt," 60–2, 64–5.

60 E.g., Bosman, *New and Accurate Description*, 391.

61 Foà, *Le Dahomey*, 249.

62 F.E. Forbes, *Dahomey and the Dahomans* (London, 1851), 2:95.

63 Dr. Repin, "Voyage au Dahomey," *Le Tour du Monde* 11, no. 1 (1863):100.

64 See Iroko, "Les cauris," 432–5.

65 Law, "On Pawning and Enslavement for Debt," 65–7.

attributing to King Glele (1858–89) an edict forbidding the extension of credit, or more precisely prohibiting, on pain of imprisonment or execution, any action by creditors to recover their debts. This prohibition applied to Europeans as well as Dahomeans: "The king told them that they would have no recourse as creditors against the debtor; it was up to them not to trust the natives."[66] It seems unlikely, however, that this edict was introduced as late as Glele' s reign; he was probably only reiterating or reinforcing a pre-existing law. There is, in fact, record of a proclamation by an earlier king of Dahomey, Kpengla, in 1781, "to forbid his people getting into white men's debts," which may allude to an earlier, similar edict.[67] Nor is the edict attributed to Glele to be understood as abolishing all recourse for creditors (and far less as outlawing all credit), but rather as prohibiting private action as opposed to action through the royal courts, which certainly continued to hear debt cases. Swanzey in the 1870s, for example, reports that in Dahomey the King "has supreme power in cases of debt," and might order the sale of the debtor and all his family into slavery.[68]

The suppression of the right to private action against debtors is consistent with the general tendency of the Dahomean monarchy to assert a monopoly of judicial authority. There is a closely parallel tradition about the treatment of theft, that private citizens had originally been allowed by law to kill thieves taken in the act, but that an early (seventeenth-century) King of Dahomey, Wegbaja, prohibited the practice and reserved the right of capital punishment to himself.[69] However, the implication in these accounts that the Kings of Dahomey innovated in prohibiting private action may be misleading. In contemporary sources the evidence for the "panyarring" of persons to recover debts related specifically to Whydah.[70] In Allada, by contrast, the French in 1670 did not venture to assume responsibility for such sanctions, but appealed to the King, who enforced payment by threatening to seize (and presumably, if necessary, sell) wives from the debtors.[71] In my earlier published study, I implicitly equated this threat of seizure by the King of Allada with the Whydah practice of "panyarring," but there is evidently a material difference between the two. It may be argued further that this difference reflected a broader contrast between the nature of judicial and political order in the two kingdoms. In Whydah, the tradition of private justice persisted: for example, private citizens there, Europeans included, were allowed to kill, or sell as

---

[66] Foà, *Le Dahomey*, 248–9.

[67] Public Record Office, London: T70/1162, Day Book, William's Fort, Whydah, 30 Nov. 1781.

[68] Swanzey, "On the trade in West Africa," 482.

[69] A. Le Herissé, *L'ancien royaume du Dahomey* (Paris, 1911), 289.

[70] For references, see Law, "On pawning and enslavement for debt," 62–3.

[71] Delbée, "Journal," 2:426.

slaves, thieves caught in the act.[72] By contrast, in Allada (as later in Dahomey) royal authority was stronger, and the King asserted a monopoly of justice, which included entailed jurisdiction over the handling of cases of debt.

In Dahomey the attractiveness of seeking redress through the King's court was mitigated by the fact that if the appeal were successful, the King retained half of the amount recovered.[73] In any case, the King's attitude toward the enforcement of debt repayment was sometimes ambivalent. In the 1780s, when Kpengla confiscated the property of a wealthy female trader at Whydah, it is reported that "her debtors were obliged to pay whatever was due to her; but her creditors demands against her were scouted "—evidently, in order to maximize the financial advantage to the king.[74] Similarly, when de Souza died in 1849, his son and successor as Chacha, Isidoro de Souza, was instructed "to pay the 'legal' debts of his father, but not his debts to slave-dealers." Although the meaning of "legal" in this context is unclear (and the British officer who reported it seems to have understood it to mean debts owed to "legitimate" [i.e. non-slave] traders), it was probably de Souza's debts to the King which were to be enforced, so as to safeguard the latter's interests.[75]

Financial Records

Another question arising from the incidence of credit in both the local economy and the overseas trade is the nature of the indigenous system of record-keeping. In Allada the local people, it was noted in 1670, in the absence of writing used knotted strings to keep records of various matters, including commercial transactions ("the price of goods").[76] Several later accounts allude to other mechanical devices for keeping financial (and fiscal) records in Dahomey. After the conquest of Allada in 1724, the King's officers counted the captives taken (over 8,000) by "giving a booge [cowrie] to every one."[77] An English trader visiting the Dahomean court in 1772 recorded that the royal gunner showed him a calabash containing fifteen pebbles to indicate the number of cannon fired in a salute in his honour.[78] When a British mission visited Abomey in 1850, in order (among other things) to assess the King's expenditure at the "Annual Customs," as a basis for estimating the compensa-

---

[72] See Law, *Slave Coast*, 90–1.

[73] Swanzey, "On the Trade in West Africa," 482; see also Burton, *Mission to Gelele*, 1:211.

[74] Dalzel, *History of Dahomy*, 210.

[75] Forbes, *Dahomey and the Dahomans*, 1:106.

[76] Delbée, "Journal," 2:440.

[77] Letter of Bulfinch Lambe, Abomey, to Jeremiah Tinker, Whydah, 27 November 1724, in William Smith, *A New Voyage to Guinea* (London, 1744), 187.

[78] Robert Norris, *Memoirs of the Reign of Bossa Ahadee, King of Dahomy* (London, 1789), 91–2.

tion which might be offered him for renouncing the slave trade, his officials offered their accounts in the form of baskets of cowries, a single shell representing each "head" of cowries (2,000) or unit of other goods distributed.[79] The British Consul Richard Burton in 1864 described the Mehu, the official in charge of state finances, as managing the affairs of Dahomey "with the poor mnemonical aid of a few beans or seeds."[80]

These accounts lend credibility to the traditions collected by Herskovits in the 1930s, of the use by Dahomean authorities of pebbles to record a census of population conducted as the basis for assessing military levies, and in the assessment and recording of tax payments.[81] For present purposes it does not matter whether the supposed census represented (as Herskovits supposed) a real count, an informed estimate, or indeed merely a conventional (or symbolic) figure.[82] No contemporary account documents the use of such methods specifically for the recording of debts. Local tradition in the Dahomey area does, however, recall the use of various devices to record debts, including knotted strings (each knot representing a bag of 20,000 cowries), wooden tallies, and pieces of cloth marked with indigo.[83]

Bills of Exchange

The European trade introduced into the Slave Coast a new kind of record for credit transactions: the written promissory note. Such written notes existed in parts of West Africa in pre-European times, being introduced from the Islamic world—as witnessed by the famous "cheque" drawn on a merchant of Awdaghost in the tenth century, seen by Ibn Hawqal.[84] By the nineteenth century, such promissory notes were evidently common in the Islamic interior of West Africa. The British explorer Clapperton, for example, was able in Kano in 1826 to settle a liability by writing a "bill of exchange" (apparently drawn on the British Consulate in Tripoli) for $500; and in Sokoto the following year his assistant Lander received in exchange for goods an "order" for 245,000 cowries drawn upon a merchant of Kano.[85] It is doubtful,

---

79 House of Commons, "Papers Relative to the Reduction of Lagos," *Sessional Papers,1852*, journal of Lieutenant Forbes, 29 May and 2 July 1850, vol. 54 enclosure 3 in no. 1; also Forbes, *Dahomey and the Dahomans*, 2:30–1, 183–4.

80 Burton, *Mission to Gelele*, 1:223.

81 Melville J. Herskovits, *Dahomey: An Ancient West African Kingdom*, (New York, 1938), 2:72–9; for the use of pebbles in the assessment and recording of taxes, see also 1:17–33.

82 For a critique of Herskovits's account of the Dahomean census, see W.J. Argyle, *The Fon of Dahomey*, (Oxford, 1966), especially 97–9.

83 Iroko, "Les cauris," 416–21.

84 Nehemia Levtzion, "Ibn Hawqal, the Cheque and Awdaghost," *Journal of African History* 9, no. 2 (1968):223–33.

85 Hugh Clapperton, *Journal of a Second Expedition into the Interior of Africa* (London, 1829), 173, 179; see also Austin, "Indigenous Credit Institutions," 104–5.

however, whether the use of such Arabic bills of exchange ever spread southwards into the Dahomey area. Literate Muslim traders certainly operated there, and one of these in 1845 gave a British explorer a written letter of introduction to another Muslim merchant trading for slaves in the interior,[86] but there is no specific evidence of commercial letters of credit in Arabic.

By the 1690s, however, traders in Whydah were accepting written "notes" from Europeans for goods due them.[87] In the immediate aftermath of the conquest of Whydah in 1727, the King of Dahomey's traders, evidently unfamiliar with this practice, showed a marked lack of confidence in such documents: "these Dahome traders would come ten times a day with their notes," declaring that "they did not like a bit of paper for their slaves, because the writing might vanish from it; or else the notes might be lost, and then they should lose their payment," and they were not mollified by assurances that their dues were recorded separately in the trader's book.[88] Subsequently, however, such written notes again became standard. The Danish account of 1784, for example, makes clear that local traders were given written "notes of credit" for the goods owed them; and the English trader of 1803 that the Whydah traders, far from insisting on immediate payment in goods, "prefer promissory notes, or books, as they call them, expressing the different articles which have been agreed upon as the price," pending settlement at the conclusion of trade.[89]

By the late nineteenth century, written promissory notes were also being accepted from European traders in Dahomey for the payment of customs duties to the king. These duties had previously been paid in cowries, but from the 1870s, King Glele ordered that his royal officials should instead take vouchers (*bons*) for the value due. These were kept in a chest at the local administrative office, and exchanged for goods at the European traders' factories as the need arose. Such vouchers were often left unredeemed for considerable periods—up to two years at Whydah and twelve at Cotonou—and at the time of the French occupation in 1892, the vouchers held by Dahomean officials at the lagoonside port of Abomey-Calavi represented an accumulated value of $1,000, equivalent to the customs duty on around 667 puncheons of palm oil.[90] This shift from payment in cowries to promissory notes was probably

[86] John Duncan, *Travels in Western Africa* (London, 1847), 2:178–9.

[87] Thomas Phillips, "Journal of a voyage in the *Hannibal* of London, ann. 1693, 1694," in *Collection of Voyages and Travels*, ed. Awnsham Churchill and John Churchill (London, 1732), 6:218; Bosman, in Van Dantzig, "English Bosman and Dutch Bosman—VI," 285.

[88] Snelgrave, *New Account*, 87–8.

[89] Isert, *Letters on West Africa*, 98; M'Leod, *Voyage to Africa*, 89.

[90] "Extraits des procès-verbaux du Conseil d'Administration de la Colonie du Dahomey et Dépendances," 17–25 August 1897, in Hélène d'Almeida-Topor, *Histoire Économique du Dahomey (Bénin) (1890–1920)* (Paris, 1995), 2:277–8.

due to the runaway inflation of the cowrie currency in the second half of the nineteenth century, which must have posed considerable fiscal problems for the state.[91]

Such written notes of credit were also acceptable in non-commercial contexts. In 1787, for example, when the Director of the French fort at Whydah arranged the ransom of some Europeans captured in a Dahomean raid on Porto-Novo to the east, the Dahomeans accepted his "notes "for the goods stipulated (amounting to the value £4,600).[92] Likewise, the British Consul Richard Burton, on a diplomatic mission to Abomey in 1864, finding himself required to provide customary gifts for some of the king's military officers at the Annual Customs, wrote out a "promissory note" for $150.[93]

Furthermore, it appears that such notes of credit were negotiable, being accepted for payment in transactions between Dahomeans; as was noted in connection with the incident of 1787, "they pass current with the natives as money."[94]

Pre-Colonial Banks?

One consequence of the introduction of the cowrie currency was to facilitate the storage of wealth, since the shells were relatively imperishable. In Dahomey, large quantities of cowries were commonly held by the wealthy. Most visibly, the King's palace at Abomey included a two-storey building called the "cowrie house" (*akuehue*), noted by several nineteenth-century European visitors.[95] Although the most frequently mentioned practice relating to this building was adorning it with strings of cowries as a display of royal wealth during the Annual Customs, it clearly served as a storehouse for the king's wealth in cowries and goods. As such, it is plausibly interpreted as a "treasury," where cowries received in taxation or through royal commercial enterprise were stored, and from which they were later disbursed for various purposes of state.[96] It is less clear, however, whether this royal "treasury" operated in any sense as a central bank. It has been suggested that the cowrie currency in Dahomey was "centrally issued," the state regulating its importation into the country, but this is unwarranted.[97] Although the royal palace is said to have had a monopoly over the issue of

---

[91] For inflation and its consequences, see further Robin Law, "Cowries, Gold and Dollars: Exchange Rate Instability and Domestic Price Inflation in Dahomey in the Eighteenth and Nineteenth Centuries," in *Money Matters*, Guyer, ed., 53–73.

[92] Dalzel, *History of Dahomy*, 195.

[93] Burton, *Mission to Gelele*, 2:225.

[94] Dalzel, *History of Dahomy*, 195.

[95] E.g., Burton, *Mission to Gelele*, 1:291–2.

[96] See Iroko, "Les cauris," 464–5.

[97] Polanyi, *Dahomey and the Slave Trade*, 187–9.

strung cowries, shells also circulated loose in Dahomey,[98] and there was certainly no royal monopoly over importing them into the country.[99]

Presumably, the royal treasury made cash advances to finance the operations of the king's own traders, since they would have required cowries to meet subsistence expenses in their travels, even if their actual trade was conducted by barter. But it is not clear whether it also made loans at interest to private traders for commercial purpose, as is said to have happened in Asante.[100] There is a conceptual problem here, however, in that Dahomean political thought represented all wealth in the kingdom as belonging to the King, whereas his subjects enjoyed only its temporary use. In expression of this principle, on the death of any chief or head of family, his wealth reverted to the king, who restored it to the heir only after deducting a share as a form of death duty. It is sometimes suggested that this royal right of inheritance was largely "fictitious," with the bulk of the estate passing to the heir,[101] but on merchant estates at least, both contemporary and traditional evidence confirms that the inheritance tax was very high. According to an account of 1848, the heir received back only "a very small portion of the estate."[102] Other sources, including local tradition recently recorded in Whydah, give the King's share as three-quarters.[103] From this perspective, all private wealth was, in a sense, on loan from the royal treasury. This concept is explicitly expressed in the contemporary account of 1848: "His headmen and others who have been amassing property by this [slave] traffic, have only been acting as so many factors to the King," and the small quantity of slaves and cowries restored to the heir "serves as a species of capital for him to commence, in like manner, his factorship."[104]

It seems clear that the royal treasury was just an especially large example of a more general phenomenon. Oral tradition recalls what might in any case be hypothesized on grounds of inherent probability, i.e., that many wealthy individuals in Dahomey kept large stores of cowries in special buildings in their compounds (called *akueho*, "cowrie huts") designed for protection against fire (with high roofs) and theft. Iroko has recently argued that such storehouses functioned as a form of banking system *(système banquaire)* in pre-colonial times. Their owners are said to have served regularly as "money-

---

98 Dalzel, *History of Dahomy*, xii.

99 See Robin Law, "Posthumous Questions for Karl Polanyi: Price Inflation in Pre-Colonial Dahomey," *Journal of African History* 33, no. 3 (1992):391–3.

100 Austin, "Indigenous Credit Institutions," 103–4.

101 Le Herissé, *L'ancien royaume du Dahomey*, 85.

102 House of Commons, "Missions to the King of Ashantee & Dahomey," *Sessional Papers*, 1849, report by B. Cruickshank, 18 November 1848, vol. 34.

103 Foà, *Le Dahomey*, 26; De Souza, *La famille de Souza*, 22, 59 (but see p. 43, where the figure is given as only two-thirds).

104 House of Commons, "Missions to the King of Ashantee."

holders" [*akuehinto* (which Iroko seeks to translate as "banker")] for others who deposited their own cowries in their wealthier neighbours' storehouses for greater security; and such deposits might be employed in turn by the money-holder in loans to third parties.[105] Even as here described, there is an obvious difference between this practice and modern banking conventions: the money-holder charged his depositors for the service of using his storehouse rather than offering interest to attract their funds. It may also be suggested that oral recollections have in this instance been influenced or distorted by the explicit analogy with modern banking.

That funds were placed on deposit with others for purposes of security is not to be doubted. One such instance is recorded in a contemporary account, in the context of the irregular expropriatory visitations by royal officials for which Dahomey became notorious in the second half of the nineteenth century. In Whydah on one occasion in the early 1860s, under threat of such official extortion, a number of people lodged their savings in cowries with the French Catholic mission (then occupying the Portuguese fort), and left them there for nearly two months.[106] But this was evidently just a temporary expedient. It is quite conceivable that similar arrangements were made with local merchants on a commercial basis for longer-term deposits, but what we know about the status and situation of merchant wealth in Whydah more generally makes it difficult to envisage how such a system of "banking" could have offered any real security during the second half of the nineteenth century, with both the heavy death duties levied on merchant wealth and the recurrent arbitrary confiscations of assets when families fell into political disfavour. The latter happened during the 1880s, for example, with both the Quénums and de Souzas, respectively the leading native Dahomean and Brazilian merchant families of Whydah.[107]

Treasures in cowries were especially vulnerable to royal attention, because their bulk made them difficult to conceal—this was indeed cited by King Gezo to a visiting French mission in 1856 as one of the reasons why he preferred to retain the cowrie currency rather than substituting metal coins.[108] Furthermore, it cannot plausibly be supposed that the Dahomean authorities would in such cases have respected the distinction between funds held on deposit for others and a merchant's own property; their attitude in the case of Jacinto da Costa Santos in 1876, cited above, suggests that they would have seized both indiscriminately. Moreover, as noted earlier Dahomey endured a catastrophic

---

105 Iroko, "Les cauris," 394–439; on the question of "banking and quasi-banking operations" by deposit-holders and money-lenders in the pre-colonial period, see also Austin, "Indigenous Credit Institutions," 105–6.

106 Abbé Laffitte, *Le Dahomé* (Tours, 1874), 81; cited in Iroko, "Les cauris," 399.

107 See Maximilien Quénum, *Les ancêtres de la famille Quénum* (Langres, 1981), 79; de Souza, *La famille de Souza*, 56.

108 A. Vallon, "Le royaume de Dahomey," *Revue Maritime et Coloniale* 2 (1860):343.

inflation of its cowrie currency in the later nineteenth century which would have rapidly devalued stocks of cowries, and would surely have discouraged both the storing and lending of money.[109]

Tontines

At a lower level of affluence, one of the principal indigenous credit institutions in West Africa in recent times has been the rotational credit association, generally referred to in francophone African usage as the "tontine." Such associations are especially strong in Yorubaland east of Dahomey, where they are known as *esusu*.[110] They certainly existed there in pre-colonial times. The missionary Samuel Crowther in 1856, for example, attested that "the system of savings clubs is universal in the Yoruba country;"[111] in one single town, Abeokuta, there were said to be no fewer than 300 such savings clubs in 1860.[112] However, the extent to which such credit associations existed elsewhere in West Africa independently of Yoruba influence, and prior to the twentieth century, may be questioned.[113] A recent study maintains that in Igboland "all sources insist that the [institution] is indigenous ... and had developed long before the establishment of colonial rule," but the name of the institution there, *isusu*, seems transparently a loanword from Yoruba.[114]

In the Dahomey area, Iroko argues on the basis of oral tradition that tontines (*gbekue*, "money clubs," in Fon) existed as early as the pre-colonial period.[115] Although there is to my knowledge no evidence of such credit associations then, this by itself in no way disproves their existence. Given the limited and haphazard documentation of the purely domestic economy in contemporary European accounts, such negative evidence can by itself hardly be decisive. The earliest known reference to the existence of tontines in Dahomey (though lacking any details of their operation) is in a work by a local scholar published in 1936.[116] It is disquieting, however, that there is no reference to credit associations in the classic ethnographic account of

[109] Late nineteenth-century inflation might possibly explain the very high interest rates (of 200–250% for two to three months) noted by Iroko, "Les cauris," 426.

[110] See Toyin Falola, "Money and Informal Credit Institutions in Colonial Western Nigeria," in *Money Matters*, Guyer, ed., 162–87.

[111] Letter of Samuel Crowther to T.J. Hutchinson, 10 September 1856, pp. 277–8 in Hutchinson, *Impressions of Western Africa* (London, 1858); see also Samuel Johnson, *The History of the Yorubas* (London, 1921), 119 (written in the 1890s).

[112] John Iliffe, *The African Poor: A History* (Cambridge, 1987), 87.

[113] See Austin, "Indigenous Credit Institutions," 102.

[114] Anthony I. Nwabughuoghu, "The *Isusu*: An Institution for Capital Formation among the Ngwa Igbo: Its Origin and Development," *Africa* 54 (1984):46–58.

[115] Iroko, "Les cauris," 389–93.

[116] Quénum, *Au pays des Fon*, 130.

Dahomey by Herskovits, based on fieldwork earlier in the 1930s, though this discusses "associations for mutual self-help" at some length.[117] Perhaps, therefore, the institution was then a recent introduction, rather than part of the traditional social order.

At a minimum, the hypothesis that the tontine did not exist in pre-colonial Dahomey deserves to be taken seriously. The absence of tontines would parallel that of other forms of private cooperation like secret societies for the suppression of theft and witchcraft, such as existed among the Yoruba. Local tradition affirms, in fact, that the king's subjects were prohibited from contracting ritual oaths with one another.[118] This stunting of private cooperative institutions seems to be correlated with the strength of the monarchy, and may indeed be the result of conscious policy. The rationale was, indeed, perceived by at least one contemporary observer of the eighteenth century, who noted in a different context that the kings of Dahomey wished "that there may be no ... associations, that might be injurious to the king's unlimited power. Hence, each individual is detached, and unconnected."[119] In any case, it should be noted that, in these as in very many other matters, extrapolation from twentieth-century conditions to the pre-colonial period is hazardous.

Conclusion

Despite the importance of credit in both overseas trade and the domestic economy, it is questionable whether specialized financial institutions ever developed in pre-colonial Dahomey. Economic relationships and transactions remained largely personal and informal, while to the extent that they were formalized, financial institutions were not sharply differentiated from others. While the state in its fiscal and judicial operations can perhaps be thought of as having features that resembled those of discrete financial institutions, its own centralizing authority left little room for the emergence of such institutions in the private sector. And the power of the state was itself circumscribed in financial matters by its effective lack of control over the money supply. In the nineteenth century, inflation due to the excessive importation of cowries created severe problems both for the financial operations of the state and for private transactions, and probably tended to undermine the operation of trade and credit in Dahomey.

---

[117] Herskovits, *Dahomey*, 1:63–77. It may be noted that there is likewise no mention of rotating credit associations in a later discussion (based on fieldwork in the 1950s) of the sources of capital to finance women's trading activities in the Dahomey area: Claudine Tardits and Claude Tardits, "Traditional Market Economy in Southern Dahomey," in *Markets in Africa*, ed. George Dalton (Evanston, 1962), 94–5.

[118] Hazoumé, *Le pacte de sang au Dahomey*, 136–7.

[119] Norris, *Memoirs of Bossa Ahadee*, 89.

Bibliography

Agbo, Casimir. *Histoire de Ouidah du XVIe au XXe siècle.* Avignon, 1959.

Akinjogbin, I.A. *Dahomey and Its Neighbours 1708–1818.* Cambridge, 1967.

Argyle, W.J. *The Fon of Dahomey.* Oxford, 1966.

Austin, Gareth. "Indigenous Credit Institutions in West Africa, c. 1750–1960," in *Local Suppliers of Credit in the Third World, 1750–1960,* ed. Gareth Austin and Kaoru Sugihara, 93–159. Basingstoke, 1993.

Boogaart, Ernst van den and Emmer, Pieter. "The Dutch Participation in the Atlantic Slave Trade, 1596–1650," in *The Uncommon Market: Essays in the Economic History of the Atlantic Slave Trade,* ed. Henry A. Gemery and Jan S. Hogedorn, 353–75. New York, 1979.

[Borghero, Francesco]. *Journal de Francesco Borghero, premier missionnaire au Dahomey (1861–1865),* ed. Renzo Mandirola and Yves Morel. Paris, 1997.

Bosman, William. *A New and Accurate Description of the Coast of Guinea.* London, 1905.

Burton, Richard. *A Mission to Gelele, King of Dahome.* Vol 1. London, 1864.

Clapperton, Hugh. *Journal of a Second Expedition into the Interior of Africa.* London, 1829.

Coquery, Catherine. "Le blocus de Whydah (1876–1877) et la rivalité franco-anglaise au Dahomey." *Cahiers d'Études Africaines* 2 (1962):373–419.

Daaku, K.Y. *Trade and Politics on the Gold Coast 1600–1720.* Oxford, 1970.

d'Almeida-Topor, Hélène. *Histoire économique du Dahomey (Bénin) (1890–1920).* Vol. 2. Paris, 1995.

Dalzel, Archibald. *The History of Dahomy.* London, 1793.

Dantzig, Albert van, ed. *The Dutch on the Guinea Coast 1674–1742: A Collection of Documents from the General State Archive at The Hague.* Accra, 1978.

—. "English Bosman and Dutch Bosman: A Comparison of Texts--VI", *History in Africa* 7 (1980):281–91.

Dapper, Olfert. *Naukeurige Beschrijvinge der Afrikaensche Gewesten.* 2d ed. Amsterdam, 1676.

[Delbée]. "Journal du voyage du Sieur Delbée," in *Relation de ce qui s'est passé dans les Isles et Terre-ferme de l'Amérique pendant la dernière guerre avec l'Angleterre.* Vol. 2. Ed. J. de Clodoré, 347–558. Paris, 1671.

Djivo, Adrien. "Le roi Glèlè et les Européens: L'échec du protectorat portugais sur le Danhomè (1885–1887)," *Cahiers du Centre de Recherches Africaines* 8 (1994):269–84.

Duncan, John. *Travels in Western Africa.* Vol. 2. London, 1847.

Falola, Toyin. "Money and Informal Credit Institutions in Colonial Western Nigeria," in *Money Matters: Instability, Values and Social Payments in the Modern History of West African Communities,* ed. Jane I. Guyer, 162–87. Portsmouth, New Hampshire, 1994.

Falola, Toyin and Paul E. Lovejoy, eds. *Pawnship in Africa: Debt Bondage in Historical Perspective.* Boulder, Colorado, 1994.

Foà, Édouard. *Le Dahomey.* Paris, 1894.

Forbes, F.E. *Dahomey and the Dahomans.* Vol. 2. London, 1851.

Guyer, Jane I., ed. *Money Matters: Instability, Values and Social Payments in the Modern History of West African Communities.* Portsmouth, New Hampshire, 1994.

Hazoumé, Paul. *Le pacte de sang au Dahomey.* Paris, 1937.

Herskovits, Melville J. *Dahomey: An Ancient West African Kingdom.* 2 vols. New York, 1938.

Hutchinson, T.J. *Impressions of Western Africa*. London, 1858.

Iliffe, John. *The African Poor: A History*. Cambridge, 1987.

Iroko, Félix Abiola. "Les cauris en Afrique occidentale du Xe au XXe siècle," Thèse de Doctorat d'État, Université de Paris I, 1987.

Isert, Paul Erdman. *Letters on West Africa and the Slave Trade*, trans. Selena Axelrod Winsnes. Oxford, 1992.

Johnson, Samuel. *The History of the Yorubas*. London, 1921.

Jones, Adam, ed. *West Africa in the Mid-Seventeenth Century: An Anonymous Dutch Manuscript*. African Studies Association Press, 1995.

Kea, Ray A. *Settlements, Trade and Polities in the Seventeenth-Century Gold Coast*, Baltimore, 1982.

Labat, Jean-Baptiste. *Voyage du Chevalier des Marchais en Guinée, isles voisines et à Cayenne*. 2d ed. Vol. 2. Amsterdam, 1731.

Laffitte, Abbé. *Le Dahomé*. Tours, 1874.

Law, Robin. "Cowries, Gold and Dollars: Exchange Rate Instability and Domestic Price Inflation in the Eighteenth and Nineteenth Centuries," in *Money Matters: Instability, Values and Social Payments in the Modern History of West African Communities*, ed. Jane I. Guyer, 53–73. Portsmouth, New Hampshire, 1994.

—. "On Pawning and Enslavement for Debt in the Pre-Colonial Slave Coast," in *Pawnship in Africa: Debt Bondage in Historical Perspective*, ed. Toyin Falola and Paul E. Lovejoy, 55–69. Boulder, Colorado, 1994

—. "The Slave Trade in Seventeenth-Century Allada: A Revision." *African Economic History* 22 (1994):59–92.

—. "Posthumous Questions for Karl Polanyi: Price Inflation in Pre-Colonial Dahomey." *Journal of African History* 33, no. 3 (1992): 387–420.

—. ed. *Further Correspondence of the Royal African Company of England relating to the "Slave Coast", 1681–1699*. Madison: African Studies Program, University of Wisconsin, 1992.

—. *The Slave Coast of West Africa 1550–1750*. Oxford, 1991.

—. ed. *Correspondence from the Royal African Company's Factories at Offra and Whydah on the Slave Coast of West Africa in the Public Record Office, London, 1678–93*. Edinburgh: Centre of African Studies, University of Edinburgh, 1990.

Le Herissé, A. *L'ancien royaume du Dahomey*. Paris, 1911.

Levtzion, Nehemia. "Ibn Hawqal, the Cheque and Awdaghost." *Journal of African History* 9, no. 2 (1968):223–33.

Manning, Patrick. *Slavery, Colonialism and Economic Growth in Dahomey 1640–1960*. Cambridge, 1982.

Marees, Pieter de. *Description and Historical Account of the Gold Kingdom of Guinea*, trans. Albert van Dantzig and Adam Jones. Oxford, 1987.

M'Leod, John. *A Voyage to Africa*. London, 1820.

Newbury, C.W. "Credit in Early Nineteenth Century West African Trade." *Journal of African History* 13, no. 1 (1972):81–95

—. *The Western Slave Coast and its Rulers*. Oxford, 1961.

Norris, Robert. *Memoirs of the Reign of Bossa Ahadee, King of Dahomy*. London, 1789.

Nwabughuoghu, Anthony. "The *Isusu*, An Institution for Capital Formation Among the Ngwa Igbo: Its Origin and Development." *Africa* 54 (1984):46–58.

Phillips, Thomas. "Journal of a voyage in the *Hannibal* of London, ann. 1693, 1694," in *Collection of Voyages & Travels.* Vol. 6. Ed. Awnsham Churchill and John Churchill, 173–239. London, 1732.

Polanyi, Karl. *Dahomey and the Slave Trade*. Seattle, 1966.

Public Record Office. *Records of the African Companies.* T70. London, 1871.

Quénum, Maximilien. *Les ancêtres de la famille Quénum.* Langres, 1981.

—. *Au pays des Fon,* 3d ed. Paris, 1983.

Repin, Dr. "Voyage au Dahomey." *Le Tour du Monde* 1, no. 1 (1863):65–112.

Ryder, A.F.C. *Benin and the Europeans 1485–1897.* London, 1969.

Smith, William. *A New Voyage to Guinea*. London, 1744.

Snelgrave, William. *A New Account of Some Parts of Guinea.* London, 1734.

Souza, Simone de. *La famille de Souza du Bénin–Togo*. Cotonou, 1992.

Swanzey, A. "On the Trade in West Africa." *Journal of the Society of Arts* 22 (1874):478–87.

Tardits, Claudine and Claude Tardits. "Traditional Market Economy in Southern Dahomey," in *Markets in Africa*, ed. George Dalton, 89–102. Evanston, 1962.

United Kingdom. House of Commons. "Missions to the King of Ashantee and Dahomey." *Sessional Papers, 1849.* Vol. 34.

United Kingdom. House of Commons. "Correspondence relating to the Slave Trade 1849–1850." *Sessional Papers, 1850.* Vol. 55.

United Kingdom. House of Commons. "Papers relative to the Reduction of Lagos." *Sessional Papers, 1852.* Vol. 54.

United Kingdom. House of Commons. "Despatches from Commodore Wilmot respecting his Visit to the King of Dahomey." *Sessional Papers, 1863.* Vol. 73.

Vallon, A. "Le royaume de Dahomey," *Revue Maritime et Coloniale* 2, (1860):332–63.

Verger, Pierre. *Les afro-américains*. Dakar, 1952.

On Currency and Credit in the Western Sahel, 1700–1850

James L.A. Webb, Jr.

The Western Sahel, situated along the southern edge of the western Sahara, was a transitional ecological region which connected the desert with the open wooded grasslands of the savannah, and displayed remarkable ecological and cultural diversity.[1] It encompassed a relatively arid northern sub-region inhabited by Arabo-Berber pastoral nomads and a more humid southern sub-region of Black African sedentary peoples.[2] By the eighteenth century, patterns of regional exchange and long-distance trade had long been established. Desert-edge exchange between pastoralists and agriculturalists probably began in a very early period, with the organization of specialized herding economies. And from the second half of the first millenium C.E. camel caravans linked the Western Sahel with North Africa as well as with the Black African states of the savannah and, to the east, the Niger Bend region. The Portuguese opened commercial relations along the Atlantic coast of the Western Sahel in the mid-fifteenth century, to be followed there by a succession of other European national trading groups.

This essay sketches out the broad outlines of the Western Sahelian experiences with currency and credit during the eighteenth and first half of the nineteenth centuries. These experiences are instructive for comparative purposes, because Western Sahelian merchants traded with North African, Black African, and Atlantic European markets, and these markets were located in distinct currency zones, where different currencies (or currency clusters) predominated. Indeed, many Western Sahelian traders carried out their commercial operations in two or three currency zones—the monetized metal zone centered in the Islamic Mediterranean to the north; the cowry zone in sub-Saharan Africa to the east and south; and the zone of mixed commodity money, principally of glassware, iron, silver coin, and cloth, along the Atlantic coast to the west. These currency zones had discrete boundaries, or frontiers, past

---

[1] The author would like to thank Ralph Austen, Sara Berry, Endre Stiansen, Jan Hogendorn, John Hunwick, Michael LaRue, Ghislaine Lydon, and Chuck Schaefer for their comments on an earlier version of this essay presented at the Seminar on Financial Institutions in Africa at Northwestern University and at the 1997 African Studies Association annual meeting. Jane Guyer and Endre Stiansen provided exceptionally close readings and valuable critiques on the final drafts.

[2] James L.A. Webb, Jr., *Desert Frontier: Ecological and Economic Change Along the Western Sahel, 1600–1850* (University of Wisconsin Press: Madison, 1995), 3–14.

which the currencies which predominated in one zone became either less culturally acceptable or too expensive due to transport costs. All three of the zones converged in the Western Sahel, where merchants and brokers could stockpile currencies and transfer value from one currency form to another, trading back and forth into the different zones.

The monetary environment was additionally complex because credit was extended across the currency frontiers to economic actors belonging to different cultural communities.[3] This pattern was due in part to cultural, climatic, and epidemiological barriers which imposed high costs on specific groups. Europeans and Black Africans who ventured into the Sahara risked enslavement by Arabo-Berber pastoral nomads. Europeans and North Africans who travelled in sub-Sahelian Africa ran grave risks from malaria and other fevers, particularly during the rainy season. Western Sahelian merchants themselves ran some of these same risks—for instance, that of heightened mortality in sub-Sahelian Africa (and upon rare occasions of enslavement by coastal Europeans)—but at a much lower level. Merchants from all three communities were acutely aware of these perils and acted to limit their exposure.

Currency Zones and Frontiers

The three currency zones had distinctive histories. Gold and silver emerged early in the premodern era as metals highly valued by societies across the breadth of the Eurasian continent, and indeed the common valuation of these metals is one indication of the early integration of the Eurasian ecumene, achieved through an increase in overland trade and the consolidation of large empires.[4] The extension of the cowry zone in the Indian Ocean and Southeast Asian tropics was a later phenomenon, but it too attests to an increasing intensity of intersocietal contact, largely as a result of an increase in maritime trade. The introduction of the cowry to West Africa, however, represents a different chapter in this history, because West Africa was not contiguous with the rest of the tropical cowry zone. The West African cowry zone began to form only in the middle centuries of the second millenium C.E., and its principal expansion took place during the heyday of the Atlantic slave trade. The Atlantic zone of glassware, iron, silver coin, and cloth evolved after the mid-fifteenth century European maritime exploration of the Western Sahelian coast. By 1700 this currency zone was of truly heterodox composition: European glassware ephemera; iron, a metal universally-valued for the production

---

[3] For an effort to draw together available evidence on West African credit during the late pre-colonial period and colonial period, see Gareth Austin, "Indigenous Credit Institutions in West Africa, c. 1750–c.1960," in *Local Suppliers of Credit in the Third World, 1750–1960*, ed. Gareth Austin and Kaoru Sugihara (London, 1993), 93–159.

[4] Jerry H. Bentley surveys other aspects of this process in "Hemispheric Integration, 500–1500 C.E.," *Journal of World History* 9, no. 2 (1998):237–254.

of weapons and agricultural implements; silver coin, valued across the Eurasian ecumene; and cotton cloth from the sub-continent of India, arguably the economic powerhouse of the early modern world.

Why the monetized metal zone of the Eurasian ecumene did not extend further into the Western Sahel or beyond into the West African savannah remains somewhat a matter for speculation. There are several plausible lines of explanation. One is that the greater concentration of wealth in the Mediterranean world simply encouraged the outflow of gold from sub-Saharan Africa in return for Mediterranean imports deemed to be of greater local utility. Another is that the collapse in 1591 of Songhai, the last great West African savannah empire, sharply fragmented economic demand and that the continuing political violence among and within the smaller, successor Black African horse cavalry states ensured a less stable political and less productive economic environment that was more conducive to the use of commodity moneys, rather than high-value monetized metal. High transport costs across the Sahara, which helped to insulate the Western Sahel from many of the broader influences of the Mediterranean world, may also explain in part why the southern desert-edge region was not fully incorporated into Eurasian monetary culture.

The cowry zone of much of sub-Saharan Africa likewise did not extend northward into the Western Sahel. One explanation hinges on the Western Sahel's intermediate location, between the two major currency zones. The seasonal trade between the Western Sahel and the savannah was almost exclusively carried out by merchants from the desert-edge. These Western Sahelian traders active in the cowry zone appear to have preferred to export their savannah earnings in exchange goods and currencies such as slaves and gold, whose value increased with distance from the point of acquisition.

Similarly, the currencies of the Atlantic zone did not extend deeply into the interior. The principal explanation for this phenomenon must be that these currencies were more purely commodity moneys that were quickly withdrawn from the money stock for use as commodities.[5] They increased in cost as a function of distance from the coast, and the zone of their use was determined by the prices of substitute goods and the strength of demand. Glassware at some point was deemed too expensive to purchase. Imported cloth could be carried into the interior until added high transport costs rendered it uncompetitive with cloth of local production. Iron bars were transformed into spear tips and the blades of knives, axes, and hoes. Silver coin was a special case: in the more humid southern sub-region it became accepted as a currency, but in the arid northern sub-region it was reworked as jewelry.

---

[5] James L.A. Webb, Jr., "Toward the Comparative Study of Money: A Reconsideration of West African Currencies and Neoclassical Monetary Concepts," *International Journal of African Historical Studies* 15, no. 3 (1982):460–461.

Did the states in the various currency zones exert significant influence over the types of currencies used? From the vantage point of the Western Sahel, there is no evidence that state power played any significant role in the formation, maintenance, or extension of the various currency zones in the period under study. The Moroccan state was unable to extend effectively its political reach into the northern reaches of the desert, let alone the southern Saharan edge. Within the Black African horse cavalry states, the political elites were engaged in repetitive attempts to extend and consolidate their powers and carried out interstate warfare and intrastate raiding toward these ends, but there is no evidence that any political elite took an interest in the types of currencies in use within its domain. This may have been due to the relative weakness of the political structures of the states and to the deep cultural division between merchants and warriors that characterized the broader region. There is likewise no evidence, to my knowledge, that African states in the immediately adjoining cowry zone either attempted to impose or succeeded in imposing a pattern of currency use. Even along the Atlantic coast, the European traders active there were not official representatives of the European states from which they hailed, and no European state regulations concerning currency use governed their behavior.

This lack of state influence left traders with a free hand, and the complex of currencies in use within the Western Sahel reflected the elaborate patterns of trade that had been developed by 1700. Traders used a measured weight of gold dust, the *mithqal*, in some trans-Saharan trade transactions along the northern frontier of the Western Sahara and in the Western Sahara proper,[6] cowry shells in the savannah and forest regions,[7] and to the west, along the Atlantic frontier, the glassware, iron, silver coin, and cloth introduced by European traders. At the crossroads of these three zones, imported moneys intermixed with a variety of Western Sahelian goods which might be used as commodity money—in particular, salt from the coastal and interior desert deposits, and grain from the sahelian farms.

This variety of currencies underscored the moderately high rate of commercial activity in the Western Sahel by the eighteenth century. This can be attributed to several factors. First, by the eighteenth century, a long-term cli-

[6] Marion Johnson, "The Nineteenth-Century Gold 'Mithqal' in West and North Africa," *Journal of African History* 9, no. 4 (1968):547–570; Philip D. Curtin, "Africa and the Wider Monetary World, 1250–1850," in *Precious Metals in the Later Medieval and Early Modern Worlds*, ed. J.F. Richards (Durham, N.C., 1983), 231–268. Important trade routes extended across these currency frontiers, and merchants at times simply stockpiled their surplus stocks of currency, particularly those needed in the seasonal desert-savannah trade. In the Western Sahelian town of Walata, for example, many merchants' houses had a special room set aside for storing cowries. Webb, *Desert Frontier*, 63

[7] Jan Hogendorn and Marion Johnson, *The Shell Money of the Slave Trade* (Cambridge, 1986).

matological trend toward increasing aridity had provoked increased exchange between herders and farmers, and some of this exchange was carried out by specialized commercial trading groups. Second, the Western Sahel was both the Atlantic and Saharan gateway to the gold mines of Bambuk on the Faleme River, and gold was of course sought as a monetary metal in both Europe and North Africa. Third, the demand for slave labor—from both the North African and Atlantic sectors and from the Black African states which paid for imported cavalry horses with slaves—made Black Africans a commodity for export. Slaves gathered in warfare became marketable goods along with other spoils of war. And fourth, an industrial demand in Europe for gum arabic mobilized desert people to harvest and market this arboreal exudate.

Transformations in Currency Use

There was significant change over time in currency use, particularly in the Atlantic zone. One notable, gradual transformation in commercial practice involved the decreasing use of "conceptual currencies" during the course of the eighteenth century, when the "bar" assortment bargaining system, which employed an ideal and somewhat abstract "bar" of goods as a standard of measure, and the *"pièce d'Inde,"* an abstract representation of the value of a healthy adult male slave for export, gradually disappeared from the historical record.

Other variations can be found in the demand for the tangible commodity moneys themselves. During the course of the eighteenth century, in the same way that the limited acceptance of the cowry had created a currency frontier between the West African savannah and the Western Sahel, the cumulative sub-regional preferences of sahelian and savannah merchants from central and southern Senegambia began to create variations in demand for particular kinds of currencies along the frontier of the Atlantic seabord. Europeans adjusted their commercial practices to accommodate these currency preferences. Some of these variations—for example, in the composition of the glassware goods which served as "small change"—were minor but had to be mastered by the successful Atlantic merchant. [8]

---

[8] The French trader Saugnier, who wrote a detailed account of commercial matters up the Senegal River and along the Atlantic seabord, described in some detail forty-four articles of glassware which were nearly essential to the trade and noted: "Pebbles, white, black, and red. This is the most current kind of glass-ware. It is useful among the Yolof [Wolof] nation to purchase millet, salt, &c. The Moors and the negro inhabitants of the interior part of the country, hold that commodity in high estimation. ... The above-mentioned articles of glass-ware, which of themselves are nothing, since their value is only ideal and momentary, are nevertheless indispensibly necessary in order to trade to advantage." (Saugnier and Brisson, *Voyages to the Coast of Africa* [1792; reprint, New York, 1969], 298, 299.) There were also variations in the value of the "bar," the fictive unit of account used for assortment bargaining in which iron bars and imported cloth figured prominently, as measured in silver coin. (Saugnier, *Voyages*, 291.)

The major variation, however, was in the acceptance or rejection of European specie as a currency during the eighteenth century. In the Gambia, the British began to introduce silver currency from the 1720s with considerable success. By the 1770–1820 period, silver coin largely replaced the diverse variety of commodities which made up the bar assortment system.[9] In contrast, French efforts to introduce silver coinage into the Senegal River trade to the north failed. Sahelian merchants rejected silver as a currency but accepted it as a trade good to be melted down to make jewelry. The use of silver coin as a circulating medium was restricted to the town of Saint-Louis.[10]

This sub-regional variation in demand for imported currencies, already marked by the 1780s, became still more pronounced in the course of the nineteenth century. Along the Gambia River, silver coin became both more deeply established and more widely used, in part as a result of the extensive growth in the groundnut export trade, in which large numbers of farmers participated.[11] Along the Senegal River, the broad outlines of a distinctively different transition are clear: assortment bargaining, with a marked emphasis on iron bars and a variety of imported cloth, gave way to the regular use of a standardized *guinée* from India (and later, elsewhere) as the staple currency in the Atlantic sector. This was not a radical departure; the use of *guinée* as a trade currency, and its role as the most important component of the trade "bar", had begun relatively early, perhaps in the 1730s. From the first half of the eighteenth century until the end of the nineteenth, this preference persisted; the French finally bowed to reality in the mid-nineteenth century in attempting to regulate the *guinée* because it was the principal medium of exchange. In 1843 the government of Senegal established quality standards and made it illegal to import or trade in *guinée* which did not bear the official stamp of quality, and four years later the government officially demonetized

[9] Philip D. Curtin, *Economic Change in Precolonial Africa* (Madison, WI, 1975), 269.

[10] Saugnier remarked on the varying utility of silver coin at the coastal markets at Saint Louis and Goree: "Dollars; a thing of the first consequence at Goree and without which it is impossible to trade; at Senegal, however, they can be dispensed with." (*Voyages*, 294.) He also remarked on the trade values of other goods and the expression of their value in silver currency: "It must be observed that there are articles at the colony, of which the price is fixed, and which cannot be refused in payment of the expences of the above voyage. ... Their price and currency is invariable ...The custom at Goree is totally different: there the value of bars is settled in money, and never in goods." (289–290.)

[11] In the British colony of the Gambia, beginning in 1923, this silver money stock came to be managed by a colonial currency board. See Jan S. Hogendorn and Hank A. Gemery, "Cash Cropping, Currency Acquisition and Seigniorage in West Africa, 1923–1950," *African Economic History* 11 (1982):15–27; Jan S. Hogendorn and Hank A. Gemery, "Continuity in West African Monetary History? An Outline of Monetary Development," in *African Economic History* 17 (1988):127–146.

silver and gold coin used in the Senegal River trade.[12] Silver coin was reintroduced late in the nineteenth century, and reinforced by the eventual introduction of paper fiat money, circulated by the French colonial government.

The Senegambian sub-regional currency preferences for silver and cloth were distinct from those along the lower coast of Guinea, where cowries and, to a lesser extent, brass manillas, were the dominant currencies during the era of the Atlantic slave trade and well into the era of the nineteenth-century "commercial revolution".[13] On the lower Guinea coast, following the great cowry inflation of the mid-nineteenth century, the British and French and German commercial firms (and later, colonial governments) banned the use of these currencies, imported monetized metal coin, and ultimately resorted to the adoption of regulated colonial currencies.

Credit Practices (1): The Late Eighteenth Century

The advance of trade goods against the promise of future repayment was a staple of Western Sahelian commerce. During the eighteenth century, credit in trade goods was extended throughout Western Sahelian trading networks and across the currency frontiers—between Western Sahelian and Maghribine merchants to the north, between Western Sahelian and southern Senegambian merchants to the south, and between Western Sahelian and Atlantic merchants in the west. The usual practice was to advance goods with the promise of future repayment, which may have served to insure against the provisioning of inferior trade goods as well as to help overcome problems of supply.[14] Among the Arabo-Berbers of the Western Sahel this practice was known as *mudaaf* (from the Arabic "*muḍa*^{cc}*af*" or "*muḍā*^{c}*fa*", to multiply). Probably this was only one of several names under which this institution was known in the savannah regions. We know little about these credit arrangements other than that they were commonplace, flexible, and unwritten, and that their stipulated form of collateral varied; among the pastoral nomads of the Western Sahel, livestock often served in this capacity.[15]

---

[12] Curtin, *Economic Change*, 268–270. The interface between the *guinée* zone and the Banque du Sénégal, created in 1844, has yet to be investigated. For a recent study of the social history of the Banque du Sénégal, see Ghislaine E. Lydon, "Les péripéties d'une institution financière: la Banque du Sénégal, 1844–1901," presented as the Commemoration du Centenaire de la Creation de l'Afrique Occidentale Française (A.O.F.), Dakar, 16–23 juin 1995 (Direction des Archives du Sénégal, Dakar, 1995).

[13] For recent studies on the nature of this "commercial revolution," see Robin Law, ed., *From Slave Trade to "Legitimate" Commerce* (Cambridge, 1995).

[14] Jan S. Hogendorn, "Economic Modeling of Price Differences in the Slave Trade Between the Central Sudan and the Coast," *Slavery and Abolition* 17 (1996):209–222.

[15] Webb, *Desert Frontier*, 63. The institutions of credit in the eighteenth-century Western Sahel might be compared in some respects to those of seventeenth-century Britain. As

The archival data concerning the mechanisms of eighteenth-century credit in the gum arabic trade are scant but suggestive. Credit was extended mutually between European traders and Western Sahelian gum merchants.[16] The practice was encouraged by the uncertain timing of the arrival of caravans and maritime transport. If one party did not have the requisite trade goods immediately at hand, transactions could still be carried out, under the obligation to pay at a future time. Withholding the transfer of one party's goods until the second party's goods had arrived could have imposed storage, maintenance, and opportunity costs that neither was willing to bear.

During the era of the Atlantic slave trade, in the late eighteenth century—the period for which we have most evidence—the granting of credit across the Atlantic frontier was an institutionalized practice. The European merchants resident on the African coast lacked immunities to many fatal tropical African diseases (in particular, malaria), and they generally tried to avoid the interior regions, where conditions were believed to be worse. In Saint-Louis du Sénégal, Europeans were often in the position of extending trade goods to prominent merchants in the Afro-European community, who agreed to undertake voyages to the Upper Senegal River Valley, on promise of future repayment. The arrangements for these deals were made publically, in the presence of at least two witnesses and two other individuals who accepted responsibility for the debt in the event of non-payment. The ultimate security for these loans was the slaves of the Afro-European inhabitants. As the French trader Saugsnier counselled in the late eighteenth century:

> If credit be given for any merchandize, it is necessary, before delivery, to enquire into the circumstances of the buyer; whether he have any negroes or not, and whether they can be made responsible for the debt; whether the slaves of this native be Tapade's slaves [negroes born of black inhabitants of the Senegal] by inheritance,

---

the principal historian of the Royal Company of Adventurers Trading to Africa wrote of British credit: "Its principal characteristic was a lack of system and organization. Specialists in the provision of credit had, it is true, made their appearance ... but in the country at large credit flowed, not along broad and clearly defined channels, but in many small rivulets which seemed to spring from the ground, crossing and recrossing one another before vanishing as mysteriously as they had arisen. Credit remained to a large extent what it had long been, a series of personal and intimate arrangements between borrowers and lenders." K.G. Davies, *The Royal African Company* (New York, 1970), 47.

16 The potential pitfalls of this practice are illustrated by the case of Mazamba Jakhumpa, an Idaw al-Hajj cleric with authority to carry on the gum trade at Portendick. When, in 1773, Abbé Demanet arrived at Portendick representing the Compagnie de Guyane to negotiate for the sale of some 500 tons of gum arabic, he had inadequate goods with which to proceed. The Idaw al-Hajj cleric authorized a large extension of credit, accepting Demanet's promissory notes. The debt was never repaid in full by Demanet or by his commercial successors, and ultimately Mazamba Jakhumpa's Western Sahelian clients, who were forced to absorb the losses, drove him into exile. Webb, *Desert Frontier*, 115.

> or have been purchased by him in the voyage to Galam. These things well ascertained, credit may be given without apprehension ...[17]

Although Saint-Louisian merchants could secure their loans by pledging either their trade slaves or house slaves ("Tapade's slaves") as collateral, in practice the latter were never sold, except in the extremely rare event of a guarantor of a breached contract refusing to substitute trade slaves for the pledged house slaves. In the case of contracts providing for the future repayment of an extension of consumable goods—either during the voyage upriver or prior to it—Saugnier counselled a different arrangement in the case of nonfulfillment of the initial contract. According to him, creditors could negotiate a second contract bearing "heavy interest," generally at 50 percent per trade season; such a prolongation of the debt rendered it "sacred," and in the event of non-fulfillment, even "Tapade's slaves" could be alienated and sold.[18] The economic rationale for the collateral was that the European traders active along the Atlantic seabord of the Western Sahel were easily able to market Africans as slaves in the Atlantic world. Europeans preferred collateral of high liquidity.

A similar logic linked the Western Sahelian political elites with the Atlantic traders. The rulers of the Black African horse cavalry states concentrated on the control of military force because their position derived from it. As was the case in feudal Europe, the ability to command trade credit could be a function of political power. In the same way that Afro-European brokers promised ultimate repayment in slave labor, the military capability of the state to deliver slaves to purchasers served as a guarantee for the extension of trade goods. Maintenance of horse cavalries was linked to predatory slave raiding which sent slaves north to desert and desert-edge markets and west to the Atlantic brokers. In this sense, the "conceptual currencies" associated with the intersection of multiple commodity currency zones shared a deep logic which knitted together different cultural worlds. Indeed, it is likely that the well-known conceptual currency (employed as a standard of measure and unit of account) based upon the prime cost of a healthy, adult male slave for export, the "*pièce*

---

[17] Saugnier, *Voyages*, 274. Saugnier went on to advise that the "Tapade's slaves" were only nominally slaves, and could generally not be sold; to caution that if trade slaves from upriver entered into marriage with the inhabitant's house slaves, the trade slaves could not be sold; to advise that an exact account of time be given for payment, goods delivered, and conditions of delivery; that all bargains be concluded publically, in the presence of three inhabitants at least; that the agreements must be signed by the mayor of the town and by the sureties and by the witnesses; that the sureties must consist of the nearest relations of the purchaser, and in the case of their default, of the most wealthy inhabitants; that as soon as the time of payment arrives, no time must be lost, otherwise the sureties and witnesses will insist upon withdrawing their names; and that it was advisable to make presents to the mayor and witnesses to ensure their goodwill. (275–277).

[18] Saugnier, *Voyages*, 279.

d'Inde," which historians have associated with Euro-African coastal trade and New World markets, may well have been employed in some Western Sahelian markets—as well as farther east in Hausaland.[19]

Yet, beyond the regular, seasonal extension of trade goods to Afro-European river merchants, in the late eighteenth century there appears to have been no regular pattern to the extension of trade goods on credit between European and African merchant communities. Trade goods were occasionally extended by Western Sahelian merchants to Europeans (or to Afro-Europeans in the employ of the Europeans), as well as vice versa; the extension of goods on credit was motivated principally by delays in the arrival of either import or export goods; and debt generally seems to have been extinguished within the trade year.[20] The venerable assumption that trade credit would "naturally" be extended from Europeans to Africans was probably rooted in an older paradigm of capitalist-precapitalist formations, or in the idea that European incomes were higher and thus trade credit would flow from the capitalized to the undercapitalized. Evidence of trade credit extended in both directions, at least in the era of the Atlantic slave trade, also undercut the argument that the slave trade was driven by a debt mechanism.[21]

In the eighteenth century, the operation of trade credit between Europeans and Africans may well have reflected the simple fact that Western Sahelian merchant diasporas and Western Sahelian states, and their European trading partners, were significantly capitalized.[22] We lack the data necessary for a

---

[19] For use of slaves as a currency in northern Nigeria, see Jan S. Hogendorn, "Slaves as Money in the Sokoto Caliphate" in this volume.

[20] On European credit needs, see Joseph E. Inikori, "The Credit Needs of the African Trade and the Development of the Credit Economy in England," *Explorations in Economic History* 27 (1990):197–231. On African and African-European credit, see Curtin, *Economic Change in Precolonial Africa*, 302–308 and Webb, *Desert Frontier*, 115, 117, 121, 127, 129.

[21] James Searing has suggested such a debt mechanism during the early eighteenth century Atlantic slave trade. He cites the extension of European goods to the damel of Kajoor and the Teen of Bawol in exchange for slaves to be paid at a later date. (James F. Searing, *West African Slavery and Atlantic Commerce* [Cambridge, 1993], 31.) Other archival evidence, however, suggests the reciprocal extension of trade credit, whereby the Damel advanced slaves to the French Company. For one example, see Archives Nationales de France, C6 6, Adition au Memoire instructif pour Monsieur de Saint Robert Directeur Commandant general a la Concession du Senegal. 6 juin 1720. André Brue. For a synthetic study of African-European relations during the era of the early Atlantic slave trade, see John Thornton, *Africa and Africans in the Making of the Atlantic World, 1400–1680* (Cambridge, 1992).

[22] On the European companies, see Henry Weber, *La Compagnie des Indes (1604–1875)* (Paris, 1904), esp. 548–580 and Davies, *Royal African Company*, esp. 47–96; on the independent eighteeenth century British gum traders, see James L.A. Webb, Jr., "The Mid-Eighteenth Century Trade in Gum Arabic and the British Conquest of Saint-Louis du Sénégal, 1758," *Journal of Imperial and Commonwealth History* 25, no.1 (1997):37–58.

close comparison of the extent of capitalization of either group of Western Sahelian actors, but it is clear that the trading diasporas of the Western Sahel—such as that of the Idaw al-Hajj which extended from the Adrar north to the Atlas mountains of Morocco, and south into the Wolof states of Kajoor and Waalo[23]—were international in scope, if constrained to a given mode of overland transport. It is also clear that the Western Sahelian states' military power and political authority were built upon their cavalries, which represented substantial investments of capital.[24]

Similarly, there is insufficient evidence to make a close comparison between North African credit which helped to underwrite the trans-Saharan caravan trade (largely in slaves), particularly from Timbuktu, and European credit which facilitated the river trade (also mostly in slaves) from the Upper Senegal River Valley. It appears that both European and North African sources of credit were concentrated within the transport sector (river boats and caravan animals, respectively) and that trade goods were advanced to travelling merchants, although fuller understanding of the impact of North African credit will have to await a thorough investigation of the documentation still extant in Timbuktu. Evidently, neither of these "external" sources of credit played a substantial role in the organization or production of non-slave goods in the Western Sahel. The organization of the gum arabic trade and of grain transport, for example, was firmly in Western Sahelian traders' control. Indeed, they moved in and out of the gum and grain trades at will, exploiting the European merchants' dependence upon them.[25] A similiar lack of European (or North African) influence can be discerned in the desert salt trade, which brought blocks of desert salt south into the Western Sahel and savannah in exchange for grain and slaves. The salt trade was built upon the labor of slaves who were stationed at the salt mines and whose maintenance was

---

[23] James L.A. Webb, Jr., "The Evolution of the Idaw al-Hajj Commercial Diaspora," *Cahiers d'Etudes Africaines*, 35 (1995):455–475.

[24] Detailed empirical evidence to reconstruct changes over time in the species composition of the horse cavalries (some horses were imported from North Africa or bred along the desert-edge; others were cross-breeds, and some had been interbred with West African ponies) is lacking, but some rough calculations are possible. Observations for the state of Kajoor indicate that in the mid-eighteenth century the state could muster 1000 horses for interstate warfare and that the damel could muster 300–400 horses for intrastate pillage. The value of this cavalry in slaves, which were the principal goods against which horses were traded, might be estimated at three slaves each, which would yield a "capitalized" horse cavalry available for pillage valued at 900–1200 slaves. This cavalry produced approximately 200–300 slaves for export annually, or a return of 15–33 percent on capital, exclusive of all costs associated with maintenance and feeding of the cavalry. The total value of the capital stock of the damel's cavalry available for pillage might thus be estimated in the range of £22,500–30,000. See Webb, *Desert Frontier*, 78, 83–84.

[25] Webb, *Desert Frontier*, 37–38, 112–114.

secured by the provisioning of grain and water by arriving caravanners. Salt was stored in the desert and in the savannah and other goods were brought to trade for it at the end of the agricultural season.[26]

European finance was, of course, essential in bringing trade goods and currencies from one part of the globe to another by integrated sea transport. European finance was also necessary to secure and market Indian cloth and to organize the logistics of the Atlantic commerce in African slave labor. Yet the historical record also indicates that European finance was not necessary for the production, storage, transportation, and marketing of Western Sahelian goods either in the interior or along the Atlantic coast: Western Sahelian trade was financed internally.

Credit Practices (2): The First Half of the Nineteenth Century

Following the abolition of the Atlantic slave trade, some of the fundaments of the reigning Atlantic trade system crumbled away early in the nineteenth century.[27] With the reoccupation of Saint-Louis du Sénégal by the French in 1817 and the creation of a greater demand for gum arabic from the expanding textile industries in Europe, the Senegal River trade was poised for expansion. Between 1818 and 1837, the population of Saint-Louis doubled and the commercial activity increased six-fold. The burgeoning growth of the river commerce wrought a transformation in the organization as well as the scale of trade. European and Afro-European firms at Saint-Louis came to dispose of more capital and more trade goods, and hence were capable of extending more goods on credit. This in turn encouraged an increasing number of independent traders to outfit their own boats. Intense competition ensued.[28]

During the explosive growth of the gum trade, a chain of credit in trade goods developed along the lower Senegal.[29] The *négociants* (principally,

---

[26] Webb, *Desert Frontier*, 47–67; E. Ann McDougall, "Salts of the Western Sahara: Myths, Mysteries, and Historical Significance," *International Journal of African Historical Studies* 23 (1990):231–257; E. Ann McDougall, "Salt, Saharans, and the Trans-Saharan Slave Trade: Nineteenth Century Developments," in *The Human Commodity. Perspectives on the Trans-Saharan Slave Trade*, Elizabeth Savage, ed., (London, 1992), 61–88.

[27] This section is based on the evidence on the commercial crisis in the gum trade presented in Webb, *Desert Frontier*, 115–131.

[28] Archives Nationales de France Section Outre-Mer, Sénégal XIII. Dossier 25. État des Batiments en traite de gomme au trois escales de 1829 à 1839 inclusivement. [n.a.] The number of boats increased from 65 in 1829 to 160 in 1839, although the increase was erratic and was influenced decisively by a variety of administratively controlled regimes of trade.

[29] The intensification of the gum trade along the lower and middle Senegal river valleys beginning in the 1820s meant that a larger volume of imported goods was available from Saint-Louis du Sénégal than had been the case in the earlier nineteenth century. At least some caravanners who otherwise would have been participated in the trans-Saharan trade chose instead to reorient their commerce along an east-west axis. Evidence

Frenchmen with capital) offered goods (principally, *guinée*) on credit to the *traitants* (Afro-European traders with boats) who in turn went upriver to court the Western Sahelian gum merchants.[30] Some *négociants* also sent their employees upriver to conduct business, and these employees then undersold the independent *traitants* without personal risk. Furious competition led to a massive extension of trade goods to the *traitants* and reached a high of 2.237 million French francs at the end of the 1839 trading season. This buildup occurred during the same years that the price of imported *guinée* dropped considerably, which gave rise to a pervasive sense of commercial crisis, and the system of river trade appeared to be near collapse. In the 1840s, the French undertook numerous efforts to reorganize the trade in order to stem the flow of credit. But the commercial crisis was finally resolved only in the 1850s, when the French colonial government in Saint-Louis fundamentally changed the rules of the river trade, allowing the larger French import-export firms to establish trading stations upriver. And in the period 1854–1858, the French conquest of the lower Senegal brought about a new balance of military and political power in the sub-region.[31] The post-conquest system allowed for the establishment of consolidated trading operations by the French import-export firms of Saint-Louis along the Senegal River, which all but eliminated the class of *traitants*; and considerably reduced the total value of the trade goods extended on credit.[32]

again is scant concerning the frequency and volume of this trade, but the official correspondance of the Governor of Senegal indicates that a merchant from Tishit by the name of Sidi Hadji Ahmed came to Saint-Louis in 1828 to trade gold for European merchandise. He left thirty camels at Podor and brought 30,000 francs worth of gold to Saint-Louis. He returned with 45,000 francs worth of merchandise, after having received a 15,000 franc credit in Saint Louis and having promised to repay it through one of his agents in Podor or Bakel. It was said to be the first example of an credit exchange of this type. More than fifty camels loaded with merchandise left the banks of the Senegal bound for Tishit. The Governor of Saint-Louis du Sénégal also wrote to the chief of Tishit to encourage further trade. The lack of follow-up evidence concerning this extension of credit suggests that the debt was indeed repaid without incident. But this single experience does not seem to have opened the door to any further, large extensions of credit. Archives Nationales du Sénégal, 2 B 12, Gouverneur au Ministre, Bureau d'Administration, 13 avril 1828.

[30] In the gum trade along the Atlantic coast—particularly at Portendick, near the site of present-day Nouakchott—there was no Afro-European system directly involved. European traders from their gum ships anchored in the Atlantic Ocean communicated directly, via skiffs, with the Arabo-Berber merchants on shore. Anonymous. "The Gum-trade renewed at Portendic, with the Moors of the Desert Sahaara [sic]," *The Royal Gazette; and Sierra Leone Advertiser*, 3, nos. 155 (1821) and 156 (1821).

[31] Webb, *Desert Frontier*, 115–124.

[32] Emile Baillaud, *Sur les routes du Soudan* (Toulouse, 1902), 35–42; Laurence Marfaing, *L'Evolution du Commerce au Sénégal, 1820–1930* (Paris, 1991).

Imported, Exported, and Internal Western Sahelian Currencies Compared

How did the indigenous Western Sahelian commodity moneys compare with those imported across the Atlantic frontier and those exported across the Saharan and Atlantic frontiers? And how did the imported Atlantic commodity moneys compare with the cowries and brass manillas imported farther to the south along the lower Guinea coast? Should the commodity currencies imported into the Western Sahel be considered as "interface moneys," a term recently coined by Jane Guyer, to describe moneys imported from the Atlantic which were both unstable in value and non-convertible to European currencies? [33]

These comparative questions are difficult to address. Indeed, it would appear that no definitive answer is possible with regard to the question of the instability of *guinée* relative to the internal Western Sahelian currencies. Evidence from the ecologically-specialized trade of the Western Sahel suggests, however, that the fluctuations occurring in the value of commodity moneys—such as salt and grain—could be quite large, especially within a given trade season. Although data do not exist to construct a continuous times series for grain or salt prices, the intra-annual market fluctuations in the prices of these humble Western Sahelian goods may well have been as large or larger than the price fluctuations in the principal exports of gum arabic and slaves, especially during periods of ecological stress.[34] Conversely, the relative stability of demand for gum arabic and slaves, which was itself a function of the strength of the larger European-controlled Atlantic market economy, probably created greater stability, measured in the value of *guinée*, both intra-annually and over the medium term.[35] It would likewise seem nearly certain that the relative stability of the value of gold in the Mediterranean world meant that Western

[33] Jane I. Guyer, "Introduction: The Currency Interface and Its Dynamics," in *Money Matters: Instability, Values, and Social Payments in the Modern History of West African Communities*, ed. Jane I. Guyer (Portsmouth, New Hampshire, 1995), 1–33.

[34] For price evidence, see Webb, *Desert Frontier*, 59, 125; Curtin, *Economic Change*, 157–159. The value of a kilogram of the principal export good, gum arabic, remained remarkably stable in nominal terms over the period from 1839 until the mid-1890s, when it suffered a marked decline. And over the course of the first half of the century, there was a marked decline in the price of guinée cloth, owing to the industrialization of cloth production. This was an economic benefit communicated directly to the desert-edge producers of gum arabic. Richard Roberts, "Guinée Cloth: Linked Transformations in Production Within France's Empire in the Nineteenth Century," *Cahiers d'Études Africaines* 32 (1992):597–627; Webb, *Desert Frontier*, [in] Table 5.8 "Prices of one pièce de guinée in French francs, c. 1776–1876," 125.

[35] Over the long term, the value of the principal imported commodity money of *guinée*, as expressed in European currencies, compared to the value of export of the principal commodity export, gum arabic, declined dramatically. Put differently, over time, the barter terms of trade moved strongly in favor of Western Sahelian traders. See Webb, *Desert Frontier*, table 5.6 "Estimated Net Barter Terms of Trade, 1718–1849," 114.

Sahelian exports of gold were more stable in value than the internal Western Sahelian currencies.

The imported currencies of the lower Guinea coast (cowries and brass manillas) can be more directly compared with those of the Atlantic frontier of the Western Sahel. Both groups of currencies could be used as commodity moneys. The major difference between the two groups lay in the length of time that they were in circulation before being consumed as goods. Cowries and manillas retained their functions as monetized goods for generations. The very fact that a substantial percentage of these imports were not retired from the money stock, in combination with a large import volume, is what accounts for the phenomenon of sustained inflation. By contrast, after initial monetization, glassware, iron, and cloth dropped rapidly out of the money supply. Indeed it is likely that the maximum lifespans of these goods as monies were on the order of two or three years, with most withdrawn from the money supply even sooner. [36] Silver, as noted above, was treated as a convertible currency along the Gambia River trading shed. Along the Senegal River, it was transformed into jewelry, although it retained its value in this form.

In what sense and to what degree were both imported and internal Western Sahelian currencies non-convertible to European currencies? This is a complex issue because of the variety of moneys in use in the Western Sahel. For heuristic purposes, one might conceive of a continuum of the convertibility of Western Sahelian to European currencies (and vice versa).[37] Along such a continuum, glassware might be found near the extreme of non-convertibility. Glassware, like cowries (delivered farther south along the West African coast), was virtually impossible to convert into European currencies, and there was certainly no demand for glassware as a currency on markets in Europe. (But neither, of course, was there demand for European currencies in the Western Sahel except for metal coins for their intrinsic value.) At the other end of the continuum might be found gold, a Western Sahelian currency much sought after by Europeans because of its monetary value on European markets. And toward the center of the continuum, arguably, one might place *guinée,* the principal imported commodity money, which was relatively easy to convert into silver or gold. Yet much depended upon where in the Western Sahel one might have wanted to effect such a conversion. Evidence suggests that at least along the Senegal River the European metal currencies had a more sharply circumscribed zone of circulation than did *guinée*—silver coin could be used as money only in Saint-Louis.[38] On the other hand, in the interior of

[36] Webb, "Toward the Comparative Study of Money," 460–461.

[37] On differential rates of transactional money use and degrees of flexibility in currency substitutions, see Webb, "Toward the Comparative Study of Money," 458–460.

[38] For comparative purposes, it is worth noting that the European merchants' experience in the Western Sahel was strikingly different from that of European merchants in

the Western Sahel, it might well have been relatively easy to convert *guinée* into gold.

Conclusion

This paper has highlighted the fact that during the period 1700–1850 Western Sahelian traders had commercial dealings across multiple regional currency frontiers— the monetized metal zone of North Africa, the cowry zone of much of sub-Saharan West Africa, and the zone of Atlantic commerce—and that these experiences with currencies (and with credit, particularly in the Atlantic zone) were complex and changed over time, even in a region without strong state structures. Within the Western Sahel, the three currency zones intersected, and Western Sahelian peoples additionally employed their own "internal" commodity currencies.

This essay has also proposed that the monetary histories of closely proximate sub-regions varied markedly. Along the Gambia River, silver coin became established as a principal trade currency during the late eighteenth century. By contrast, along the Senegal River, both during the eras of the eighteenth-century Atlantic slave trade and of the booming trade in gum arabic during the first half of the nineteenth century, *guinée* became accepted as the principal imported commodity currency. In this light, the Western Sahelian evidence indicates that the general model of transition in currency use along the Atlantic frontier from the pre-colonial period through the colonial period—from commodity money to silver coin to the colonial fiat moneys regulated by currency boards—took place with variations of up to a century or more in timing among the sub-regions.

This paper has also presented evidence of different Western Sahelian experiences with international credit along the Atlantic frontier. Indications of the extension of credit in the eighteenth century between European traders and Western Sahelian states, or between European traders and local merchants, suggests that such practices were seasonal and could be employed by either party. This indicates that the Western Sahelian states and merchant groupings were significantly capitalized. During the late eighteenth century, the extension of trade credit in goods took place principally from Europeans to Afro-European traders at Saint-Louis, which facilitated the organization of river transport, particularly on the upper Senegal River. During the first-half of the nineteenth century, a boom in the gum trade provoked a large-scale extension of trade goods, leading to a commercial crisis and French military conquest. In the latter half of the nineteenth century, the political power of Western Sahelian states and merchants was circumscribed, while the French import-export enterprises consolidated their influence and extended their activities upriver.

---

the Indian Ocean world, where Asian merchants *required* silver in exchange for export commodities, and the Europeans resented this drain on their resources of bullion.

This essay has also posed some broad comparative questions for the study of imported, exported, and internal currencies. It has suggested that the principal imported and exported commodity currencies (*guinée* and gold, respectively) were likely more stable than the internal commodity currencies of the Western Sahel (grain and salt), at least in the short-run; that the imported currencies of glassware, iron, cloth, and silver (along the Senegal River) had short lifespans as currencies and were consumed as commodities within a few years, a fact that distinguishes these currencies from the principal imported currencies of the lower Guinea coast; and that variations in convertibility among the imported, exported, and internal currencies might be usefully conceptualized as lying along a continuum between full and non-convertibility. Taken together, these approaches suggest some new lines for the further exploration of Western Sahelian and other African moneys.

Bibliography

Austin, Gareth. "Indigenous Credit Institutions in West Africa, c. 1750–c.1960," in *Local Suppliers of Credit in the Third World, 1750–1960,* ed. Gareth Austin and Kaoru Sugihara, 93–159. London, 1993.

Baillaud, Emile. *Sur les routes du Soudan.* Toulouse, 1904.

Bentley, Jerry H. "Hemispheric Integration, 500–1500 C.E." *Journal of World History,* 9, no. 2 (1998):237–254.

Curtin, Philip D. "Africa and the Wider Monetary World, 1250–1850," in *Precious Metals in the Later Medieval and Early Modern Worlds,* ed. J.F. Richards, 231–68. Durham, North Carolina, 1983.

—. *Economic Change in Pre-colonial Africa.* Madison, 1975.

Davies, K.G. *The Royal African Company.* New York, 1970.

"The Gum-trade renewed at Portendic, with the Moors of the Desert Sahaara," *The Royal Gazette; and Sierra Leone Advertiser* 3, nos. 155, 156 (1821).

Guyer, Jane I., ed. *Money Matters: Instability, Values and Social Payments in the Modern History of West African Communities.* Portsmouth, New Hampshire, 1995.

Hogendorn, Jan S. "Economic Modelling of Price Differences in the Slave Trade between the Central Sudan and the Coast." *Slavery and Abolition,* 17, no. 3 (1996):209–22.

—. "Slaves as Money in the Sokoto Caliphate," in *Credit, Currencies and Culture: African Financial Institutions in Historical Perspective,* ed. Endre Stiansen and Jane I. Guyer. Uppsala, 1999.

Hogendorn, Jan S. and Henry A. Gemery. "Cash Cropping, Currency Acquisition and Seignorage in West Africa, 1923–1950." *African Economic History* 11 (1982):15–27.

Hogendorn, Jan S. and Henry A. Gemery. "Continuity in West African Monetary History? An Outline of Monetary Development." *African Economic History* 17 (1998):127–46.

Hogendorn, Jan S. and Marion Johnson. *The Shell Money of the Slave Trade*. Cambridge, 1986.

Inikori, Joseph E. "The Credit Needs of the African Trade and the Development of the Credit Economy in England." *Explorations in Economic History* 27 (1990):197–231.

Johnson, Marion. "The Nineteenth-Century Gold 'Mithqal' in West and North Africa." *Journal of African History* 9, no. 4 (1968):547–570.

Law, Robin, ed. *From Slave Trade to "Legitimate" Commerce*. Cambridge, 1995.

Lydon, Ghislaine E. "Les péripéties d'une institution financière: la Banque du Sénégal, 1844–1901," presented at the Commemoration du Centenaire de la Creation de l'Afrique Occidentale Française. Dakar, 1995.

Marfaing, Laurence. *L'évolution du commerce au Sénégal, 1820–1930*. Paris, 1991.

McDougall, E. Ann. "Salts of the Western Sahara: Myths, Mysteries, and Historical Significance." *International Journal of African Historical Studies* 23 (1990):231–257.

—. "Salt, Saharans, and the Trans-Saharan Slave Trade: Nineteenth Century Developments," in *The Human Commodity: Perspectives on the Trans-Sahara SlaveTrade*, ed. Elizabeth Savage, 61–88. London, 1992.

Roberts, Richard. "Guinée Cloth: Linked Transformations in Production Within France's Empire in the Nineteenth Century." *Cahiers d'Etudes Africaines* 32 (1992):597–627.

Saugnier and Brisson. *Voyages to the Coast of Africa*. 1792. Reprint, New York, 1969.

Searing, James F. *West African Slavery and Atlantic Commerce*. Cambridge, 1993.

Thornton, John. *Africa and Africans in the Making of the Atlantic World, 1400–1680*. Cambridge, 1992.

Webb, Jr., James L. A. *Desert Frontier: Ecological and Economic Change Along the Western Sahel ,1600–1850*. Madison, 1995.

—. "The Evolution of the Idaw al-Hajj Commercial Diaspora." *Cahiers d'Etudes Africaines* 35 (1995):455–75.

—. "The Mid-Eighteenth Century Trade in Gum Arabic and the British Conquest of Saint-Louis du Sénégal, 1758." *Journal of Imperial and Commonwealth History* 25, no. 1 (1997):37–58.

—. "Toward the Comparative Study of Money: A Reconsideration of West African Currencies and Neoclassical Monetary Concepts." *International Journal of African Historical Studies* 15, no. 3 (1982):455–66.

Weber, Henry. *La Compagnie des Indes (1604–1875)*. Paris, 1904.

Slaves as Money in the Sokoto Caliphate

Jan Hogendorn

In economics, money is said to serve as a medium of exchange, a unit of account, a store of value, and a standard of deferred payment.[1] Anthropologists emphasize one other function of money, as a means of unilateral payment outside usual commercial relations, for such purposes as paying fines, taxes, tributes, compensations for wrongs, dowries, and the like.[2] Most economists would probably agree that the function of greatest importance is to "settle transactions," which encompasses the medium-of-exchange role in the commercial domain and means of payment in the non-commercial sector. More than the other functions, money as a medium of exchange and means of payment is the test of whether a money is "important," and the others are not by themselves sufficient to qualify an article as money in the formal sense.[3] This paper applies such a standard by concentrating on the transactions-settlement (medium-of-exchange and means-of payment) function of money.[4]

The questions addressed here are whether slaves *could* have served as a high-denomination medium of exchange and means of payment in the Sokoto Caliphate and whether they actually did so in the late nineteenth century. The tentative answer to both questions is yes, on the grounds of economic theory in regard to the first question and the historical record in the second. The historical evidence cited here is admittedly the result of a relatively brief search,

---

[1] See virtually any textbook on the principles of economics. Key works in the development of the tradition were W.S. Jevons, *Money and the Mechanism of Exchange* (London, 1875), and Gustav Cassel, *The Theory of Social Economy* (London, 1923).

[2] Jacques Melitz, "The Polanyi School of Anthropology on Money: An Economist's View," *American Anthropologist* 72, no. 5 (October, 1970):1020–1.

[3] Jacques Melitz, *Primitive and Modern Money: An Interdisciplinary Approach* (Reading, Massachusetts, 1974), 11. There has been a recent resurgence of interest in the theory of money used for exchange purposes. Two recent contributions include Shouyong Shi, "Money and Prices: A Model of Search and Bargaining," *Journal of Economic Theory* 67, no. 2 (1995):467–96, and Alberto Trejos and Randall Wright, "Search, Bargaining, Money, and Prices," *Journal of Political Economy* 103, no. 1 (1995):118–41.

[4] In many parts of Africa (Nilotic Sudan, western Sudan, coastal Dahomey) slaves functioned as a unit of account. For specific discussions see Paul Einzig, *Primitive Money* (London, 1949): 121, 144, and Marion Johnson, "The Ounce in Eighteenth-Century West African Trade," *Journal of African History* 2 (1966):197–214. The practice was indicated by the well-known terms *captif, peça das Indias,* and *pièce des Indes* used at or near the coast. In the Sokoto Caliphate, however, cowries were the favored unit of account.

and it is to be hoped that the concept of slaves as a medium of exchange and payment will encourage historians to examine the subject in greater depth.

If a good case can be made that slaves served as a form of money in the Sokoto Caliphate, there would be several major ramifications for the economic history of that region. The demand for slaves would accordingly have been higher than otherwise, leading to an enhanced effort to acquire them. A monetary function for slaves would have meant that the colonial authorities must have faced greater resistance to the abolition of slavery than previously understood. Under the circumstances, if no other feasible high-denomination medium of exchange and payment were available, we could expect abolition to entail greater difficulty in accomplishing high-value transactions, with probable contractionary results for the economy until a substitute could be found.

Very little work has been done on how slaves could serve as high-denomination currency, in the Sokoto Caliphate or indeed anywhere else.[5] The basic problem is a difficult one: how to differentiate between an item that is highly salable, and with which "real money" can be obtained, and an item that is understood to be usable by itself as a means for transacting business.[6] To a large degree the difference is only semantic, with no fixed dividing line. But it can be agreed that the criterion for determining if slaves served to settle transactions (medium of exchange and means of payment) is whether they could be directly exchanged as payment, whether they had this characteristic more than most other items, and whether they served frequently in this transfer function. Beyond a certain point the reduced scope of an item's monetary role would qualify it only as a liquid asset easily disposable for cash, and not as a way to settle transactions.[7]

The Problem with the Cowrie Currency

The cowrie currency of the Caliphate was admirably suited to the low-value transactions that made up most of the day-to-day market activity of that area.[8] At a time when a British penny was worth about 125 cowries and when a person's food supply for a whole day cost perhaps eighty cowries, buying just a single banana would have posed insuperable difficulty if other moneys were used. (A single banana costing five cowries would be worth only one twenty-fifth of a penny.) Indeed, cowrie values fell as imports of *C. annulus* from East

---

[5] J. Deutsch, *Die Zahlungsmittel der Naturvolker in Afrika* (Marburg, 1957), 17.

[6] See Joseph A. Schumpeter, *History of Economic Analysis* (New York, 1954), 1086.

[7] Frederic L. Pryor, *The Origins of the Economy: A Comparative Study of Distribution in Primitive and Peasant Economies* (New York, 1977), 153; Einzig, *Primitive Money*, 324, 328; W. Gerloff, *Die Entsehung des Geldes und die Anfänge des Geldwesens* (Frankfurt, 1947), 322.

[8] See the introduction and chapter one, and seven through ten, of Jan Hogendorn and Marion Johnson, *The Shell Money of the Slave Trade* (Cambridge, 1986).

Africa were added to the already very large stocks of *C. moneta* imported from the Maldive Islands. The late nineteenth century devaluation of the cowrie cut its value by more than half.[9]

Dealing with huge numbers of cowries was inconvenient and expensive. Accurately counting 100,000 cowries (the sterling equivalent of less than £4) was a day's work for a specialist. The 100,000 shells weighed about 250 pounds if they were *C. moneta,* and nearly double that if most of the shells were *C. annulus.* A weight of 250 pounds was the equivalent an entire camel load, or two donkey loads, or five carrier head loads.[10] The difficulties were exacerbated by the rising weight as C. *annulus* gained ground and by the unimproved nature of many tracks and paths which lengthened the duration of journeys and put extra wear and tear on the means of transport. Carrying costs ran up even further. Not surprisingly, a given quantity of cowries at Lagos was usually about twice as expensive at the confluence of the Niger and Benue (Lokoja).[11] They were forty percent more than the Lokoja price at Zaria, and sixty percent above the Lokoja price at Kano.[12] Further north, in the Caliphate's northern hinterland, they could be double the Lokoja price.

Those who attempted to carry cowries on long journeys faced daunting difficulties. Hugh Clapperton's ready cash of 212,000 cowries must have weighed about 500 pounds, moving which required the purchase of an additional camel.[13] C.H. Robinson calculated his cost of moving cowries from Zaria to Kano, a distance of less than 100 miles, to be about 8,000 cowries per bag of 20,000, if not prohibitive then at least a damaging forty percent subtraction from value. (Given the cowrie price differentials between Zaria and Kano cited in the preceding paragraph, Robinson's transport costs were greater than those incurred by indigenous traders.) Caravan tolls payable in cowries posed a real obstacle. The toll of 400,000 cowries payable on the Kano to Birnin Gwari route would have weighed about half a ton of *C. moneta* and as much as a ton if the total contained a large proportion of *C. annulus*.

The dilemma facing merchants and travelers who wanted a portable means of exchange and payment was well captured by Robinson and his much-quoted story of the sick horse which he would have liked to sell. The cowrie proceeds of the sale would have required fifteen extra porters whose wages for the carriage would have more than exceeded the amount received.[14]

---

[9] Hogendorn and Johnson, *Shell Money of the Slave Trade,* chapter 9.

[10] Hogendorn and Johnson, *Shell Money of the Slave Trade,* 126–8.

[11] See W. Ibekwe Ofonagoro, *Trade and Imperialism in Southern Nigeria 1881–1929* (New York, 1979), 250.

[12] C.H. Robinson, *Hausaland* (London, 1896), 86.

[13] Hugh Clapperton, *Journal of a Second Expedition into the Interior of Africa from the Bight of Benin to Soccatoo* (London, 1829), 258.

[14] Robinson, *Hausaland,* 46.

In short, the cowrie currency's combination of heavy (and rising) weight, low (and falling) value, and high transport costs meant that the shell money was poorly and decreasingly suited for middle- or long-distance trade.[15] The larger the cowrie amount, the worse the problem in making large purchases or payments, and in transporting money over any distance.

A Large Denomination Currency in the Caliphate?

The Sokoto Caliphate's economy encompassed a very extensive trade in many different commodities, a thriving textile sector, and a widespread network of transport services, all involving many wealthy merchants. It maintained a substantial flow of tribute payments that supported a large cadre of titled officials and a military establishment that regularly mounted major expeditions. Cowries might be a fine unit of account, but they could not serve well in the settlement function (medium of exchange and means of payment) when large sums were involved. If some more valuable item were commonly used in transactions, both directly and to acquire cowries for daily use, then the suspicion would arise that the item had a monetary role, serving as a high-denomination currency.

In the late nineteenth century, did any such item exist in the Sokoto Caliphate? According to C.H. Robinson in 1896, there was no large denomination money available to him. The closest he could come was the Maria Theresa dollar (thaler).[16] This silver coin, taken out of Austrian circulation in 1854 but minted as a trade dollar for over a hundred years thereafter, always bore the date 1780 after the death of the empress in that year.[17] It was in use over a wide area that stretched as far as Madagascar in the south, the Turkish Black Sea coast in the northeast, and the Barbary states of northwest Africa. Areas of heavy circulation were the Eastern Sudan, East Africa, and Arabia.[18]

---

[15] A conclusion also reached by Einzig, *Primitive Money*, 148.

[16] Robinson, *Hausaland*, 85–6.

[17] The standard works on the Maria Theresa dollar are Carl Peez and Josef Raudnitz, *Geschichte des M. Theresien-Thaler* (Vienna, 1898), and Marcel-Maurice Fischel, *Le Thaler de Marie-Thérèse* (Dijon, 1912). In English, see Raymond Gervais, "Pre-Colonial Currencies: A Note on the Maria Theresa Thaler," *African Economic History* 11 (1982):147–52; H.G. Stride, "The Maria Theresa Thaler," *The Numismatic Chronicle* 16 (1956) 339–43; H.B. Thomas, "The Maria Theresa Dollar," *Uganda Journal* 16 (1952):96–8, and the details on the coin given in Chester L. Krause and Clifford Mishler, *Standard Catalog of World Coins*, 13th ed. (Iola, Wisconsin, 1987), 86. For many years, in practice anyone who brought silver to a mint that produced M.T. dollars could obtain them on payment of a coinage charge. See Gervais, "Pre-Colonial Currencies," 149.

[18] The wide range of the Maria Theresa dollar is discussed by Lars Sundström, *The Exchange Economy of Pre-Colonial Tropical Africa* (New York, 1974), 97. From 1751, at various times the coins were minted at Halle, Günzburg, Kremnitz, Karlsburg, Milan, Venice, and Prague, as well as at Vienna which became the only source after 1866. (That is, until 1935 when Austria was persuaded to turn the dies over to Italy for minting in connection with the Ethiopian war. That led Britain, France, and Belgium to break the

The coin's ornamental design was attractive and its silver content and fineness were strictly maintained. (It weighed 28.0668 grams, was .8333 fine, and contained 23.39 grams of pure silver. The silver content was about three percent less than a U. S. dollar.) Clipping and shaving were very difficult because it had a lettered edge.[19] About five Maria Theresa dollars were equal to one pound sterling. A few Spanish dollars could also be found. The Spanish dollar was worth about one percent more than a Maria Theresa dollar.[20] There were no gold coins.

Maria Theresa dollars could have served as a high denomination currency, and to some extent they did, but they were in short supply. Though they had had a presence in the Caliphate since at least the start of the nineteenth century, they were scarce, and often those that did circulate were melted down as a source of silver jewelry.[21] Evidence of their limited circulation is clear from C.H. Robinson's testimony that his spending of only 140 Maria Theresa dollars in Zaria caused the dollar to depreciate by twenty percent from 5,000 cowries per dollar to 4,000. Before Maria Theresa dollars could serve well for large transactions, he suggested that much greater quantities would have to be introduced.[22]

Italian monopoly by preparing dies for striking their own Maria Theresa dollars. The Vienna monopoly was restored in 1960.) See Gervais, "Pre-Colonial Currencies," 148–49.

[19] It read "*JUSTICIA ET CLEMENTIA*." with various symbols in the spaces. The obverse (with a bust, pun intended, of the empress), was inscribed "Maria *THERESIA* Dei Gratia Romanorum *IMP*eratrix *HU*ngariae et *BO*hemiae *REG*ina." On the reverse was a coat of arms and the legend "*ARCHID*ux *AUST*riae *DUX BURG*undiae *CO*mes *TYR*oli 1780."

[20] For values see Krause and Mishler, *Standard Catalog of World Coins*, 86, 1245, 1422–24. Caution must be exercised in evaluating the weight of this coin: when the figures are in ounces, they are usually Troy ounces, which are heavier than the avoirdupois ounce.

[21] My thanks to Paul Lovejoy, whose unpublished note, "Currency and Credit," makes these points. Also see Deutsch, *Zahlungsmittel*, 140. In his book of 1860, General Daumas went so far as to say that silver coins did not circulate at all. General E. Daumas, *Le Grand Désert. Itinéraire d'une caravane du Sahara au pays des négres, royaume de Haoussa*, 4th ed. (Paris, 1860), extracted English translation of portions of pp. 199–247 by John Hunwick, MS, p. 3.

[22] Robinson, *Hausaland*, 85–6, 135. Assuming that Robinson was correct in claiming that his dollars were the cause of the depreciation, the information is sufficient to make a rough calculation of the number of M.T. dollars in the Zaria market at the time. Use the standard formula for the price elasticity of demand. ε_d is the numerical elasticity, ΔQ is the percentage change in quantity, Q is the original quantity, ΔP is the percentage change in price, and P is the original price.

$$\varepsilon_d = \frac{\%\Delta Q / Q}{\%\Delta P / P}$$

Assume that the elasticity of demand for M.T. dollars was likely to be no lower than 0.5 or higher than 2.0. Given these bounds, solve for Q. If the price elasticity of demand

An economist would then want to know why, if dollars were the only large-denomination currency, they did not command a premium, flow in across the desert, and fill the need. One explanation would be the existence of other media for accomplishing high-value exchange. Letters or bills of credit were available by the last half of the nineteenth century, and these too might have served the purpose. Money or goods were paid at one location against a check-equivalent of money or goods payable at another location.[23] (Sometimes these letters of credit were actually payable in slaves.)[24] But the high cost of such transactions (one hundred percent of the shipment's value is reported) and the risk of default, together with not very systematic legal support of regulatory law to enforce the collection of such letters and bills, made them impracticable for ordinary high-value transactions. Arguably, only very wealthy travelers, officials, and merchants had the connections and could afford the terms involved in using such letters as a medium of exchange and means of payment.

Aside from slaves, what other means were available? About the only reasonable possibilities with sufficiently large value were the useful animals (horses, donkeys, cows). I have seen no indication that donkeys and cows had a monetary role, and only tenuous evidence that horses served in this regard. (Several emirates included horses as part of the regular tribute payments to Sokoto and Gwandu).[25] But no one has claimed, insofar as I am aware, that horses were actually used as a medium of exchange and payment.

Slaves As Medium of Exchange and Means of Payment

That leaves the case of slaves to be examined. Could they have passed the threshold to become a high-denomination money in the latter half of the nineteenth century?

$\varepsilon_d=1$, then $1=\frac{140/Q}{20\%}$ therefore Q=140x5=700. That is, with $\varepsilon_d=1$ the formula predicts that there were 700 M.T. dollars in the market. If the elasticity were half this ($\varepsilon_d=0.5$), there would be 1400 dollars in the market. If double ($\varepsilon_d=2.0$), 350 dollars. Even the high figure is very small. Moreover, we would expect the elasticity of demand for M.T. dollars to be relatively high given the available opportunity for substituting one form of money for another.

[23] See the reports of letters and bills in Denham and Clapperton, *Narrative*, 2:268, 273; Heinrich Barth, *Travels and Discoveries in Northern and Central Africa, Being a Journal of an Expedition Undertaken under the Auspices of Her Majesty's Government in the Years 1849–1855*, vol. 3 (London, 1857), chapter 83; Robinson, *Hausaland*, 106. There is a general discussion covering West Africa in Sundström, *Exchange Economy of Pre-Colonial Tropical Africa*, 36–40.

[24] C. Vicars Boyle, "Historical Notes on the Yola Fulani," *Journal of the African Society* 10, no. 37 (1910), 82.

[25] H.A.S. Johnston, *The Fulani Empire of Sokoto* (London, 1967), 176–7.

Some of the characteristics of slaves made them well suited to serve as the Sokoto Caliphate's high-denomination money. These characteristics fit Keynes' definition of money as an item with great liquidity in relation to carrying costs.[26] Slaves were self-transporting, which reduced transit costs. In effect, they bore interest in that they did useful work and were capable of reproduction. New supplies were regularly available and reasonably controllable as part of the Caliphate's slave acquisitions. (When there was reluctance to sell household slaves considered part of the family, such slaves would be far less liable to transfer.) Most households capable of dealing in large sums of money owned slaves, sometimes many, and there were at least a million people in bondange, perhaps as many as two-and-a-half million. So accomodating payments in slaves would not pose special difficulties or require any unusual arrangements.[27]

Other characteristics reduced slaves' effectiveness as money, including their costs of subsistence, the need to police against their escape, the possibility that they might sicken or die, and their lack of uniformity so that there was no single standard of value and every transaction had to be valued separately.[28]

The ability of slaves to provide their own transport was a particularly important feature in an economy with otherwise relatively high transport costs.[29] Slaves combined high value (a representative local slave price of £2 in Caliphate markets was the equivalent of over 50,000 cowries) with substantial weight-saving in transport. The 50,000 cowries would have weighed at minimum 125 pounds and up to nearly double that depending on the *C. annulus* content. In valuing this attribute, the net gain would be the opportunity cost of carrying cowries as against any costs of holding slaves for a monetary purpose.

An additional advantage of slaves held as a stock of money is that the money bore interest in the form of slave productivity (agricultural commodities, porterage, household services, etc.), and in the form of occasional offspring. This had to be netted against aging, sickness and death, costs of subsis-

---

[26] J.M. Keynes, *Treatise on Money* (London, 1930), 1:3.

[27] This last point about special difficulties and arrangements was emphasized by Cassel, *The Theory of Social Economy*, 350. The population of slaves is estimated by Paul E. Lovejoy and Jan S. Hogendorn, *Slow Death for Slavery* (Cambridge, 1993), 1.

[28] All of these traits were shared by monetary systems based on cattle. See Harold K. Schneider, *Economic Man: The Anthropology of Economics* (London, 1974), 172–4, for a discussion of cattle money in Africa. There were famous cattle moneys in Europe, including ancient Rome (Latin *pecus* = cow, hence pecuniary) and Germany (Germanic *fehu* = cattle, hence the English word "fee" and the modern German *Vieh*. See Pryor, *The Origins of the Economy*, 158–9.

[29] Einzig, *Primitive Money*, 413, stresses the importance of transport costs.

tence, and costs of policing.[30] It should be noted that the interest involved was in real terms and so did not violate Islamic religious scruples on the payment of interest.[31]

Evidence of the Monetary Role of Slaves

Slaves had a monetary role in several parts of the world.[32] Did they do so in the Sokoto Caliphate? The testimony of some observers points to an affirmative answer. The evidence here is limited, but many other references could probably be found with further research. My information includes no local account books, court records, or Hausa memoirs, and only a few scholarly dissertations that touch on the subject. Even so, the evidence includes observations by contemporary visitors, including Heinrich Barth, Paul Staudinger, and C.H. Robinson, and it does indicate that later analysts believed it was possible that slaves had a monetary role.

The Early Travelers

Despite the scarce and fragmentary first-hand testimony supporting this conclusion, the statements we do have from early travelers are clear, and based on direct observation. In the absence of evidence to the contrary, they must be regarded as credible.

Heinrich Barth's observation comes in the form of a complaint that his visit to the area was hindered by the absence of any usable high-denomination currency. He wrote that "All business in these countries is transacted on two or three months' credit, and, after all, payment is made, not in ready money, but chiefly in slaves."[33] Paul Staudinger concurred: "There are only a few means of paying for expensive goods. These can sometimes only be bought by kings who pay with slaves."[34] Robinson came to the same conclusion. He stated that "Slaves form to a great extent the currency of the country, where larger amounts are involved than can be conveniently paid in cowries."[35] Sir George Goldie's informants gave him similar information. The Royal Niger Company's founder testified as follows before the Barbour Committee in 1899:

---

[30] The assumption here is that the interest was positive. The interest could conceivably have been negative, which would have reduced but possibly not eliminated the advantage of slaves over cowries as money for high-value transactions.

[31] For references to slaves and interest, see Sundström, *Exchange Economy of Pre-Colonial Tropical Africa*, 116. Deutsch, *Die Zahlungsmittel*, 19, posits that "slaves' offspring were a greater gain than using the slaves as workers."

[32] Einzig, *Primitive Money*, 18, 121, 144, 148–67, 176, 247–9, 324, 402–3, 430, 433.

[33] Heinrich Barth, *Travels and Discoveries*, 2:228.

[34] Paul Staudinger, *In the Heart of the Hausa States*, trans. Johanna E. Moody, (Athens, Ohio, 1990), 2:112.

[35] Robinson, *Hausaland*, 131. He went over the same ground in Robinson, *Nigeria, Our Latest Protectorate* (London, 1900), 204.

> 783. Were the cowries used for making very large payments? — No; I should say that slaves were the means of large payments in some parts ...
>
> 841. You explained that slaves in some parts are used as currency? —Yes, in the north.
>
> 842. Has not that system encouraged slavery? —Yes, I think it has.[36]

Later Writers on "Primitive Moneys," the Northern Nigerian Economy, and the Caliphate

Later writers viewing the historical record include those on the general subject of pre-modern moneys and analysts of the early Nigerian economy. Paul Einzig's comprehensive survey has attracted the most attention among economists. He notes that

> Second only in importance to cowries as a primitive currency were slaves. While cowries were essential for everyday requirements, slaves were equally essential for large transactions. Their use was particularly developed in communities lacking a valuable staple commodity which could be used as currency for big payments.[37]

The German analyst J. Deutsch also held that slaves had a monetary role, and he included the Sokoto Caliphate in his comment.[38] The comprehensive work on money in British colonial Africa by W.T. Newlyn and D.C. Rowan concluded that at the end of the nineteenth century slaves were being used as money in the area.[39] The historian of Nigeria, A.C. Burns, stated much the same.[40] Allan McPhee's view of the Nigerian economy in the 1890s was that

> In addition to cowries [other moneys included] most important of all, slaves ... The lack of valuable exchange commodity was the reason for the use of slaves as currency ...[41]

A.F. Mockler-Ferryman's turn-of-the-century works also refer to the monetary role of slaves in the Caliphate. He recounts the following example:

> ... the reader must bear in mind three things, viz. that in these countries there is no free labour, no portable currency worth speaking of, except on the heads of natives. For these reasons the traveling merchant is obliged to use slaves, and we will give

[36] Report of the Barbour Committee, "Minutes of Evidence taken before the Committee on the Currency of the West African Colonies," 21 November, 1899. Examination of Sir George Taubman Goldie.

[37] Einzig, *Primitive Money*, 148.

[38] Deutsch, *Zahlungsmittel*, 17.

[39] W.T. Newlyn and D.C. Rowan, *Money and Banking in British Colonial Africa* (Oxford, 1954).

[40] A.C. Burns, *History of Nigeria* (London, 1929), 208.

[41] Allan McPhee, *The Economic Revolution in British West Africa* (1926; reprint, London, 1971), 234. McPhee's often-cited comment that the slave "has been the cheque book of the country, and has been necessary for all large payments" does not, however, refer directly to the Caliphate. It was based on the "Report on Lagos 1891," 58.

> an example. A merchant is going from Kano to the ivory markets in German Adamawa, and proposes taking with him a stock of tobes and cotton goods, and a supply of cowries for making small purchases on the road—all bulky articles. Accordingly, he goes to the slave market and purchases the number of slaves necessary to carry his merchandise and provisions for the journey. After traveling for a few days he finds that the consumption of the provisions has reduced the loads of his carriers, and he is able to dispense with the services of one or two of them, and for these he can always obtain a fair price. At Bautshi or Yola he stays for several days ... and pays his bill by dropping a slave. Thus in reality slaves are a currency—fluctuating, perhaps, but portable—far more so than their value in cowries, the only other universal currency of the country.[42]

E.D. Morel, the gadfly of government, wrote that one of the motives behind slave raids was the use of slaves as money.[43] Sir Charles Orr also referred to slaves as currency.[44] Governor Lugard in his *Political Memoranda*, No. 6 on Slavery, noted that prior to his assumption of office "almost literally ... slaves were a form of currency." He instructed officials that debts in slaves recorded in account books were not recoverable.[45]

Among the modern works on the Caliphate, there are statements by Adamu Fika, Joseph Smaldone, and Lucie Colvin. According to Fika,

> War captives, who were usually enslaved, were invaluable for two reasons. Slaves were used in Kano, as elsewhere in the central Sudan, as currency where any large sum was involved. They were also used as carriers which meant that this medium of exchange could transport itself. This contrasted sharply with the cowrie currency which was the primary medium of exchange in Hausaland.[46]

Smaldone adds:

> Slaves were also a universally accepted currency for large commercial and credit transactions in domestic and regional trade. Cowrie shells, the only other common currency, were unsuitable for such transactions because of their bulk and the consequent costs of porterage. The unique advantage of slaves was their simultaneous economic role as currency, commodity, and porter. The utility of slaves as currency increased during the nineteenth century because of the progressive devaluation of cowries.[47]

According to Colvin, slaves "could also be used as a means of payment ..."[48]

---

[42] A.F. Mockler-Ferryman, *British Nigeria* (London, 1902), 243. See also A.F. Mockler-Ferryman, *British West Africa* (London, 1900), 371, and the same author's *Imperial Africa* (London, 1899), 371.

[43] E.D. Morel, *Affairs of West Africa* (London, 1902), 100.

[44] Sir Charles Orr, *The Making of Northern Nigeria* (London, 1911), 157.

[45] Lord Lugard, *Political Memoranda 1913–1918*, 3d ed. (London, 1970), Memorandum No. 6, 219, 240.

[46] Adamu Fika, *The Kano Civil War and British Over-Rule 1882–1940* (Ibadan, 1978), 40.

[47] Joseph P. Smaldone, *Warfare in the Sokoto Caliphate: Historical and Sociological Perspectives* (Cambridge, 1977), 148.

[48] Lucie G. Colvin, "The Commerce of Hausaland, 1780–1833," in *Aspects of West African Islam*, Boston University Papers on Africa, ed. Daniel F. McCall and Norman R. Bennett

Slaves as Tribute

Perhaps the best circumstantial evidence that slaves had a monetary role in the Caliphate is the payment of the tribute to the emirates and to Sokoto (and Gwandu). Frederic Pryor advises us that a nice tell-tale of the presence of a money function is when payment of taxes, tribute, and fines is made in a standardized stuff.[49]

Though the accounting of the Caliphate's network of tribute payments is incomplete, there is no reason to doubt that several thousand slaves were involved by the middle of the nineteenth century.[50] Robinson reported in the 1890s that slaves made up at least three-quarters of the Sultan's tribute. He noted that only one emirate, Kano, was at the time not paying any slaves as part of its tribute, and that some (Bauchi and Adamawa) paid entirely in slaves.[51] Take as examples the tribute payment from Katsina and Adamawa emirates. Katsina paid 100 slaves annually. If these slaves had a value of £2 each, the total value involved would have been the equivalent of about ten million cowries weighing over twelve tons and requiring 500 porters to carry. In years when Adamawa paid 2000 slaves, the cowrie amounts would have been over 240 tons requiring 10,000 porters to carry them over a much longer distance.[52] The figures assume that all the shells were the lighter C. *moneta*. High C. *annulus* content would have raised the weight and need for porters considerably.

Characteristics of Slaves as Money: Limited Function

To this point, the case has been made that in the late nineteenth century, slaves could have and arguably did function as a medium of exchange and means of payment for the Caliphate's high-value transactions. Assuming that this case is plausible, what characteristics would such a system have? A slave medium of exchange and means of payment would obviously be limited to large value transactions. The major ones would be settlements of accounts between merchants, obtaining large quantities of cowries, payment of substantial bills, and payment of tribute, taxes, and fines. Some anthropologists have argued that the use of "money" only for special purposes is a disqualifying factor. In reply, it should be pointed out that $1000 currency notes (some still

(Boston, 1971). She comments that the use of slaves as a medium of exchange was rare, which, compared to the number of transactions carried out with cowries, is undoubtedly correct. By number, very high value transactions are always rare compared to those of low value.

49 Pryor, *The Origins of the Economy*, 154.

50 For this estimate see Paul E. Lovejoy, "Problems of Slave Control in the Sokoto Caliphate," in *Africans in Bondage*, ed. Paul E. Lovejoy (Madison, Wisconsin, 1986), 240.

51 Robinson, *Hausaland*, 105, 134.

52 The figure of 2000 for Adamawa is frequently repeated. See Boyle, "Historical Notes on the Yola Fulani," 82.

exist in the United States, though they have not been printed for years) are called money by economists even though as a medium of exchange they are obviously useful only to make large payments or to acquire lower-denomination, and hence more useful, notes.[53]

The limited function and high value of the transactions would imply that the velocity of circulation was low. That is, slaves would presumably change hands for monetary reasons on few occasions.[54]

Characteristics of Slaves as Money: A Floating Currency

Slaves are not a uniform unit of exchange. To the extent that they served as a high-denomination money, they had to be valued separately in every transaction. The age, size, sex, physical characteristics, health and strength, and so on, of an individual slave would all need to be assessed in a transaction. Moreover, the demand for slaves would not be the same in all markets, so variability in value could be expected. That undoubtedly opened the door to sharp practices, such as paying tribute with as poor a quality of slave as could pass without objection.[55] Obviously, however, the scope for dishonest dealing was

---

53 For discussions, see George Dalton, "Primitive Money," in *Tribal and Peasant Economies: Readings in Economic Anthropology*, ed. George Dalton (Garden City, New York, 1967), 254–84; Deutsch, *Zahlungsmittel*, 17; Einzig, *Primitive Money*, 18; M. J. Herskovits, *The Economic Life of Primitive People* (New York, 1940), 228; E.E. Hoyt, *Primitive Trade* (London, 1926), 85; and A.M. Quiggin, *A Survey of Primitive Money* (London, 1949), 4.

54 A similar comment is in Einzig, *Primitive Money*, 403. His statement on page 433 is worth noting: "If separate currencies are used for big, medium-sized and small purchases, then changes in the quantity of any one of them only affects the prices of the categories of goods and services which can be bought with it. In that case there may be conflicting tendencies between the various sections of the price levels. If the use of a currency is limited to the purchase of a small range of goods—for instance, luxuries only—then the goods factor tending to affect prices is liable to assume considerable relative importance. The wider the range of goods which can be bought with the same currency, the higher is the relative importance of the money factor as against the goods factor. In other words, if a money can be used for buying anything, then changes in the supply of some of the categories of goods are not liable to effect its value to a high extent unless the total supply of goods is affected. If, on the other hand, the money can only buy a few kinds of goods, then changes in one or two kinds of goods are liable to affect the supply of goods to a relatively high degree, and for this reason they are apt to produce a pronounced effect on the average value of the monetary unit."

55 See Richard Lander's roadside observation (June 8, 1827) of the poor condition of slaves being sent as tribute to Sultan Bello, in Clapperton, *Second Expedition*, 292. For a general discussion of how differences in the quality of slaves led to a wide variety of prices, see Patrick Manning, *Slavery and African Life: Occidental, Oriental, and African Slave Trades* (Cambridge, 1990), 103.

limited by the high level of expertise possessed by many in judging slave quality in a slave economy as big as the Sokoto Caliphate's.[56]

Such considerations lead some authorities to disqualify slaves as money. But economists might reply that individual assessment typified transactions even in coins until a quite late date, with weighing and assaying the norm and with floating values in different markets. Acceptance by tale was not common until relatively late in the history of coinage.[57]

Characteristics of Slaves as Money: Demand Enhancement

To the degree that slaves had a monetary use and earned a positive real rate of interest for the holder, the demand for slaves would be enhanced. This effect would be non-existent or weak for household slaves not often transferred, but stronger for new captives who were sent to market. The predictable economic pressures would be for a slave price higher than otherwise because of the increased demand, and a response in quantity supplied in the form of a greater effort to acquire slaves and a greater overall quantity of slaves. Also, demand would have been enhanced to the extent that the Caliphate's economy grew and trade expanded in the late nineteenth century,. As McPhee put it,

> commerce, which had been regarded as a liberator, was actually forging the chains more firmly on the slaves ...[58]

Characteristics of Slaves as Money: Control of Supply

It is essential that any article used as money not be available without cost and in unlimited quantity, for with the growth in money supply prices would inflate and the money would lose value. The Caliphate's slave supply, being the product of a system of political and military pressure that yielded slaves through both tribute and capture, was at least to some degree controllable. The variations in volume that would have caused price fluctuations and exchange rate changes could be dampened by the conscious choice of how many slaves to acquire.[59]

---

[56] Armen Alchian makes the relevant point that the existence of reliable specialists with sound judgment of quality is vital if an item is to have a monetary role. If the quality of a money item is difficult and expensive for a recipient to assess, then the item will tend to be held longer in inventories awaiting transfer and the bid-ask spread will be larger. See Armen A. Alchian, "Why Money?" *Journal of Money, Credit and Banking* 9, no. 1, part 2 (February 1997):133–40.

[57] See Einzig, *Primitive Money*, 324–5.

[58] McPhee, *Economic Revolution*, 251.

[59] Smaldone makes the point explicitly in *Warfare in the Sokoto Caliphate*, 149.

Conclusion

If slaves did indeed perform a monetary function in the Caliphate, three corollaries would apparently follow. First, abolition of the exchange of slaves immediately after the imposition of colonial rule would have been more provocative and would have generated more resistance than otherwise. Second, the need to make high-value payments in a different way, at least until substitutes were available, would (all other things being equal) have damaged the economy. Third, the introduction of colonial moneys suitable for high-value transactions would have minimized this damage.[60] In historical situations where data is lacking, it is difficult or impossible to prove conclusively that an article of commerce was used often enough in making payments to have monetary significance. An economist's role can properly be to make a prima facie case based on theory and evidence supporting it, and then invite historians to take an interest in the subject and fill in the historical record. That has been my purpose. The conclusion that slaves played a monetary role as a medium of exchange and a means of payment in the Sokoto Caliphate's high-value transactions would not basically change our views of that region's economy or society, but it *would* reinforce our knowledge that slavery was a prominent feature of the Sokoto Caliphate, and that eradicating it was an exceptionally difficult endeavor.

Bibliography

Alchian, Armen A. "Why Money?" *Journal of Money, Credit and Banking* 9, no. 1, part 2 (1997):133–40.

Barth, Heinrich. *Travels and Discoveries in Northern and Central Africa, Being a Journal of an Expedition Undertaken Under the Auspices of Her Majesty's Government in the Years 1849–1855*. Vols. 2 and 3. London, 1857.

Boyle, C. Vicars. "Historical Notes on the Yola Fulani," *Journal of the African Society* 10, no. 37 (1910).

Burns, A. C. *History of Nigeria*. London, 1929.

Cassel, Gustav. *The Theory of Social Economy*. London, 1923.

Clapperton, Hugh. *Journal of a Second Expedition into the Interior of Africa from the Bight of Benin to Soccatoo*. London, 1829

Colvin, Lucie. "The Commerce of Hausaland, 1780–1833," in *Aspects of West African Islam*. Boston University Papers on Africa, vol. 5, ed. Daniel F. McCall and Norman Bennett, 101–36. Boston, 1971.

[60] Among the writers who make this case are Einzig, *Primitive Money*, 149; McPhee, *Economic Revolution*, 252; Sir George Goldie in the "Report of the Barbour Committee," sections 842–3; and Robinson, *Hausaland*, 134.

Dalton, George. "Primitive Money," in *Tribal and Peasant Economies: Readings in Economic Anthropology*, ed. George Dalton, 254–84. Garden City, New York, 1967.

Daumas, General E. *Le Grand Désert: Itinéraire d'une caravane du Sahara au pays des négre, royaume de Haoussa.* 4th ed. Paris, 1860.

Deutsch, J. *Die Zahlungsmittel der Naturvölker in Afrika.* Marburg, 1957.

Einzig, Paul. *Primitive Money.* London, 1949.

Fika, Adamu. *The Kano Civil War and British Over-Rule 1882–1940.* Ibadan, 1978.

Fischel, Marcel-Maurice. *Le Thaler de Marie-Thèrése.* Dijon, 1912.

Gerloff, W. *Die Entsehung des Geldes und die Anfange des Geldwesens.* Frankfurt, 1947.

Gervais, Raymond. "Pre-Colonial Currencies: A Note on the Maria Theresa Thaler," *African Economic History* 11 (1982):147–52.

Herskovits, Melville J. *The Economic Life of Primitive People.* New York, 1940.

Hogendorn, Jan and Marion Johnson. *The Shell Money of the Slave Trade.* Cambridge, 1986.

Hoyt, E.E. *Primitive Trade.* London, 1926.

Jevons, W.S. *Money and the Mechanism of Exchange.* London, 1875.

Johnson, Marion. "The Ounce in Eighteenth-Century West African Trade," *Journal of African History* 2 (1966):197–214.

Johnston, H.A.S. *The Fulani Empire of Sokoto.* London, 1967.

Keynes, John Meynard. *Treatise on Money.* Vol. 1. London, 1930

Krause, Chester L. and Clifford Mishler. *Standard Catalog of World Coins.* 13th ed. Iola, Wisconsin, 1987.

Lovejoy, Paul E. *Africans in Bondage.* Madison, Wisconsin, 1986.

—. "Problems of Slave Control in the Sokoto Caliphate," in *Africans in Bondage*, ed. Paul E. Lovejoy. Madison, Wisconsin, 1986.

Lovejoy, Paul E. and Jan S. Hogendorn. *Slow Death for Slavery.* Cambridge, 1993.

Lugard, Lord. *Political Memoranda 1913–1918.* 3d ed. London, 1970.

Manning, Patrick. *Slavery and African Life: Occidental, Oriental, and African Slave Trades.* Cambridge, 1990.

McCall, Daniel and Norman R. Bennett, ed. *Aspects of West African Islam.* Boston University Papers on Africa, vol. 5. Boston, 1971.

McPhee, Allan. *The Economic Revolution in British West Africa.* London, 1971.

Melitz, Jacques. "The Polanyi School of Anthropology on Money: An Economist's View." *American Anthropologist* 70, no. 5 (1970):1020–1.

—. *Primitive and Modern Money: An Interdisciplinary Approach.* Reading, Massachusetts, 1974.

Mockler-Ferryman, A. F. *British Nigeria.* London, 1902.

—. *British West Africa.* London, 1900.

—. *Imperial Africa.* London, 1899.

Morel, E. D. *Affairs of West Africa.* London, 1902.

Newlyn, W.T. and D.C. Rowan. *Money and Banking in British Colonial Africa.* Oxford, 1954.

Ofonagoro, W. Ibekwe. *Trade and Imperialism in Southern Nigeria 1881–1929.* New York, 1979.

Orr, Sir Charles. *The Making of Northern Nigeria.* London, 1911.

Peez, Carl and Josef Raudnitz. *Geschichte des M. Theresien-Thalers.* Vienna, 1898.

Pryor, Frederic L. *The Origins of the Economy: A Comparative Study of Distribution in Primitive and Peasant Economies.* New York, 1977.

Quiggin, A. M. *A Survey of Primitive Money.* London, 1949.

Robinson, C. H. *Hausaland.* London, 1896.

—. *Nigeria, Our Latest Protectorate.* London, 1890.

Schneider, Harold K. *Economic Man: The Anthropology of Economics.* London, 1974.

Schumpeter, Joseph A. *A History of Economic Analysis.* New York, 1954.

Shi, Shouyong. "Money and Prices: A Model of Search and Bargaining," *Journal of Economic Theory* 67, no. 2 (1995):467–96.

Smaldone, Joseph P. *Warfare in the Sokoto Caliphate: Historical and Sociological Perspectives.* Cambridge, 1977.

Staudinger Paul. *In the Heart of the Hausa States.* Trans. Johanna E. Moody. 2 vols. Athens, Ohio, 1990.

Stride, H.G. "The Maria Theresa Thaler." *The Numismatic Chronicle.* Sixth Series, vol. 16 (1956): 339–43.

Sundström, Lars. *The Exchange Economy of Pre-Colonial Tropical Africa.* New York, 1974.

Thomas, H.B. "The Maria Theresa Dollar." *Uganda Journal* 16 (1952):96–8.

Trejos, Alberto and Randall Wright. "Search, Bargaining, Money, and Prices," *Journal of Political Economy* 103, no. 1 (1995):118–41.

Islamic Financial Institutions: Theoretical Structures and Aspects of Their Application in Sub-Saharan Africa*

John Hunwick

It is something of a cliché to point out the symbiotic relationship of Islam and trade. Although the political kingdom of Islam was established largely through the military energy of former nomads, the sinews of the Islamic œcumene (*umma*) were the mercantile networks that stretched across Asia and Africa and, though largely through intermediaries, deep into Europe. The West African Sahel was from the tenth century firmly plugged into this vast network whose tentacles stretched into Central Asia and eventually China.

But Islam did not become a mercantile civilization simply through the circumstances of its expansion. It was born into a mercantile environment in Mecca where the urban leaders of the Quraysh, the Prophet Muḥammad's kin group, were engaged in long-distance trading to southern Arabia on the one hand, and the eastern Mediterranean on the other. Muḥammad himself engaged in trade as a young man, and married a widow, Khadīja, who was a businesswoman. The intimate association of Islam with commerce goes deeper still. It is not merely one of historical precedent and Prophetic practice; it is inherent in the words of the sacred scripture of Islam, the Qurʾān, and thus has, for Muslims, the stamp of divine authority.

Trade in the Qurʾān

The Qurʾān is replete with mercantile metaphors, and we may trace within it what may be characterized as a moral economy of salvation. Belief in God, and the practice of worship and alms-giving constitute a profitable commerce (*tijāra*),[1] whereas the hypocrites who "purchase error with right guidance"

---

* I am grateful to Endre Stiansen for his judicious comments on drafts of this paper. I am, however, the sole source of its errors and inadequacies.

[1] Qurʾān 35:28–9: "Those who recite the book of God and perform worship and give away part of what we have bestowed on them, secretly and openly, hope for a commerce that will never fail, that He may pay them their wages in full and give them an increase out of His bounty."

Qurʾān 61:10: "O you who believe. Shall I guide you to a commerce that will save you from a painful chastisement? You should believe in Allah and His messenger, and strive hard in Allah's way with your wealth (*māl*) and your lives. That is better for you, did you but know."

pursue a commerce that brings no profit.[2] The believers are warned that on the Day of Judgment there shall be no trading (*bay*^{c}); each individual is responsible for his or her sins and no one can bargain them away.[3] We may note also that the metaphor of a trading bargain is implicit in the oath of loyalty (*bay*^{c}*a*) that the believer owes to the caliph as supreme head of the Islamic community. The term *bay*^{c}*a* means literally a sale which is concluded by the clasping of hands. God's granting of the pleasures of Paradise is a bargain he strikes with believers in exchange for "purchasing" their persons and their wealth.[4] It is also the wage of those who fight and are slain in a *jihād,* who "sell" their lives in exchange for the life of the Hereafter.[5] The believer's devotion to God, expressed through fighting in His path, is described as a "goodly loan" which God shall pay back twofold.[6] Commercial metaphors are also employed to explain the judgment process on the Last Day. The believers' earthly actions will be weighed and "those whose balances are heavy [with good deeds] on that day are the successful ones; and those who balances are light are those who have wasted themselves."[7]

The Qur'ān also supplies both moral injunctions and practical guidance for the believer in matters of worldly commerce. Believers are enjoined not to let interest in commerce override religious obligations, and to cease business when Friday communal prayer is called.[8] However, business may be resumed immediately thereafter, since there is no sense of sacredness about the day itself. Most importantly, as far as commercial dealings are concerned, *ribā* is to be avoided at all costs. *Ribā* means "increase," and covers any unjustified accumulation of capital; hence it is generally translated as "interest," though "unlawful gain" might be more appropriate. Islamic law pays close attention to the interpretation of this term, and merchants took much legal advice on ways to avoid the full rigor of the law. But the Qur'ān is unequivocal: "Those who eat up *ribā* shall only stand as would one who has been touched by Satan. That is because they say 'Trading is just like *ribā*.' Allah has permitted trading and has forbidden *ribā*."[9] "O believers, devour not *ribā,* doubling and redoubling, and keep your duty to Allah that you may be successful. And guard yourselves against the Fire which has been prepared for the disbelievers."[10] *Ribā* is contrasted with making charitable donations: "God wipes out *ribā* and

[2] Qur'ān 2:16.
[3] Qur'ān 2:254.
[4] Qur'ān 9:111.
[5] Qur'ān 4:74.
[6] Qur'ān 2:245, 57:11.
[7] Qur'ān 7:8–9.
[8] Qur'ān 62:10–11.
[9] Qur'ān 2:275.
[10] Qur'ān 3:129.

makes charitable donations profitable."[11] "Gaining through *ribā* is not profitable with God, but giving out *zakāt* for the sake of God is."[12]

In a general sense, wealth (*māl*) should be used in the service of God, and believers should be wary lest wealth (or other worldly lures such as wives and children) distract them from this noble purpose. It should be obtained through lawful means, and one should avoid dealing with those known to have obtained their wealth in wronging others. This was a live issue on the desert frontiers of West Africa, where Arab and Berber nomads frequently obtained infusions of "capital" in the form of livestock seized from other groups during raids. The eleventh-century Almoravid teacher of the western Sahara, ᶜAbd Allāh b. Yāsīn, came up with a strange ruling: groups whom he accused of gaining illicit wealth were allowed to keep two-thirds of it, and the other third was to be given to the movement, thus "purifying" the larger portion. When he stayed among one of the tribes he refused to eat their food because he thought their wealth was "impure."[13] The issue was still being debated in the late eighteenth-early nineteenth century when al-Mukhtār al-Kuntī gave rulings on it.[14]

Credit is also regulated by the Qurʾān. Large or small, a debt engaged for a fixed term must be recorded in writing, and witnessed. If no scribe is available, a security for the debt may be taken.[15] A debtor who has difficulty in repaying his debt at the appointed time should be given additional time, though it is recommended that the debt be written off as charity.[16] This injunction to keep written records of credit given is invaluable for the student of economic history; if nothing more, it increases the possibility of historians discovering raw data.[17]

---

[11] Qurʾān 2:276.

[12] Qurʾān 30:39

[13] See J.F.P. Hopkins and Nehemiah Levtzion, *Corpus of Early Arabic Sources for West African History* (Cambridge, 1981), 74.

[14] See Bibliothèque Nationale, Paris, MSS Arabes, 5599, ff. 40r–43v; Centre de Documentation et de Recherches Historiques Ahmad Baba (CEDRAB), Timbuktu, 968, 1077, 2566, 2716, 3848. See also the ruling of al-Maghīlī in John Hunwick, *Sharīᶜa in Songhay: The Replies of al-Maghīlī to the Questions of Askia al-Hājj Muhammad* (Oxford, 1985), 83.

[15] Qurʾān 2:282–3.

[16] Qurʾān 2:280.

[17] Little of this has been done in sub-Saharan Africa, but for the northern sectors of the trade see, for example, Paul Pascon et. al., *La Maison d'Iligh et l'histoire du Tazerwalt* (Rabat, 1984); Daniel J. Schroeter, *Merchants of Essaouira: Urban Society and Imperialism in Southwestern Morocco 1844–1886* (Cambridge, 1988), Ulrich Harmann, "The dead ostrich: life and trade in Ghadames (Libya) in the nineteenth century," *Die Welt des Islams* 38 (1998): 9-94, and for the Sudan, Anders Bjørkelo, *Prelude to the Mahdiyya: Peasants and Traders in the Shendi Region, 1821–1885* (Cambridge, 1989). The documentation center at Timbuktu (CEDRAB) contains a good number of merchant documents, two of which are translated in the appendix below.

The Public Sector

So much for the private sector. In the public sector, not only was Islam a political religion from the time of Muḥammad's relocation to Madina, but state economics also became intimately bound up with pious practice: alms (*zakāt*) are always conjoined in the Qurʾān with worship (*ṣalāt*). *Zakāt* (or *ṣadaqa* to use the alternative Qurʾānic term) is an obligation for every adult free male, and constitutes the third of the five pillars of the faith. Following the Prophet's death, the rejection of the obligation to pay *zakāt* by some nomadic tribes of Arabia was regarded as an act of apostasy (*ridda*), and became a cause for war. While the Qurʾān says nothing about *zakāt* in an institutional sense, it does lay down how it should be distributed once it has been collected.[18] Historically we know very little about how it was assessed, gathered, or distributed, and this is true in regard to Africa as elsewhere.[19] Quite early on in West Africa the Islamic rules on revenue collection and disbursement were outlined by the North African jurist al-Maghīlī in a treatise he wrote for Sarki Muḥammad Rumfa of Kano (r. 1463–99).[20] We do not, of course, know how he or succeeding rulers of Kano engaged with such rules, or if the rules remained no more than a pious ideal. On the other hand, one may legitimately assume that states that had as their justification the implementation of the *sharīʿa*, such as the so-called Sokoto Caliphate or the Mahdist state in the Sudan, did undertake official collection and disbursement of *zakāt* at the state level, though in other times and places it may have been collected and disbursed at the level of town or mosque. It is rarely the subject of *fatwās* or polemics, a notable exception being the debate that took place in Ibadan in the 1940s over the definition of the minimum sum (*niṣāb*) on which it was to be paid.[21] It is likely that the institution of *zakāt* has undergone creative transformations in various African societies. One clear example comes to mind: in the Murīd rural communities of Senegal the annual fees paid by farmers to the founding "saint" of a village to "allocate" them plots of land is called *zakāt*.[22] Research would no doubt

---

[18] Qurʾān 9:58–60. "The *ṣadaqāt* are for the poor the indigent, those who collect it, those whose hearts are to be softened [new "converts" among the Quraysh], for slaves [to ransom them], debtors, and in the path of Allah [usually interpreted as *jihād*, or simply support of Islam], and for the wayfarer. [This is] an ordinance from God."

[19] But see Ahmad Ibrahim Abu Shouk and Anders Bjørkelo, ed. and trans., *The Public Treasury of the Muslims: Monthly Budgets of the Mahdist State in the Sudan, 1897*, (Leiden, 1996), xvii–xix.

[20] See K.I. Bedri and P.E. Starratt, "*Tāj al-dīn fi mā yajib ʿalā 'l-mulūk*, or 'The Crown of Religion concerning the obligations of princes,'" *Kano Studies* n. s., 1, no. 2 (1974/77):15–28. Al-Maghīlī also touched on these matters in his replies to Askiya *al-ḥājj* Muḥammad of Songhay; see Hunwick, *Sharīʿa in Songhay*, 84–5.

[21] See J.O. Hunwick et. al., comp., *Arabic Literature of Africa*, vol. 2, *The Writings of Central Sudanic Africa* (Leiden, 1995), 489–90, 501, and references cited there. There are some *fatwās* and *responsa* on *zakāt* in the CEDRAB collection.

[22] See Donal Cruise O'Brien, *Saints and Politicians* (Cambridge, 1975), 69–70.

uncover many other ways in which this institution has been appropriated by African societies to serve local needs whilst retaining an aura of orthodoxy.

The Muslim state had other sources of revenue: the poll-tax (*jizya*) paid by non-Muslims, booty of war (*ghanīma*), and land-tax, the first two of which are mentioned in the Qurʾān. The poll-tax was an annual tax payable by adult non-Muslim males. In principal, it was an acknowledgment of the right of People of the Scripture (*ahl al-kitāb*) to dwell in the lands of Islam, but the privilege was in practice extended to others such as the *majūs*—originally the Magians of Persia, and later a broad category of persons whom Muslims did not wish to treat as outright "pagans," who should be fought in *jihād*, and could thereafter be enslaved. *Jizya* was either a fixed amount agreed upon at the time such persons were conquered by Muslim armies, or, if no such agreement existed, an amount fixed later by the "imam" (in practice the local political authority). It was to be paid in cash individually in a public ceremony of humiliation, and lapsed upon conversion to Islam. People of the Scripture were often also obliged to provide hospitality to Muslim travelers for up to three days.

In Africa *jizya* became a subject of great contention in the late fifteenth century in the central Saharan oasis of Tuwat where Jews (many of whom were engaged in the trans-Saharan trade) were accused of giving presents to chiefs in lieu of *jizya*. A protracted dispute ensued in which *fatwās* were called for from North African scholars. The upshot was that the Jewish community was considered guilty of breaking its pact with the Muslims, it was attacked, and the synagogue it had long maintained was destroyed. Jews were forbidden to trade in the Songhay empire, and their effective participation in trans-Saharan trade came to an end.[23] In the nineteenth-century Sokoto Caliphate, non-Muslim Fulani, living near Sokoto, were called upon to pay *jizya*, as were some pagans of Bauchi who could not be subdued.[24] The same was also true of the Maguzawa—whose very name (sing. *Ba-Majūsi*) proclaimed that they were assimilated to the *majūs*. The Sokoto rulers also made the National African Company pay *jizya* in return for trading rights and jurisdiction over foreigners.[25] Similarly, Al-Ḥājj ʿUmar called on the French to pay *jizya*, and the tolls they remitted for trading at stations on the middle/upper Senegal were referred to in the Arabic texts of treaties as *jizya*.[26]

Booty of war was naturally a contentious issue. The Qurʾān mandated that one-fifth (*al-khums*) of what was taken in battle should go to "God and His Messenger"—in effect to the state's coffers—to be used for "God's apostle, his

---

23 See Hunwick, *Sharīʿa in Songhay*, 31–8.

24 D.M. Last, *The Sokoto Caliphate* (London, 1967), 106; R.A. Adeleye *Power and Diplomacy in Northern Nigeria, 1804–1906* (London, 1971), 32.

25 See Adeleye, *Power and Diplomacy in Northern Nigeria*, 132–3.

26 See David Robinson, *The Holy War of Umar Tal* (Oxford, 1985), 147 n. 1, 163.

family, the orphan, the needy and the traveler."[27] What was to happen to the remaining eighty percent was not precisely stated, though since in ancient Arabian practice *all* booty of war had belonged to those who obtained it, such practice was enshrined in Islamic law as regards the portion not assigned the state. Booty was defined as spoils which had been obtained in a *jihād,* and *jihād* itself had a strict legal definition. The matter only became a substantive issue in African history in the course of movements such as the Sokoto *jihād.* We do not know the details of how booty was administered, much less what kinds and how much of it was obtained in various engagements. What we do know is that in practice the strict Islamic rules for reporting and distributing booty were most often observed in the breach. Muḥammad Bello (ruled 1817–1837) had to write half a dozen treatises aimed at correcting malpractice. A key issue from the historical point of view was the "wealth in people" that resulted from the *jihād* wars and other military engagements and "pacification" activities undertaken by individual emirs. Non-Muslim captives of war were a legitimate part of booty and could be retained as slaves. Certainly *jihād* and post-*jihād* military activity produced large numbers of slaves, but who profited from them and in what degree—individual soldiers who captured them, merchants to whom the slaves might be sold, or the ruling class who might appropriate them—is far from clear.[28]

During the Mahdist period (1881–1898) in the Sudan some booty clearly was handed over to the state coffers.[29] The Mahdist treasury (the *bayt al-māl*) contained a number of items brought back from the battlefield.[30] A related but somewhat different issue arose in Songhay in the late fifteenth century. Askiya *al-Ḥājj* Muḥammad (reigned 1493–1529) was anxious to show that his predecessor Sunni ᶜAlī had effectively been an unbeliever. From this it followed that his wealth and the wealth of those who had supported him was to be treated like booty, though since such wealth was not spoils of war no division among soldiers was called for and everything went to the Public Treasury. Askiya Muḥammad could then decide how to use it. Although he no doubt made such a decision for himself and acted upon it when he came to power, the rulings of the North African jurist al-Maghīlī a few years later

[27] Qurʾān 8:41.

[28] Louis Brenner, "The North African Trading Community in the Nineteenth Century Central Sudan," in *Aspects of West African Islam,* Boston University Papers on Africa, vol. 5, ed. Daniel F. McCall and Norman Bennett (Boston, 1971), 142–3, provides some evidence from nineteenth-century Bornu suggesting that the soldiers who took part in "raids" (the dominant method of slave acquisition rather than the *jihād*) probably got rather little. From his field work in 1966 he learned that "the only booty which filtered down to the troops was 'blind, lame and broken-horned cattle.'"

[29] See Abu Shouk and Bjørkelo, *Public Treasury of the Muslims,* xxvii–xxviii.

[30] See below. p. 11.

were an important legitimation, both of his rule and of his right to confiscate property and persons owned by Sunni ᶜAlī and his defeated supporters.[31]

Land tax (*kharāj*) was instituted during the early Muslim conquests of the seventh century as a tax on the produce of the lands in conquered territories. Originally it was imposed on lands left in the hands of their non-Muslim owners, but as so many of these converted to Islam (and were only liable for *zakāt*) by the beginning of the second Islamic century, it was decreed that the land paid the tax, no matter the religion of the owner. Al-Maghīlī ruled that Askiya Muḥammad could "impose ... such tax (*kharāj*) as will bring benefit to the Muslims and development to the land without hardship," though property intended for the general well-being of the community was exempt.[32] This has a very modern ring about it, and, like the *zakāt, kharāj* is in certain respects a precursor of modern income tax. According to Last, *kharāj* was paid in the emirates of Kano and Zaria in the nineteenth century.[33] Lord Lugard, as High Commissioner of Northern Nigeria, later capitalized on this to legitimize his revenue-raising strategy. He adopted both the tax and the terminology in his Memorandum No. 5 of 1906. His flat-rate General Tax levied on agricultural and industrial products was to be called *haraji* (the Hausaization of the Arabic *kharāj*) in the Muslim areas, since this terminology was thought to be "justifiable to the Moslem mind."[34] Early tax receipts were issued in Arabic with parallel *ajami* (Hausa written in Arabic script), and only in the 1930s was Arabic replaced by English, and *ajami* with *boko* (Hausa in the Latin alphabet).[35] The *haraji* was paid into another Islamic institution appropriated by the British—the Beit-el-Mal [*bayt al-māl*]—known in northern Nigeria as the Native Treasury. First introduced by H.R. Palmer in Katsina in 1909, it was soon adopted by C.L.Temple at Kano, and in 1911 the governor of Northern Nigeria, Sir Hesketh Bell, reported that the institution had been adopted in all emirates.[36]

Any taxation over and above *zakāt* and *kharāj* on Muslims and *jizya* and *kharāj* on non-Muslims, was theoretically *ultra vires*. In practice, a wide variety of taxes were imposed in different times and places. Such taxes are generally called *maks* (pl. *mukūs*), a word with a very negative connotation. As early as the 1490s a Muslim reformer in the Agades region was complaining about seasonal taxes on livestock, market dues payable on livestock, slaves, clothes

---

31 See Hunwick, *Sharīᶜa in Songhay*, 75–8, 82–3. The only proviso was that property identifiable as having been seized from specific persons should be returned to those persons.

32 Ibid., 84.

33 Last, *Sokoto Caliphate*, 104.

34 See Lord Lugard, *Political Memoranda*, 3d ed., with introduction by A.M.H. Kirk-Greene (London, 1970), 191.

35 Examples are preserved in the Falke Collection of the Melville J. Herskovits Library of Africana, Northwestern University, Evanston, IL (U.S.A.).

36 See M.G. Smith, *Government in Kano, 1350–1950*, (Boulder, Colorado, 1997), 428–9.

and food, and city gate taxes on entry and exit.[37] Such taxes roused the ire of Muslim reformers such as al-Maghīlī and Usuman dan Fodiyo. The latter listed a wide range of illegal taxes which Hausa rulers (*sarakuna*) used to levy, and he declared that levying such taxes was reason for them to be adjudged unbelievers who should be overthrown in a *jihād*.[38] One especially hated tax, the *jangali* (a tax on cattle) was abolished, but later crept back in, and was collected in the twentieth century by British colonial authorities and in independent Nigeria.[39] In nineteenth-century Timbuktu North African merchants entering from the northern gate paid no city gate taxes, but African traders approaching through the southern Kabara gate paid some four percent.[40]

In theory all revenue of the Islamic state was handled through the *bayt al-māl* (literally, "house of wealth"), the Public Treasury, a broad state institution rather than just a physical structure. There might, indeed, be store-houses where cash or certain items were held, but in a larger sense *bayt al-māl* signified state-owned property, or rather property jointly owned by all Muslims, to be used on their behalf by the imam or his representative. It could include camels pasturing, slaves carrying out labor on behalf of the state, or public utilities, such as the government lithograph machines taken over by the Mahdists of the Sudan from the Turco-Egyptian regime, or boats on the Nile, and so forth.

With one single exception, we have no clear idea how the Public Treasury functioned in any African Muslim state. That exception is the *bayt al-māl* created by Muḥammad Aḥmad, the Mahdī of the Sudan, for the short-lived state (1881–1898) presided over by himself and his successor the Khalīfa ᶜAbdullāhi. The ledger of this institution covering a single year (1897) has survived,[41] and we have a description of the *bayt al-māl* by a Christian prisoner when it was under the stewardship of Ibrāhīm wad ᶜAdlān (*amīn bayt al-māl*

---

37 J.O. Hunwick, "Notes on a Late Fifteenth-Century Document Concerning 'al-Takrūr,'" in *African Perspectives: Papers in the History, Politics and Economics of Africa Presented to Thomas Hodgkin*, ed. Christopher Allen and R.W. Johnson (Cambridge, 1970), 12–3.

38 See M. Hiskett, "The *Kitāb al-farq*: A Work on the Habe Kingdoms Attributed to 'Uthmān dan Fodio," *Bulletin of the School of Oriental and African Studies* 23 (1960):567, 574–5.

39 See Charles Franz, "Contraction and Expansion in Nigerian Bovine Pastoralism," in *Pastoralism in Tropical Africa*, ed. Théodore Monod (London, 1975), 342–3, where it is noted that pastoral Fulbe often incur debts to pay the *jangali*.

40 James Grey Jackson, *An Account of Timbuctoo and Housa, Territories in the Interior of Africa by El Hadge Abd Salam Shabeeny* (London, 1820), 14. Nineteenth-century travel literature contains a wealth of detail on taxes levied by various African Muslim rulers. For an example of an African system of taxes and fines, see R.S. O'Fahey, *State and Society in Dār Fūr* (London, 1980), 101–14.

41 See Abu Shouk and Bjørkelo, *The Public Treasury of the Muslims*.

1886–90).[42] An actual building in Omdurman contained stores for grain, a yard with rooms for slaves, who were fed on grain from the *bayt al-māl*, and auctioned there—mainly females, as males were attached to the army—and a large pen for livestock. The mint was a sub-department, issuing gold and silver coins stamped "By order of the Mahdi," imitating Egyptian golden guineas and Turkish silver Majīdī dollars. Pieces of twilled cotton fabric were used at that time for small change, due to a shortage of small coins, but these were often rejected by merchants and had to be withdrawn. In addition to the silver *maqbūl* ("accepted"—but often in theory only) dollar (*riyāl*) there were five and ten piastre pieces and some one piastre pieces. English sovereigns and Egyptian gold pounds also circulated, as well as the Maria Theresa dollar *(abū nuqṭa)*,[43] especially in trade with Ethiopia and in the Red Sea ports. The so-called Maria Theresa dollar (*thaler*) was first minted in Austria in the reign of Maria Theresa, and continued to be minted after her death in 1780, always bearing this latter date, and was widely used throughout Sudanic Africa.[44] Also circulating in the Mahdist state were the French five-franc piece, the Spanish dollar (*douro*) and the Austrian quarter-gulden piece (*fiorini*, equal to two piastres). The *bayt al-māl* also contained a curio house, with objects brought in from battles (e.g., King John of Ethiopia's throne), a printing and lithograph press, and a dispensary.

We turn now to two financial institutions in the private domain, but which have implications in the public sphere: the *waqf* or *ḥubus* ("charitable endowment") and the highly regulated inheritance procedure. The *waqf* may be either *pro bono publico* (Arabic: *khayrī*), or familial (*ahlī*). It generally consists of a piece of property capable of producing "benefit", usually financial, on a perpetual basis (or at least for the very long term), typically a block of productive land, or a house or store that might be rented to produce income. From a legal point of view it must be donated unencumbered, in perpetuity, and it may not thereafter be sold, inherited, given away or otherwise disposed of. The usufruct of the property thus endowed goes either to support a public institution—typically a mosque and/or college (*madrasa*), or a public fountain or hospital—or to pay salaries, provide lighting, or pay for maintenance and cleaning of the endowed building; in the case of a *waqf ahlī*, it is used for the benefit of a person's descendants. The *waqf ahlī* may be stipulated to include all such descendants, or only males, or only females, and other conditions could also be laid down.

---

[42] See Fr. Joseph Ohrwalder, *Ten Years' Captivity in the Mahdi's Camp, 1881–1892*, 13th ed. (London, n. d.), 227–30.

[43] The name *abū nuqṭa* ("possessing a dot") may refer to the brooch on the bust of the empress, which, according to R. Gervais, "Pre-Colonial Currencies: A Note on the Maria Theresa Thaler," *African Economic History* 11 (1982):147–52, "had to be intact to be accepted at full value." The coin was also called *abū ṭayra* ("possessing a bird"), referring to the eagle on the reverse side.

[44] See Gervais, "Pre-Colonial Currencies," 147–52.

The *waqf* is rare in sub-Saharan Africa, partly because there is little building of a (more or less) permanent nature, i.e., little in stone. Some examples of *waqf* property other than buildings come to mind: in Lamu in East Africa there seems to have been a practice of making a *waqf* of copies of the Qurʾān and other books, both for the donor's descendants or for a mosque.[45] In Timbuktu there is a record (probably dating from the late nineteenth century) of a woman making a female slave and her daughter into a *waqf* for her daughter and the daughter's female descendants.[46] Al-Maghīlī had earlier ruled that possession of "slaves of the sultanate"—probably servile people perpetually held in thrall by the Askiya—was lawful, on the grounds that they were like a *waqf* for the Askiya and his descendants.[47] One of the great benefits of the *waqf* institution is that it enables a wealthy person to dispose of part of his property to his family or others outside of the laws of inheritance which strictly regulate to whom an inheritance may or must pass. To the best of my knowledge, no study of the *waqf* institution in sub-Saharan Africa exists, either from a general perspective or of a particular instance of its operation.

Inheritance is strictly regulated by the Qurʾān, 4:11–12. A basic rule is that where there are both males and females involved, the female gets half the share of the male. Husbands inherit wives—one-half the value if there are no children, or a quarter if there are;[48] wives similarly inherit husbands, but only in the amount of one-quarter or one-eighth (if there are several this must be further split). The rules are many and complex, and division of inheritance became a specialized branch of the legal profession, usually commanding a fee—not least because property had to be reduced to a monetary value, on the basis of which fractions could be established. In a case in nineteenth-century Timbuktu, a widow died, leaving a house and some slaves. She had one daughter, a brother, and two sisters. The house and the slaves were evaluated, and the total estate was eighty-five *mithqāls* (mq.), less three-and-a-half mq. for funeral and legal expenses, leaving eighty-one-and-a-half mq. The daughter got half, the brother a quarter, and each of the sisters one-eighth.[49]

---

[45] J.O. Hunwick and R.S. O'Fahey, "Some Waqf Documents from Lamu," *Bulletin d'Information* [Fontes Historiae Africanae] 6 (1981):26–43.

[46] See Document No. 1 below. In another document (CEDRAB, 3851/11) a woman makes a *ḥubus* of a slave women for her children, both male and female.

[47] Hunwick, *Sharīʿa in Songhay*, 86, 88.

[48] It should be recalled that Islamic law allows women to own property in their own right. An investigation of Muslim women's roles as property owners in Africa is overdue.

[49] See Document No. 2 below. See also M. Hiskett, "Materials Relating to the Cowrie Currency of the Western Sudan—I: A Late Nineteenth-Century Schedule of Inheritance from Kano," *Bulletin of the School of Oriental and African Studies* 29 (1966):122–142, where a large estate including slaves, cattle, a great deal of cloth and garments, and many other miscellaneous items is valued, item by item, in cowries for the purpose of division among the heirs.

In accordance with the laws of inheritance, libraries were split up, land was divided into small parcels, and slaves sometimes ended up being jointly owned. A person was allowed to make a bequest or bequests of up to one-third of the value of the estate, but only to persons not their mandatory heirs. The value of the estate was calculated after payment of lawful debts and funeral expenses, but the value of slaves who had been promised freedom upon their owner's death was deducted from the one-third of the estate which could be freely disposed of.

Although Islamic law does not blatantly advocate fines as a means of punishment, certain religious transgressions call for "fines" in kind as expiation. For example, expiation for breaking an oath is the freeing of a slave, or feeding or clothing ten needy persons;[50] the use of a particular divorce formula (the *ẓihār*) is to be expiated by feeding sixty destitute persons, or two months of fasting.[51] Unintentional homicide calls for the freeing of a slave and payment of blood-wite (*diya*), generally fixed at one hundred camels for a male and fifty for a female.[52]

Commercial Law

Islamic commercial law is highly developed, and is in most cases an outgrowth of the commercial law that Arabs found in place in the lands they conquered in the Middle East and North Africa (i.e., aspects of Roman provincial law, and Jewish law).[53] The cardinal principles of commercial transactions are (1) to avoid *ribā*, and (2) to avoid the appearance of gambling or speculation—both strictly forbidden by the Qurʾān. Since these are integral to most commercial practice, many stratagems were devised to get round them, generating a whole literature of "lawful" stratagems (*ḥiyal*). *Ribā* is defined by Schacht as "any advantage to be derived from the granting of a loan." This means not merely paying back more than was borrowed, but for example, receiving any favors from the debtor—food, the use of his property, horse, or even (in theory) sitting under the shade of his tree.

One way to make a loan at interest is through fictitious sale (*bayᶜ al-ᶜīn* or *bayᶜ al-ᶜayniyya*). The debtor sells the creditor an item and immediately repur-

---

50 Qurʾān 5:89. In practice, many Muslim states did impose fines. A complex system of "traditional" fines operated in the Muslim sultanate of Dār Fūr in the eighteenth- nineteenth centuries; see R.S. O'Fahey and M.I. Abu Salim, *Land in Dār Fūr Charters and Related Documents from the Dar Fur Sultanate,* (Cambridge, 1983), and R.S. O'Fahey, *State and Society in Dār Fūr* (see n. 40 above).

51 Qurʾān 58:4.

52 Qurʾān 4:92. For a case study of the workings of *diya* and its contestation in an African context, see Raymond Taylor, "Warriors, Tributaries, Blood Money and Political Transformation in Nineteenth-Century Mauritania," *Journal of African History* 36, no. 3 (1995):419–41.

53 The theoretical material in this section is based mainly on Joseph Schacht, *An Introduction to Islamic Law* (Oxford, 1964).

chases it for a higher sum, payable at a later date. The difference represents the cost of the loan (the "interest") and the object is retained by the creditor as security. The loan could also be unsecured through a fictional sale. The creditor sells the debtor an item for a sum $(x + y)$ representing the base price plus interest, the total amount to be paid at some future date. He then buys back the object at its base price (x) which he pays to the creditor immediately. The debtor thus ends up with the sum he wants (x), and later repays the originally agreed price $(x + y)$.

In order to raise money or provide goods for a commercial venture—in particular long-distance trade—the sleeping partnership (*muḍāraba* or *qirāḍ*—commenda) evolved. It is a partnership in profit only, a fiduciary relationship (*amāna*),[54] in which one partner supplies the capital or goods, shares in the profits, and bears any losses. The other partner does the actual work of commerce, traveling if necessary and selling the goods at the best profit he can. He shares in the profits but does not share in losses. Large caravans would carry goods provided by many merchants; their partners sold the goods by themselves or through agents in the towns they visited, and bought other goods which were taken back and sold at base.[55] The provider of initial capital could not stipulate a sum of money to be repaid, and could only share in the profit accruing from the venture. Profit-sharing is, in fact, the principle on which Islamic banks are supposed to work—they are investment banks and investors may earn a profit on their investment, or may lose money on it. The *muḍāraba* partnership is thus a useful way to make money work without getting ensnared in *ribā* dealings.

There were, of course, other kinds of business partnerships both limited and unlimited. In a limited liability partnership (*sharikat ᶜinān*), each partner is responsible to third parties for his own transactions only and has the right of recourse against his partner to the extent of the share he invested. Each partner puts in any amount of capital. The profits are shared proportionally, though if their labor varies, their share in profits may also vary. In the unlimited partnership (*sharikat mufāwaḍa*) each partner has full power and liability and makes available his entire capital.

Clearly liability and trust are two essential elements of business transactions, especially when time and distance are involved in a trading venture. Goods would frequently be entrusted to a person to take and sell at a distant location. He, in turn, might leave all or some of them in the trust of a third party (host/landlord) to store on his behalf, or to sell. Numerous examples

---

54 For *amāna*, see Qur᾿ān 2:283, 23:8, and 33:72.

55 See Terence Walz, *Trade between Egypt and Bilād al-Sūdān, 1700–1820* (Cairo, 1978), 107–8, for an example from eighteenth century Egypt, trading with the Sudan. See Stephen Baier, *An Economic History Central Niger* (Oxford, 1980), 71–6, for an account of how trans-Saharan trade from Tripoli to the central Bilād al-Sūdān was financed in the nineteenth century.

are to be found in merchant archives of Timbuktu.[56] The person entrusted is not liable for accidental loss, but is liable for failure to perform the contract agreed upon, or for wilfully transgressing the trust. Obligations—towards goods in trust or payment of debts—cease upon fulfilment of the specified terms, or upon the agent being acquitted unconditionally by the person providing the goods or money through some new arrangement that satisfies the creditor. The obligation can be unilaterally relinquished by the creditor, or satisfied in consideration of some other compensation. Debts may also be transferred to a third party. For example, X owes me 100 mq. I wish to pay Y 90 mq, so I charge X to pay this out of the sum he owes me. The acceptance of the obligation by X extinguishes my obligation towards Y. Or it could be a simple matter of debt collection: I charge X to collect the debt which Y owes me. Such assignments of claims to third parties are called *ḥawāla* (transfer), and may involve both money and goods.[57]

This has important consequences, since it enables payments to be made over long distances without the physical transfer of funds or goods, thus obviating any risk of loss. This type of bill of exchange was known as a *suftaja* (Farsi: *suftaha*), and is an important banking-type financial transaction, clearly of importance for trans-Saharan trade, for example. In fact, Western banking owes one of its most fundamental term—"check"—to the Arabic word *ṣakk*,[58] which means a document or more especially a document acknowledging a financial obligation. These were widely used in the Muslim world, and were evidently of importance in the trans-Saharan trade. As early as the tenth century there is a record of a promissory note for 40,000 *dīnār*s owed by a Sijilmasa merchant trading in Awdaghast (southern Mauritania) to another merchant of Sijilmasa.[59] In the early nineteenth century the Moroccan trader ᶜAbd al-Salām Shabaynī [Shabeeni] noted: "The merchants of Timbuctoo have agents or other correspondents in other countries; and are themselves agents in return. ... A principal source of their wealth is lending gold-dust and slaves at high interest to foreign merchants, which is repaid with goods from Marocco [*sic*] and other countries to which the gold-dust and slaves are carried."[60]

In Islamic law business is subject to contract, spoken or written, except on minor purchases where gesture may suffice (such as buying fruit at a fruit stall). The meeting of buyer and seller to negotiate a price and conditions of sale is called a "session" (*majlis*), and recision of the sale is automatically

---

[56] See, for example documents three and four in the appendix below. For another example, see Abner Cohen, *Custom and Politics in Urban West Africa: A Study of Hausa Migrants in Yoruba Towns* (Berkeley, 1969).

[57] Hence the French *aval*—guarantee, endorsement of a bill of exchange.

[58] Probably from the Persian word *chakk*.

[59] Hopkins and Levtzion, *Corpus of Early Arabic Sources*, 47.

[60] Jackson, *An Account of Timbuctoo and Housa*, 22.

allowed during the session, i.e., until the two part company. Recision may also be a stipulation (as, for example, within a stated period). There is an automatic right to return defective goods with pre-existing faults (*ᶜayb qadīm*), for example, a bale of cloth eaten away in the middle, or a slave concubine who snores, within three days. Written contracts are accepted in court in evidence only if witnessed, and the witness can be made to testify.

It is a principle of trading in the Islamic system that there be no unjustified enrichment—no monetary advantage is to be received without giving counter value. It is not permitted to purchase an item and resell it immediately before paying the first owner his money. This amounts to *ribā*. Items that can be weighed or measured cannot be exchanged for items of the same type in greater or lesser quantity, nor should there be a delay in performance of the contract. For example gold, if worked, can only be sold for the equivalent weight in gold, which means that the artisan receives no wage for his work. The solution is to pay for the worked object in silver, or to supply the raw gold and hire the artisan to work it. Contracting parties should have sure knowledge of the counter-values intended for exchange as a result of their transaction. These values should be determined at the "session". As a general rule (to which, naturally, there are exceptions) one cannot arrange the sale of things at a future date, since this involves "risk" (*gharar*), and may entail dealing in non-existent commodities. For example, one cannot sell crops that have not been harvested, animals that are as yet unborn, salt that has not yet been mined. Insurance has thus been regarded with some suspicion, since this is selling a commodity (an accident claim) that does not yet, and may never, exist.

Currencies

The use of coinage is as old as Islamic civilization. In ancient Arabia no local coinage was issued, but merchants were familiar with Byzantine and Sasanian gold and silver specie. The earliest Islamic coins were modeled on these and stamped with a simple Arabic inscription. Islamic coinage is comprised essentially of the gold *dīnār* and the silver *dirham*,[61] though later, copper coins of one sort or another were issued in some places. The gold *dīnār* was equivalent in weight and value to the *mithqāl*. Its weight varied from 3.8–4.7 gr., an average weight being 4.25 gr. or three-twentieths of an ounce, i.e., six-and-two-thirds mq. equals one ounce.[62] Silver coinage was not used in Sudanic

[61] The term *dirhem* is the Greek *drachme*, while *dīnār* is the Roman *denarius* (*aureus*). One or other of these terms is used by various Arab countries for units of modern currency: the *dirhem* is used in Morocco and the United Arab Emirates, the *dīnār* in Iraq, Kuwait, Jordan, the Sudan. Mauritania uses the *ougeya*, which is the Arabic *ūqiya* (ounce). The notional relationship of the "classical" *dirham* to the *dīnār* was 10:7.

[62] See Leo Africanus, *Description de l'Afrique*, trans. E. Epaulard (Paris, 1956), 2:469. Ibn Baṭṭūṭa was given the seemingly odd amount of thirty-three-and-one-third *mithqāl*s of

Africa, at least before the early nineteenth century. There were no sources of silver, so whatever circulated was imported (e.g., the Maria Theresa dollar, the Spanish dollar and various other European coins). Most imported silver was recycled into ornaments; silver jewelry was popular, especially among Tuareg women. In West Africa, at any rate, there seems to have been little or no minting of gold coins. In the eleventh century al-Bakrī refers to unstamped gold coins (*dīnārs*) in use at Tādmakka,[63] and mentions import and export dues in Ancient Ghana in terms of *dīnārs/mithqāls*, though it is not clear whether he is referring to actual coins or to equivalent weights of gold.[64] In the fourteenth century Ibn Baṭṭūṭa makes several casual references to *mithqāls*, but again these may refer to a weight of gold (dust) rather than a coin, unless Moroccan *dīnārs* were circulating.[65] There are also several references to large sums of *mithqāls* both in his account and in the Timbuktu chronicles, but again these are also probably weight measurements rather than coins; though Leo Africanus mentions pieces of unstamped gold, which he says were exchanged for cowries at the rate of 1:400.[66] Timbuktu commercial documents of the nineteenth century also refer to *mithqāls*–and, of course, to cowries. Dupuis reported a stamped *mithqāl* minted at Nikki in Borgu (a way-station of the Wangara gold route from Asante to Hausaland) in the early nineteenth century, but no sample has survived, though it was said to have wide currency.[67] Caillié reported that at Arawān, 150 miles north of Timbuktu, "on ne connait

gold by Mansa Sulayman, but this, of course, was five ounces, just as the 100 mq. he was given on departure was fifteen ounces. See Hopkins and Levtzion, *Corpus*, 290. According to Garrard, "The earliest *dīnārs* of 4.25 gr. had been reckoned at seven to the *ūqiya* of 29.7 grams, and Arab *dirhems* of 2.97 gr. were reckoned at ten to the same ounce. Seven gold *dinars* or *mitkals* therefore had the same weight as ten silver dirhems, and this relationship, according to the scholar Ibn Khaldun (born 1332), had been fixed since the beginning of Islam. The reckoning of seven *dinars* to the ounce was not used for long, however. By the late tenth century, when North African *dinars* had fallen to 4.1 grams or less, these lighter coins could not be reckoned at 7 to the ounce of 29.7 grams; instead they were reckoned at 6⅔ to a widely used trade ounce of 27.0 grams. This was the old Roman-Byzantine ounce from which the original solidus standard had been derived, and it was to become of major importance in the trans-Saharan gold trade". See Timothy Garrard, *Akan Weights and the Gold Trade* (London,1980), 215. Marion Johnson, however, draws attention to the varying real weights of the *mithqāl*, dependent on time and place, and to differences between the "trade" *mithqāl* and the "legal" *mithqāl*. "The Nineteenth-Century Gold 'Mithqal' in West and North Africa," *Journal of African History* 9, no. 4 (1968):547–569,

[63] Hopkins and Levtzion, *Corpus*, 85.

[64] Ibid., 81.

[65] Ibid., pp. 290, 293 (specifically mentioned as gold dust), 295 (large amounts equivalent to 450 and 600 oz.), 298 (4, 000 mq. equals 600 oz), 302, 303.

[66] Leo Africanus, *Description de l'Afrique*, 2:469. This is an extremely low exchange rate—in fact a "famine" rate.

[67] Joseph Dupuis, *A Journal of a Residence in Ashantee*, 2d ed. (London,1824), cxii–cxiii; Johnson, "Nineteenth-Century Gold 'Mithqal' in West and North Africa," 552–5.

d'autre matière représentative que l'or et l'argent, qu'on devise par pièces de la valeur d'un mithkal, à l'imitation de la monnaie de Maroc."[68] In Bornu Shehu Muḥammad al-Amīn al-Kānemī requested Denham to procure for him from England a die for stamping coins, but apparently nothing came of it.[69]

Since there was virtually no gold coinage in West Africa, the question arises as to how transactions involving *mithqāls* were conducted. Was gold dust actually weighed out on such occasions? Perhaps so. Al-Maghīlī gives detailed instructions as to how to weigh gold-dust, suggesting that it was an important skill in fifteenth century Timbuktu.[70] Jackson speaks of "skins" of gold dust (*tibr wangarī*), each containing four ounces of gold, and bars weighing twenty ounces each (*sibkat dhahab wangarī*),[71] while threads of twisted gold are mentioned by al-Bakrī (eleventh-century Awdaghast),[72] and Barth (nineteenth-century Timbuktu).[73] On the other hand, given the large number of transactions taking place in a commercial emporium such as Timbuktu, constant weighing would have been tedious and vulnerable to loss. It is possible then that the *mithqāl* was under most circumstances merely a money of account, to be realized as actual gold dust only under special circumstances.[74] In the meantime credit and debit notes would have served to keep accounts straight.

Other items, such as cloth strips and pieces of rock salt, were, from the eleventh century right down to the nineteenth, used as units of value against which other items could be valued.[75] However, the most widely used cur-

---

68 Réné Caillié, *Journal d'un voyage à Temboctou et à Jenné dans l'Afrique centrale* (Paris, 1830), 2:377.

69 Denham and Clapperton, *Travels and Discoveries,* 2:534.

70 Hunwick, *Songhay in Sharīʿa,* 92.

71 Jackson, *Account of Timbuctoo and Housa,* 347. In Kano in the early sixteenth century, there were said to be "purses" of 500 mq. (equals 2⅛ kg.). The visiting scholar ʿAbd al-Raḥmān Suqqayn of Fez was allegedly given fifty such purses; see Muḥammad b. Jaʿfar al-Kattānī, *Salwat al-anfās* (Fez, 1898–9), 2:160.

72 See Levtzion and Hopkins, *Corpus, 69.*

73 See Heinrich Barth, *Travels and Discoveries in Northern and Central Africa, Being a Journal of an Expedition Undertaken Under the Auspices of Her Majesty's Government in the Years 1849–1855* (1857–9; reprint, London, 1965), 3:360. He remarks that he did not see the "tibber" (*tibr*) mentioned by Shabayni. Jackson, *Empire of Morocco,* 290, mentions "twisted gold rings of Wangara" and "gold rings made at Jinnie [Jenne]" among articles imported into Morocco from West Africa.

74 Pascon, *La Maison d'Iligh,* 61, n. 15, notes that in nineteenth-century Morocco the *mithqāl* was a money of account rather than a real money, no doubt reflecting the scarcity of gold reaching Morocco from across the Sahara.

75 In the eleventh century al-Bakrī mentions short pieces of red cloth in the purchase of slaves in Zawīla (Fezzan), the slaves no doubt coming from Kanem. He says salt was the currency at Kawkaw (Gao); see Hopkins and Levtzion, *Corpus,* 64, 87. In late nineteenth- century Bornu cotton strips five to six centimeters wide and three to four meters long called *gabag* were still "the most acceptable purchasing medium in Bornu"; see Gustav Nachtigal, *Sahara and Sudan,* trans A.G.B. Fisher and H.J. Fisher, 4 vols. (London,

rency and unit of account in the Sudanic regions, as well as on the West African coast, was the cowrie shell.[76] It is first mentioned by al-Bakrī (eleventh century) as an import into Kūgha (close to Ancient Ghana), along with salt, copper and euphorbium, and in the following century al-Zuhrī reported that cowries were imported into Zāfun (Diafunu), but neither writer says that cowries were used as currency.[77] Cowries are first mentioned as currency in Kanem and Mali in the mid-fourteenth century. Al-ᶜUmarī reports that, while the standard currency of Kanem was a cloth called *dandī*, the people also used "cowries, beads, copper in round pieces, and coined silver as currency, but all [are] valued in terms of that cloth."[78] The second reference is even more interesting, since it reveals where cowries were imported from and indicates that their importation was a considerable source of profit for North African merchants. Al-ᶜUmarī reports: "The currency in the land of Takrūr consists of cowries, and the merchants, whose principal import these are, make big profits on them."[79] In reference to the North African caravan station of Sijilmāsa, he says: "[I]t is Sijilmāsa that the merchants set out from for the land of the Sūdān with salt, copper and cowries, and return to with gold. [They cross the perilous deserts and risk dangers] impelled ... only by the great profits which they make out of the Sūdān, for they set out with valueless articles and return with bullion."[80]

These cowries did not, of course, originate in Morocco. As is well known, cowries are harvested in the Indian Ocean, especially in the waters around the Maldives. In the fourteenth century they were exchanged for rice with Bengali merchants, and some were then sent then via Afghanistan and Persia to the Mediterranean; others were taken by Yemeni ships as ballast.[81] Leo Africanus may be referring to this first route when he says that at Timbuktu they use

1971– 87), 2:111, 223. For a detailed survey of sources for trade in both salt and textiles, as well as their monetary usage, see Lars Sundström, *The Exchange Economy of Pre-Colonial Africa*, 2d ed. (London, 1974).

76 The most detailed work on cowrie currency in Africa is Jan Hogendorn and Marion Johnson, *The Shell Money of the Slave Trade* (Cambridge, 1986). The shell most used was the small *Cypraea moneta*, but the larger *Cypraea annulus* was also used. For a short time at Timbuktu in the late eighteenth century these were substituted for with the West African *Marginella*, owing to a shortage of *Cypraea*; see idem., *Shell Money and the Slave Trade*, 130–1.

77 Hopkins and Levtzion, *Corpus*, 83, 100.

78 Ibid., 260. The reference to coined silver is unique. If accurate, it would probably indicate *dirham* coins minted in North Africa.

79 Ibid., 269. In this context "Takrūr" evidently means the Malian empire (Mansā Mūsā was known as the "king of Takrūr").

80 Ibid., 276.

81 See *The Travels of Ibn Baṭṭūṭa, A.D. 1325–1354*, vol. 4, trans. H.A.R. Gibb and C.F. Beckingham, Hakluyt Society Publications, 2d ser., vol. 178 (Cambridge, 1994), 827; A.M.H. Kirk-Greene, "The Major Currencies of Nigerian History," *Journal of the Historical Society of Nigeria* 2, no. 1 (1960):132–50.

small shells brought from Persia for petty transactions.[82] When early Portuguese navigators made their way down the Mauritanian coast they found cowries in use among the Sanhaja. The shells had been obtained from Venice whence they had been imported from "the Levant."[83] Later, after the route around the Cape was opened up by the Portuguese, the merchants of various European countries imported cowries, often as ballast, taking them first to European ports and then re-exporting them to West African ports and, it would seem, to some North African ports as well, especially in Morocco. In 1805, for example, Jackson reported that 32,000 lbs of cowries were imported into Mogador from Amsterdam, clearly for re-exportation to West Africa.[84] Other reports confirm this.[85] Cowries were also exported to the Middle Niger from Egypt. Walz documents this from archival records for the seventeenth century, when the term used is *kūda* (or *kawda*), the form which may have given rise to the Hausa term *kudi*,[86] and demonstrates that they were already known by this name in Egypt in the fifteenth century and equated with *wad*ᶜ*a*—the most widely used term.[87] An anonymous Spaniard, writing in 1591, claims that Songhay switched its source for cowries from Morocco to Egypt in the sixteenth century, and that the defeated Askiya Isḥāq II suggested a return to Moroccan supply as part of his negotiations with his conqueror, Pasha Jawdār.[88] However, the larger picture of the importation of cowries across the Sahara remains far from clear.

---

82 Leo Africanus, *Description*, 2:469.

83 See F. Iroko, "Les marchards vénitiens et le commerce des cauris entre le XIIIe et le XVe siècle," *Africa* [Rome] 45, no. 3 (1990):480–4. He cites the voyage of Cadamosto; see *The Voyages of Cadamosto and Other Documents on Western Africa in the Second Half of the XVth Century*, ed. G.R. Crone, 25–6.

84 Jackson, *Account of the Empire of Morocco*, 247.

85 E.g., a report from the British consul in Morocco, James Matra (1789), who listed cowries among caravan goods going to Timbuktu, and the report of Shabeni [Shabayni] (1792), who said that the cowries used at Timbuktu were bought at Fez by the pound; see *Records of the African Association, 1788–1831*, ed. Robin Hallett (London, 1964), 80, 108. Writing in 1697, the French dragoman Pétis de la Croix reported cowries going south from Tripoli; see John Lavers, "Trans-Saharan Trade Before 1800: Towards Quantification," *Paideuma* 40 (1994):252.

86 But the singular *wuri* remains problematic.

87 See Terence Walz, "Trade between Egypt and Bilād al-Takrūr in the XVIII Century" (Unpublished paper presented to the International Seminar on the History of Kano, Bayero University, 1976), 11. Hogendorn and Johnson, *Shell Money of the Slave Trade*, 15, say that while it is likely that "by the Middle Ages" a major market for cowries existed in Cairo, "the case is largely circumstantial and by no means certain." However, it is not clear what they mean by "the Middle Ages" in the context of the Middle East.

88 According to him, Songhay used to import cowries from Morocco, but abandoned this for the cheaper cowries of Cairo and Mecca. The ruler forbade the entry of Moroccan cowries. As part of Pasha Jawdār's negotiations with Askiya Isḥāq it was said that the king (Mūlāy al-Manṣūr) agreed that Songhay could import salt and cowries without

We know little about how this cowrie currency was regulated. Once a caravan of cowries arrived, say, in Timbuktu, there must have been some buyers there who essentially acted as bankers, setting an initial exchange rate for the cowrie against the gold *mithqāl*, and exchanging the cowries for goods that they wanted to purchase on the local market. The exchange rate, apart from times of famine, remained extraordinarily steady over three centuries (sixteenth through nineteenth), at around 3,000 cowries to the *mithqāl* of gold, though the cowrie became devalued later in the century. At source in the Maldives one mq. could buy 400,000 cowries (and apparently on occasion as many as one million).[89] No matter what the transport costs were, many middlemen must have made considerable profits in this trade.

We are a little better informed as regards Bornu, thanks to Nachtigal. There the exchange rate of the recently introduced cowrie against the silver dollar was periodically fixed by royal decree, and in Nachtigal's day (1870) it was about 4,000.[90] As he observed, this rate fluctuated according to the number of dollars in circulation, so that towards the end of his stay the exchange rate was some fifty percent higher. This suggests that control by the ruler was not very effective, unless he was himself engaged in manipulating the rate, as his minister Hajj Beshir apparently was.[91] In Hausaland, too, there was some attempt by rulers to intervene in the money market. The "sheikh of the soug" (*sarkin kasuwa*) who was an agent of the emir, fixed the prices of goods, and thus had control over the purchasing power of the cowrie.[92] In Katsina in the early 1830s the sultan maintained a monopoly over cowries, and imposed heavy customs duties on any individual who tried to import cowries.[93]

---

tax; see H. de Castries "La conquête du Soudan par el Mansour (1591)," *Hespéris* 3 (1923):433–88.

89 See Gibb and Beckingham, *Travels of Ibn Baṭṭūṭa*, 2:827. In Mali and the Niger Bend the cowrie was very expensive in Ibn Baṭṭūṭa's day. He reports an exchange rate of one mq. for 1,500 cowries, twice the price of the period extending from the sixteenth through nineteenth centuries. Perhaps the price reflects the cost of a land route through Asia, whereas later prices reflect the cheaper costs of a direct sea route in European ships.

90 Nachtigal, *Sahara and Sudan*, 2:224.

91 Ibid., note 1.

92 Clapperton gives the name of the cowrie as "whydah," which led his editor, E.W. Bovill, to remark in a note that this was because Whydah was the principal port for the importation of cowries; see Denham and Clapperton, *Travels and Discoveries*, 651. Earlier, Lucas had mentioned that the Arabs of Hausaland called cowries "Hueda," which led Colvin to make a similar assumption; see Lucie Colvin "The Commerce of Hausaland, 1780–1833," in *Aspects of West African Islam*, 123. In fact, in both cases, the word is more likely to be a rendering of the Arabic *wadaᶜa*.

93 General E. Daumas, *Le Grand Désert: Itinéraire d'une caravane du Sahara au pays des nègres, royaume de Haoussa*, 4th ed., (Paris, 1860), 204. According to this account, cowries were then being brought from the river Niger, presumably shipped upriver by local traders who obtained them from European importations into the Niger Delta area.

Salt and cloth have both been mentioned as currencies. While in the Timbuktu region in the nineteenth century they could no longer really be considered as "currencies," they did play an important role in commercial dealings that otherwise involved gold and cowries. Barth gives us a fascinating insight into the complexity of trading operations involving salt, cloth, cowries and gold.[94] Trade in salt on a large scale was conducted through cloth—the *turkedi*—used for female attire, which was manufactured in Kano. There a piece was bought for 1,800 cowries.[95] This was equivalent notionally to roughly one-half mq. of gold, though in Kano the money of commerce was the Austrian (Maria Theresa), or the Spanish, silver dollar. *Turkedi* were then taken from Kano to Ghat, thence to Tuwat and from there to Timbuktu. Ghadames merchants bartered in the market of Arawān six turkedi for nine slabs of salt prepared for the market (i.e., one slab equals 1,200 cowries valued at four-tenths mq. at the Timbuktu rate; this allows 600 cowries or one-third of the selling price for cost of transportation and profit). The minimum price of a middle-sized slab at Timbuktu was no more than 3,000 cowries (or one mq. of gold), though under certain conditions it could, in Barth's day, rise to twice as much.[96] If the merchants transported it to Timbuktu, says Barth, they sold it there at eight slabs for six mq. (i.e., one slab equal three-quarters mq. or 2,250 cowries). In Sansani near Segu one slab fetched two mq.[97] The cost of transportation to Sansandi was augmented by the taxes (*ᶜushūr*) paid to the Fulani and transportation by donkey from Jafarabe where they were obliged to unload. Transportation costs amounted to one-third of the total cost. An investment of 1,200 cowries in Kano thus yielded 6,000 or more cowries at Sansani (assuming the cowrie/mq. rate to be not less than at Timbuktu),[98] but this must be offset by the costs of transportation of the *turkedi* and the salt over very long distances, the taxes that were to be paid en route, and variations in the price of salt and in the cowrie/mq. exchange rate.

Cowries and gold, of course, became obsolete in trading transactions in the twentieth century as the use of colonial currencies was established

---

[94] Barth, *Travels and Discoveries*, 361–2.

[95] According to Clapperton, in 1824 the *turkedi* sold for 2–3,000 cowries, but merchants could no doubt get a lower bulk purchase price. See Denham and Clapperton, *Travels and Discoveries*, 659.

[96] Barth, as a foreigner, paid a mark up of twenty-five percent. He exchanged gold for cowries at a rate of 3,750.

[97] In document three below, the average price of a slab of salt sold at Sansandi would be 2.83 mq.

[98] Or, at the price deducible from document three, 8,490 cowries per slab. Richard Roberts, *Warriors, Merchants and Slaves: The State and the Economy in the Middle Niger Valley, 1700–1914* (Stanford, 1987), gives the price of a bar of salt in the middle Niger valley as 8,000 cowries in 1805, and 10,000–12,000 in 1828. All of these figures are, of course, no more than rough guides to prices. There would have been considerable variation due to the quality and exact weight of a salt slab, transportation costs, scarcity at a particular time, etc. The same is true of the other commodities involved in such exchanges.

through the demands of taxation. Cowries became rapidly devalued against gold and silver in the late nineteenth century, though as late as the 1950s they were still used in some remote areas for very small transactions.

What was the "Islamic" reaction to the introduction of colonial currencies in the late nineteenth and early twentieth centuries? Insofar as Muslims in Africa had been using the money of the unbelievers for a long time (on the western coasts since the sixteenth century, one would suppose, and throughout the nineteenth century in the Sahel), there was no recorded opposition to infidel coinage. But questions did arise in regard to the use of paper money. A pamphlet written in Medina (Saudi Arabia) in 1348/1929, authored by Alfa Hāshim (d. 1932), a nephew of al-Ḥājj ᶜUmar, the founder of the Muslim state of Segu, deals with how paper money (*awrāq al-fulūs*) is to be regarded in the light of Islamic law.[99]

He discusses paper money within the framework of *zakāt* and *ribā*, asking whether it liable to *zakāt*, and if transactions with it fall under the law of *ribā*? The answer seems to be that paper money is treated essentially as a material object which can be traded, rather than as currency per se. As such it is not subject to *zakāt*, just as copper coin (*fulūs*) is not. However, some authorities thought it could be subject to *zakāt* if it is widely used,[100] and if its face value was equivalent to the taxable minimum (*niṣāb*) for gold and silver. It could also be treated as a promissory note, and provided nothing more than its stated value (in gold or silver) was eventually paid, there would be no question of *ribā*.[101] No doubt a combing of *fatwā* literature in the nineteenth and twentieth centuries would throw light on the way Muslims have looked at money issues, and perhaps specifically colonial currencies.

As for banking, there is, of course, a great deal that has been written on this issue in the Muslim world at large, especially in the past twenty years. Again, the specifically African literature has not been explored.[102] In concluding this brief survey, let me allude to a small book by the contemporary Tijānī shaykh of Bornu, Shaykh Sharīf Ibrāhīm Ṣāliḥ, published apparently in Nigeria in 1993.[103] In it he refers to a meeting of the Fatwa Committee of the Higher Council of Muslim Affairs (of which he is the chair), which met in Sokoto under the patronage of the then Sultan of Sokoto, Ibrāhīm Dasūqī (a well-known commercial banker). This body concluded that the interest paid by banks on deposits is forbidden. Nevertheless, given the current insecure conditions in Nigeria, there was no alternative to depositing money in

---

99 See *Imtāᶜ al-aḥdāq wa'l-nufūs bi-muṭālaᶜat aḥkām awrāq al-fulūs* (Khartoum, 1351/ 1933). See especially the summing up on pp. 22–3.

100 The same seems to be true of cowries (see ibid.,70).

101 Nor, presumably, could it be liable to *zakāt* since it is only a promise to pay, and *not* an actual payment of gold or silver—the two metals on which *zakāt* is liable.

102 But see the contribution of Endre Stiansen in this volume.

103 *al-Bunūk: ḍarūratuhā— ᶜā'idatuhā.*

banks—an argument used in the juridical literature to defend the bill of exchange (*suftaja*), which otherwise might be seen as a form of unlawful profit, that is, money which benefits from being transferred without loss or payment, or which is "increased" by being established in one type of currency and paid out in another. The principle that necessity makes the forbidden allowable is also invoked. Interest on money is unlawful, and such unlawful gain should be returned to its "owners" if they are known. If they are not, this unlawful profit should be given out as charity—technically through the *bayt al-māl*, which receives money whose owners are unknown, but in practice through the individual concerned. The solution with which the book concludes, however, is the "classical" one, namely that investment banks, where depositors can place money to be invested in projects, should be established. Depositors/investors would then take profit or loss according to the fate of the project, in an agreed proportion with the bank. This arrangement is reflective of the *muḍāraba* contract in operation in regular commercial transactions.

Conclusion

In closing, let me apologize to economic historians and anthropologists to whom this paper may appear both unadventurous and inconclusive. What I have tried to do, in the absence of sustained empirical studies of the financial institutions of Muslim polities in Africa, or any detailed examination of the structures of trans-Saharan trade, is to draw attention to the research potential of such topics and thereby to suggest that they deserve greater consideration.[104] Muslim ways of conducting business, grounded in, if not always well reflecting, Islamic law and social ethics, have been a factor in sub-Saharan African commerce for a millennium. Muslim polities there have come and gone for almost as long, yet we still do not have a clear notion of how business was conducted in Timbuktu, Ghadames, Kano and Kuka; the account books and merchant correspondence have not been studied—though at least for the nineteenth century some do exist. Nor do we know how Muslim states made use of the resources of Islamic financial theory in the collection and disbursement of revenue, how the niceties of the *sharīʿa* were observed, adapted, or ignored, either in the pre-colonial period, or the

[104] This is not to ignore some excellent broad studies that have been made of trans-Saharan trade, such as Baier, *Economic History*; Jean-Louis Miège, "Le commerce trans-Saharien au XIXe siècle: essai de quantification," *Revue de l'occident et de la méditerranée* 32, no. 2(1981), 93–119; Zahra Akhchichine-Tamouh, "Le Maroc et le Soudan au XIXe siecle, (1830–1894): contribution à une histoire inter-régionale de l'Afrique," (thèse de troisième cycle, Université de Paris I, 1982); Dennis Cordell, *Dar al-Kuti and the Last Years of the Trans-Saharan Slave Trade* (Madison, 1985); Rita Aouad, "Les incidences de la colonisation française sur les relations entre le Maroc et l'Afrique noire (1875–1935)," (doctorat d'état, Université d'Aix en Provence, 1994), and the review of it in *Newsletter* [Saharan Studies Association] 4, no. 2 (1996), 2–6; James L.A. Webb, Jr., *Desert Frontier: Ecological and Economic Change along the Western Sahel, 1600–1850* (Madison, 1995).

colonial period when British and French authorities appropriated some of the discourse of Islam for their own purposes. Above all, we do not yet fully understand how the culture of Islam affected the ways in which African Muslims conceptualized trade, or the ways in which such conceptualizations influenced how they actually conducted their business on a day-to-day, year-to-year basis. These, I would suggest, are among the matters to which researchers should turn their attention.

Bibliography

Abu Shouk, Ahmad Ibrahim and Anders Bjørkelo, ed. and trans. *The Public Treasury of the Muslims. Monthly Budgets of the Mahdist State in the Sudan, 1897.* Leiden, 1996.

Adeleye, R.A. *Power and Diplomacy in Northern Nigeria, 1804–1906.* London, 1971.

Akhchichine-Tamouh, Zahra. "Le Maroc et le Soudan au XIXe siecle, (1830–1894): contribution à une histoire inter-régionale de l'Afrique." Thèse de troisième cycle. Université de Paris I, 1982.

Aouad, Rita. "Les incidences de la colonisation française sur les relations entre le Maroc et l'Afrique noire (1875–1935)." Doctorat d'état. Université d'Aix en Provence, 1994.

Baier, Stephen. *An Economic History of Central Niger.* Oxford, 1980.

Barth, Heinrich. *Travels and Discoveries in Northern and Central Africa, Being a Journal of an Expedition Undertaken under the Auspices of Her Majesty's Government in the Years 1849–1855.* Vol. 3. 1857. Reprint, London, 1965.

Bedri, K.I. and P.E. Starratt. "*Tāj al-dīn fī mā yajib ᶜalā 'l-mulūk*, or 'The Crown of Religion concerning the obligations of princes'," *Kano Studies* n. s., 1, no. 2 (1974/77):15–28.

Bjørkelo, Anders. *Prelude to the Mahdiyya: Peasants and Traders in the Shendi Region, 1821–1885.* Cambridge, 1989.

Brenner, Louis. "The North African Trading Community in the Nineteenth Century Central Sudan", in *Aspects of West African Islam,* ed. Daniel F. McCall and Norman Bennett, 137–50. Boston, 1971.

Caillié, René. *Journal d'un voyage à Temboctou et à Jenné dans l'Afrique centrale.* Paris, 1830.

Colvin, Lucy. "The Commerce of Hausaland, 1780–1833," in *Aspects of West African Islam,* ed. Daniel F. McCall and Norman Bennett, 101–36. Boston, 1971.

Cordell, Dennis. *Dar al-Kuti and the Last Years of the Trans-Saharan Slave Trade.* Madison, 1985.

Crone, G.R., ed. *The Voyages of Cadamosto and other Documents on Western Africa in the Second Half of the XVth Century.* London, 1937.

Daumas, General E. *Le Grand Désert: Itinéraire d'une caravane du Sahara au pays des nègres, royaume de Haoussa.* 4th ed. Paris, 1860.

Denham, D. and Hugh Clapperton. *Travels and Discoveries in Northern and Central Africa.* 2d ed. London, 1826. Reprinted in *Missions to the Niger,* ed. E. W. Bovill. Vols. 2–4. London, 1966.

Dupuis, Joseph. *A Journal of a Residence in Ashantee.* 2d ed. London, 1824.

Franz, Charles. "Contraction and Expansion in Nigerian Bovine Pastoralism," in *Pastoralism in Tropical Africa,* ed. Théodore. Monod, 338–53. London, 1975.

Garrard, Timothy. *Akan Weights and the Gold Trade*. London, 1980.

Gervais, R. "Pre-Colonial Currencies: A Note on the Maria Theresa Thaler," *African Economic History* 11, (1982):147–52.

Harmann, Ulrich. "The dead ostrich: life and trade in Ghadames (Libya) in the nineteenth century", *Die Welt des Islams* 38 (1998):9–94.

Hiskett, M. "The *Kitāb al-farq*: A Work on the Habe Kingdoms Attributed to ᶜUthmān dan Fodio," *Bulletin of the School of Oriental and African Studies* 23 (1960):558–79.

—. "Materials Relating to the Cowrie Currency of the Western Sudan—I: A Late Nineteenth-Century Schedule of Inheritance from Kano," *Bulletin of the School of Oriental and African Studies* 29, no. 1 (1966):122–42.

—. "Materials Relating to the Cowrie Currency of the Western Sudan—II: Reflections on the Provenance and Diffusion of the Cowrie in the Sahara and the Sudan," *Bulletin of the School of Oriental and African Studies* 29, no. 2 (1966):339–66.

Hogendorn, Jan and Marion Johnson. *The Shell Money of the Slave Trade*. Cambridge, 1986.

Hopkins, J.F.P. and Nehemiah Levtzion. *Corpus of Early Arabic Sources for West African History*. Cambridge, 1981.

Hunwick, John. "Notes on a Late Fifteenth-Century Document Concerning 'al-Takrūr,'" in *African Perspectives: Papers in the History, Politics and Economics of Africa Presented to Thomas Hodgkin*, ed. Christopher Allen and R.W. Johnson, 7–34. Cambridge, 1970.

—. *Sharīᶜa in Songhay:The Replies of al-Maghīlī to the Questions of Askia al-Hājj Muḥammad*. Oxford, 1985.

Hunwick, J.O. and R.S. O'Fahey. "Some Waqf Documents from Lamu," *Bulletin d'Information* [Fontes Historiae Africanae] 6, (1981):26–43.

Hunwick, J.O. et. al., comp. *Arabic Literature of Africa*. Vol. 2, *The Writings of Central Sudanic Africa*. Leiden, 1995.

Ibn Baṭṭūṭa. *The Travels of Ibn Baṭṭūṭa, A.D. 1325–1354*. Vol. 4. Trans. H.A.R. Gibb and C.F. Beckingham, Hakluyt Society Publications, 2d ser., vol. 178. Cambridge, 1994.

Iroko, F. "Les marchards vénitiens et le commerce des cauris entre le XIIIe et le XVe siècle," *Africa* [Rome] 45, no. 3 (1990):480–4.

Jackson, James Grey. *An Account of the Empire of Morocco and the Districts of Suse and Tafilelt*. London, 1809.

—. *An Account of Timbuctoo and Housa, Territories in the Interior of Africa by El Hadge Abd Salam Shabeeny*. London, 1820.

Johnson, Marion. "The Nineteenth-Century Gold 'Mithqal' in West and North Africa," *Journal of African History* 9, no. 4 (1968):547–69.

—. "The Cowrie Currencies of West Africa," *Journal of African History* 11 (1970):17–49, 331–53.

Kirk-Greene, A.M.H. "The Major Currencies of Nigerian History," *Journal of the Historical Society of Nigeria* 2, no. 1 (1960):132–50.

Last, D.M. *The Sokoto Caliphate*. London, 1967.

Lavers, John E. "Trans-Saharan Trade before 1800: Towards Quantification," *Paideuma*, 40 (1994):243–278.

Leo Africanus. *Description de l'Afrique*. Trans. E. Epaulard. Vol. 2. Paris, 1956.

Lugard, Lord. *Political Memoranda*. 3d ed. Introduction by A.M.H. Kirk-Greene. London, 1970.

Miège, Jean-Louis. "Le commerce trans-Saharien au XIXe siècle: essai de quantification," *Revue de l'occident et de la méditerranée* 32, no. 2 (1981), 93–119.

Nachtigal, Gustav. *Sahara and Sudan*. Trans. A.G.B. Fisher and H.J. Fisher. Vol. 2. London, 1980.

O'Brien, Donal Cruise. *Saints and Politicians*. Cambridge, 1975.

O'Fahey, R.S. *State and Society in Dār Fūr*. London, 1980.

O'Fahey, R.S. & M.I. Abu Salim. *Land in Dār Fūr: Charters and Related Documents from the Dar Fur Sultanate.* Translated with an introduction by R.S. O'Fahey and M.I. Abu Salim with M.-J. and J. Tubiana. Cambridge, 1983.

Ohrwalder, Fr. Joseph. *Ten Years' Captivity in the Mahdi's Camp, 1881–1892*. 13th ed. London, n. d.

Pascon, Paul, et. al. *La Maison d'Iligh et l'histoire du Tazerwalt*. Rabat, 1984.

Roberts, Richard. *Warriors, Merchants and Slaves: The State and the Economy in the Middle Niger Valley, 1700–1914*. Stanford, 1987.

Robinson, David. *The Holy War of Umar Tal*. Oxford, 1985.

Schacht, Joseph. *An Introduction to Islamic Law*. Oxford, 1964.

Schroeter, Daniel J. *Merchants of Essaouira: Urban Society and Imperialism in Southwestern Morocco 1844–1886*. Cambridge, 1988.

Smith, M.G. *Government in Kano, 1350–1950*. Boulder, Colorado, 1997.

Sundström, Lars. *The Exchange Economy of Pre-Colonial Africa*. 2d ed. London, 1974.

Taylor, Raymond. "Warriors, Tributaries, Blood Money and Political Transformation in Nineteenth-Century Mauritania," *Journal of African History* 36, no. 3 (1995):419–41.

Walz, Terence. "Trade between Egypt and Bilād al-Takrūr in the XVIII Century." Unpublished paper presented to the International Seminar on the History of Kano, Bayero University, 1976.

—. *Trade between Egypt and Bilād al-Sūdān, 1700–1820*. Cairo, 1978.

Webb, James L.A., Jr., *Desert Frontier: Ecological and Economic Change along the Western Sahel, 1600–1850*. Madison, 1995.

Wilks, Ivor, and Phyllis Ferguson. "In Vindication of Sīdī al-Ḥājj ᶜAbd al-Salīm Shabayni", in *African Perspectives*, ed. Christopher Allen and R.W. Johnson, 35–52. Cambridge, 1970.

APPENDIX

DOCUMENTS ON FINANCIAL TRANSACTIONS FROM NINETEENTH CENTURY TIMBUKTU

Translated by John Hunwick

All the documents translated below are from the collection of the Centre de Documentation et de Recherche Ahmad Bāba (CEDRAB) at Timbuktu. The translations are all provisional.

DOCUMENT NO. 1. *Waqf* of a slave woman. CEDRAB, 3851/9

1. Praise be to God alone, and may God bless
2. him who through prayer for him major sins are forgiven,
3. Next: know and bear witness
4. to this document all who read it
5. among Muslims of high and low status,
6. that Nādda daughter of Batāka endowed
7. for her daughters a slave woman called Tadāy
8. in perpetuity for her offspring,
9. the females to the exclusion of the males. Witness
10. to that is the writer of the document al-Ḥasan
11. son of the qāḍī Hamma, and Sālah (sic) son of
12. the jurist Ḥammū, and Muḥammad son of Ḥamma.
13. Peace.

DOCUMENT NO. 2. Division of the estate of a woman. CEDRAB 3851/14

1. In the name of God, the Beneficent, the Merciful, and may God bless our master Muḥammad and his Family and his Companions most fully.
2. Let the one who sees this document know that the estate of Nāna ᶜĀʾisha daughter of *al-ḥājj* Muḥammad Awzāl was valued,
3. and the total was 85.5 mq., after deducting funeral expenses and the payment of debts.
4. From this was taken 4 mq. as wage for the witnesses. Then the rest, being 81.5 mq., was divided up thereafter
5. among the inheritors who had a right to an inheritance. They were her daughter Fāṭima and her brother Sanber,
6. and her two sisters Nāna Khadīja and Nāna Ber. The daughter was apportioned half of it, which is 40.75 mq.
7. She took half the house valued at 22.5 mq. Then she took
8. the slave woman called Bunkān with her daughter, and they were valued at 18 mq. This was one half [of the inheritance].
9. Then the second half was divided among the brother and the two aforementioned sisters.
10. The brother was apportioned 20.25 mq, and each of the daughters was apportioned 10 mq. and 3 qīrāṭs.

11. The aforementioned brother took half of the house at its value, and the slave called al-Manṣūr and 10 mq.
12. for himself, and for his two sisters was the value of half the aforementioned house, 22.5 mq. and the slave at 18 mq.
13. [Continuation missing]

DOCUMENT NO. 3. Sale of salt. CEDRAB, 5519/1

1. A Register (*zimām*) for remembrance and to counter forgetfulness. Sublime is He who forgets not.
2. The salt with which Fanda G-m entered the land—i.e. Sansanding[1]—is 200 *salāmiyya* slabs
3. and 19 slabs (*ḥajarāt*).[2] Of it he sold 141 *salāmiyya*
4. slabs, whose price was 399.5 mq.
5. which we are sending with the blessed al-Ḥājj al-Tuwāt(i), and 42 slabs
6. I sold for 119 mq, the price
7. [per piece] being $2\frac{5}{6}$ mq.[2.833 mq], which we are sending with Farāj, the slave boy of ᶜĪsā.
8. And we are sending with him 21 mq. for ᶜĪsā, to whom I owe
9. 32 mq, and I still owe him 11
10. mq. And seven slabs I sold for a price [per piece] of 2.75 mq.,
11. and six blocks I sold at $2\frac{5}{6}$ mq. each,
12. so the price of all was 36.75 mq.
13. I gave back to the "people of gold" (*ahl al-dhahab*)[3] 0.5 mq, so there remains 35.75.
14. I purchased a young slave boy for 6.75 mq., which comes out of that
15. 35.75 mq, since it was *min dafᶜihā*.[4] And there comes out of it
16. Our expenses of 14. Its changing (*ṣarf*) was 3.5 mq.[5]
17. With ᶜUbayd walad Aᶜlī walad al-Bahandāwī is 8 *ajāl*.

DOCUMENT NO. 4. Accounting of goods deposited on trust (*amāna*). CEDRAB, 5516/2

1. Know that the total of what reached you from me of your first and second trusts (*amāna*) was 2283 mq. and 2 *qirāṭ*.[6]

---

[1] Although this salt probably passed through Timbuktu, there was a direct trade in salt between Arawān and Sansanding, according to Caillié, *Journal d'un voyage*, 2:376.

[2] The difference between *salāmiyya* slabs and other undefined slabs is not clear, since both were sold at 2.833 mq. each. The somewhat confused Arabic of the text could be construed to mean that all the slabs were *salāmiyya*.

[3] Perhaps those who weigh gold professionally.

[4] Not entirely clear, but the phrase would seem to mean that the price of the slave boy was to be counted as part of the expenses.

[5] This seems to indicate that the actual trading was conducted with another currency, presumably cowries.

[6] Spelled throughout the document thus, although the correct form is *qīrāṭ*. A *qīrāṭ* (carat) is four grains, that is about one-sixteenth of a *mithqāl* (one mq = 4.25 gr. = 65.5 grains)

2. Of this amount 333$^{1}/_{3}$ came to you with Muḥammad al-Ṣaghīr in the first year,
3. in gold. And with al-Ṣāliḥ b. Aḥmad al-Khlīf there came to you in the year 1291/1874–5
4. 765 [pounds of ostrich] feathers. And there came to you with al-ᶜAbd b. ᶜĀl in the year 92
5. and 1200,[7] 1184$^{3}/_{4}$ [pounds of ostrich] feathers, of which two *qinṭār* [200 lbs] were *tajakjākat,*[8]
6. and one *qinṭār* [100 lbs.] *ẓlīm,*[9] and 1$^{1}/_{2}$ lbs. *salāṭīn*.[10] In the load were also 3 lbs. of *tajakjākat* not included
7. in the total [amount in trust], being the price of three boxes of sugar. The account of the second [trust] with come to you later, God willing. And I sent
8. to you among these feathers, by way of a trust, $^{2}/_{3}$ lb of *salāṭīn* belonging to me. What I desire [in exchange] for them is in the kettle
9. which is in the hands of al-ᶜAbd b. ᶜĀl. Next, know that the first trust has been executed from my side, and I sent it to you.
10. No part of it remains with me. Of the second you have received 696 mq and 2 qirāṭ.
11. I gave to al-Ṣāliḥ b. Aḥmad al-Akhlīf 16$^{2}/_{3}$ mq. for hiring [camels?],
12. and I gave 2 mq. to the dyer and the tailor.
13. Next al-Bakkāy paid from the register to al-Wāli b. Bahī, the agent of the provider of the capital, through the agency of the writer, 132 mq. and we wrote it [?] on 10 Rabīᶜ II in the year
15. 1297/21 March 1880 Muḥammad al-Raḥim b. Muḥammad al-Khalīl, may he be forgiven. Amen.
16. Then he also paid to the agent 40 mq. in consideration of the $^{2}/_{3}$ lb.
17. which my father sent to you as a trust, and 10 *qirāṭ*. Then he handed over to him ten
18. pounds of *ẓalīm* for 95 mq. This is the last of what remained with ᶜĪsā (?), and the remainder
19. of what is enumerated in the registrar is in the record (*rasm*) of Aḥmad al-Yaḥyāwī—may God have mercy on him.

---

[7] The year 1292 of the *hijra* corresponds to 1875–6 C.E.

[8] Pascon, *La maison d'Iligh*, 76–7, mentions *tajakjikt* as small feather of inferior quality, taken from the female ostrich. Earlier (p. 7) he had referred to these feathers as *tajekjijt*.

[9] Written ʾ*ẓlīm,* that is, *ẓalīm* (pronounced *dlim* in Morocco), the Arabic term for the male ostrich, and by extension, for its feathers.

[10] The precise meaning of this term has not been discovered. However, given the small amounts traded, we may assume it was of the highest quality. Its name—*salāṭīn*, meaning "sultans", would also indicate this.

Islamic Banking in the Sudan: Aspects of the Laws and the Debate

Endre Stiansen

Modern banking techniques such as the bill of exchange and the check were pioneered in the Near East, but merchants specializing in foreign exchange and credit and debt instruments did not establish institutions comparable to the banking houses that emerged in Europe in the early modern period—to borrow a phrase from Abraham Udovitch, in the Islamic heartland there were many bankers yet no banks.[1] The first banks in Muslim countries were founded in the nineteenth century. While none of the early banks have survived as autonomous institutions, their legacy of banking based on European models and legislation went without serious challenge until after World War II, when some political activists and religious scholars began designing "Islamic" banking systems that rejected the modus operandi of conventional banking: namely, that deposits earn interest and loans are repaid with interest. To date, three countries—Pakistan, Iran and the Sudan—have tried to implement Islamic banking on a national scale. Of the three, the Sudan's is the most interesting because it is both the most comprehensive and enduring experiment (in Pakistan the full "Islamization" of the financial sector is still pending,[2] while in Iran after 1979 interest rates have largely been replaced with service charges on loans and bonuses on deposits[3]). The Sudan, therefore,

---

[1] Abraham L. Udovitch, "Bankers without Banks: Commerce, Banking, and Society in the Islamic World of the Middle Ages," in *The Dawn of Modern Banking*, Center for Medieval and Renaissance Studies, UCLA (New Haven, 1979), 255–73.

[2] While in May 1991 the National Assembly established a committee to "oversee the process of elimination of *Riba* from every sphere of economic activity in the shortest possible time", in November 1991, Pakistan's Federal Sharia Court independently declared interest un-Islamic and therefore illegal, and demanded that by 30 June 1992 all financial legislation should have been amended to conform with the Koran and the Sunna. If the necessary changes were not made, the laws "held [to be] repugnant to the injunctions of Islam [would] cease to have effect." A commercial bank, the Muslim Commerce Bank, probably with the tacit approval of the government, appealed the decision to the Supreme Court and thereby prevented the prohibition of interest to come into effect. The Supreme Court has yet to rule on the issue. See "Pakistan: Islam's interest", *The Economist*, 18 January 1992; Izzud-Din Pal, "Pakistan and the Question of Riba," *Middle Eastern Studies* 30, No. 1 (1994), 64–78; and "Pakistan banks face lottery ban", *Financial Times*, 14 May 1999.

[3] Shortly after the 1979 revolution nationalized banks in Iran started substituting "interest" for words like "service charge" and "profit", and in August 1983 the "Law of

provides a unique example of a modern attempt to recreate the banking system according to Islamic principles.

The raison d'être for Islamic banking is the Koranic prohibition of *ribā*. In classical Arabic, *ribā* (from the root *r, b, w*) means to grow, prosper, or increase. In the Koran, the word is used in different contexts, and sections from suras Āl ᶜUmrān (verse 130) and al-Baqara (in particular verses 274-80) contain the key passages regarding lending and borrowing. While there is agreement among Muslim scholars on the absolute prohibition of *ribā*, opinions differ with regard to how the term should be understood. Broadly speaking, there are two "schools": one argues for a historical interpretation, and one sees the issue in more theoretical terms. An exponent of the first school is Fazlur Rahman, who considers the *ribā* verses to refer to unethical commercial practices common in Arabia at the time of the Prophet. Specifically he sees the prohibition as addressing the wide-spread practice of doubling and redoubling the principal when borrowers could not repay loans. Moreover, he argues for the necessity of differentiating between (legal) interest and (illegal) usury, and therefore dismisses as historically invalid any analogy between *ribā* and bank-interest.[4]

The second school also sees prohibition of *ribā* within the framework of Islam's social message, but does not accept any distinction between usury and interest. In an eloquent elaboration of this position, Iqbal and Mirakhor relate the *ribā* verses to the Islamic perspective on individuals' claims to property, and suggest that Islam only recognizes property that is the result of creative labor and (fair) exchange. Interest, therefore, is illegal because it gives a lender an unearned claim on the property of a borrower. Similarly, all material gains from hoarding, speculation, gambling and fraud are illegitimate because such activities do not contribute to the production of real assets.[5]

To the historical school, there is not necessarily any contradiction between conventional banking and banking according to Islamic principles, provided the banks follow basic ethical principles and do not finance un-Islamic activities. The theoretical school cannot agree, and the Islamic banking movement is therefore based on the equation of *ribā* and interest. For instance, one of the leading Islamic banks in the Sudan, the Tadamon Islamic Bank, defines *ribā* as any increase on the principal of a loan, whether it is "interest simple or com-

---

the Interest-Free Banking System" prohibited banks from charging interest. Consequently fees (on loans) and bonuses (on deposits) replaced interest in the formal sector of the economy; the difference between straight interest rates and fees/bonuses was largely semantic since the Central Bank fixed the bonuses paid to depositors, and returns on Islamic investment contracts. See Ali Rahnema and Farhad Nomani, *The Secular Miracle: Religion, Politics and Economic Policy in Iran* (London, 1990), 241, 281–82, 286.

4 Fazlur Rahman, "*Ribā* and Interest," *Islamic Studies* 3, No. 4 (1964): 6–8. The Koran quotations are from this article.

5 Zubair Iqbal and Abbas Mirakhor, *Islamic Banking*, International Monetary Fund, Occasional Paper, no. 49 (Washington, D C, 1987), 2.

pound, real or monetary."[6] It is important to note, however, that even rigid interpretations of the *ribā* verses do not lead to rejection of profits (from fair business transactions) as morally unjustifiable. Moreover, it is commonly accepted that lenders have the right to shares of the income generated by loans if the returns are not decided in advance—in such contexts loans should be regarded as investments that may bring profit or loss. Leasing is also legal because the lessor sells to the lessee the right to use a property or an asset at an agreed price, and the same reasoning applies to rent contracts. Such contracts would, on the other hand, be illegal if the parties did not enter contracts on equal terms, or if owners of capital goods sought to gain additional benefits over and above the agreed rent.[7]

Islamic banks aim to provide the public with all types of banking services and in many respects are quite similar to conventional banks: they offer checking services, underwrite letters of credit, have branch networks and correspondent banks (not always Islamic banks), buy and sell foreign exchange, and are often organized as joint stock companies. This is as can be expected since none of these services are necessarily affected by the prohibition of interest. Business involving deposit accounts, and borrowing and lending, are different matters.

Typically Islamic banks offer customers a choice of three types of accounts. By far the most common is the *current account*. Deposits in current accounts do not earn interest but may be guaranteed. Usually, the banks charge current account holders for services such as checking and transfers, and also use deposits to fund other banking activities. Most banks require customers to deposit a minimum amount to open accounts. *Savings accounts* are basically the same as current accounts, but are designed for customers who wish to qualify for loans. Often there are no restrictions on withdrawal, and account holders may not have to pay service charges. Savings accounts, of course, do not earn interest. The third alternative is called an *investment account* and is similar to a share in a mutual fund. Basically, the depositor can choose between earmarking his money for one or more ventures organized by the bank, and letting his deposit be part of the bank's general portfolio for trade and investment. In the

---

[6] "Memorandum and Articles of Association," Tadamon Islamic Bank, Khartoum, March 1983, 29. Here "real" must be understood as compensation in kind rather than cash. *Taḍāmun* means solidarity.

[7] On this point it can be added that some Muslims regard all forms of profit and rent as *ribā*, and a few even reject private property because inevitably it leads to inequality. See Farhad Nomani and Ali Rahnema, *Islamic Economic Systems*, (London, 1994), 76. It is important to stress, however, that these views do not have much support. Given the acceptance of conventional banking among Muslims, it can even be argued that the present Islamic banking movement represents a minority position, and the situation in the Islamic world may not be very different from Catholic Europe before the Church, in the late nineteenth century, finally accepted a formal distinction between usury and interest.

first case, income or loss on the accounts will depend on the success or failure of the venture(s), while in the second case profit or loss will depend on the bank's overall performance. Customers with investment accounts commit their money for specific periods of time, and usually do not have to pay service charges. Since they are used for investments which may lead to profits or losses, in principle neither savings accounts nor investment accounts can be guaranteed.

Perhaps the most interesting aspect of Islamic banking is the repertoire of techniques developed to enable customers to acquire capital and the banks to invest. Again, there are three basic models available:

Mushāraka

Equity participation of two or more partners, usually for a limited period of time and with a specific purpose. Profits, or losses, are shared in proportion to each partner's investment.

Muḍāraba

An agreement of two persons or more whereby one or more of them provide finance, while the other provides entrepreneurship and management, for agreed business ventures. Profits are shared according to a predetermined key (often 50:50), but monetary losses are born by the financier alone; the contract is therefore neither a loan proper nor a partnership.

Murābaḥa

Sale agreements whereby the seller, at the request of the buyer, purchases a commodity that is resold at a marked-up price; payment can, according to agreement, be settled in one transaction or in instalments within an agreed time frame.

While none of these financial techniques are incompatible with conventional commercial practices (the *mushāraka* resembles limited liability joint-stock companies, the *muḍāraba* is identical to the medieval European *commenda* and the *murābaḥa* functions as a letter of credit), they represent conscious efforts at drawing on the Islamic heritage to avoid interest while meeting the needs of contemporary economies.

Islamic Banking in the Sudan: Legislative Changes in 1983

In the Sudan efforts to make the constitution and laws more Islamic have been on the political agenda since before Independence in 1956.[8] But while a majority of establishment politicians may have agreed on the goal of giving the new

[8] I am grateful to Muḥammad Abū Sabīb for help in translating the Arabic text referred to in this section.

state a distinct Islamic identity, they could not agree either on (a) the expression of the Islamic nature of the state or (b) the formulation of the laws governing the envisioned state. When Prime Minister for the first time in 1966-1967, Ṣādiq al-Mahdī prepared an Islamic constitution, but it was not ratified by the parliament before he was forced to relinquish office, and the constitutional issue was left unresolved. The Muslim Brothers, at roughly the same time, prepared their own Islamic constitution. In 1972 Jaᶜfar Nimayrī, by then undisputed leader of the country, introduced a "Permanent Constitution" that represented a radical break with the recent past as it drew more inspiration from the French Revolution and "third-world" socialism than from Islam, but its secular nature was eroded in the process of National Reconciliation begun in the mid-seventies. From 1977 several groups began working to amend existing laws, or introduce new laws, to bring the judicial system in line with the sharia, and the Committee for the Revision of Laws, chaired by Ḥasan al-Turābī, came up with specific suggestions such as prohibition of alcohol, interest on loans and economic corruption.

None of these suggestions were implemented, and in general the President did not give much attention to legal reform before early 1983, when in a secret meeting with Sufi leaders, he " ... made a covenant to implement [the] Shariah at no matter what cost".[9] The President approved establishment of a new three-member committee entrusted to prepare sharia laws for all aspects of public life.[10] The committee worked in the Palace in the greatest secrecy, and the public and the other committees working on Islamization of the judicial system, as well as the political establishment, were caught by surprise when Nimayrī introduced the new body of law by presidential decree.

Only one brief section in the new Supplement to the Civil Procedure Act (1983) dealt with the banking system:

> *Section 110: No decree of interest*
> The court shall under no circumstance whatsoever make a decree ordering payment of interest on the principal sum adjudged.[11]

In the Arabic text, the word used for "interest" is *fāʾida* and not *ribā*. This choice of terminology is curious. *Fāʾida* (from the root *f, y, d*) means to gain and is translated as "interest," "advantage," "profit," or "benefit." Unlike *ribā*,

---

[9] Abdelwahab El-Affendi, *Turabi's Revolution: Islam and Power in Sudan* (London, 1991), 122.

[10] The committee members were al-Nayyal Abū Qurūn, ᶜAwaḍ al-Jīd Muḥammad and Badriyya Sulaymān.

[11] Civil Procedure Act [*Qanūn al-Ijrāʾāt Madaniyya*] 1983, section 110. Arabic text: "*ᶜadam al-ḥakm bi-l-fāʾida. La taḥakum al-maḥkama bi-l-fāʾida bi-āyyi ḥāl min al-ʾaḥwāl.*" The English wording of the subheading, which is rendered as published by the Justice Department, does not really convey the meaning of the Arabic; a better translation would be "no enforcement of interest" or "no judgements in support of interest." This act was issued as a supplement to the Private Law (*Mulḥaq al-Tashrīᶜ al-Khāṣ*).

the term does not have any religious connotation and is free of association with exploitation; often writers use the two words conjointly to bring out the difference between "interest" and "usury." By using *fāʾida*, the committee did not leave any room for compromise between "liberals" who differentiated between usury and interest, and the "orthodox" who regarded all gain over and above the principal as illegal—in a sense, by using non-religious language to enforce a religious principle (however understood or defined) they removed the possibility of a secular debate over how best to interpret the prohibition of *ribā* in the contemporary context. But by *not* situating the interest ban within its religious context, the law lacked both motivation and natural authority, and in any case it needed clarification since it did not give any direction for non-interest banking. The law's major flaw, however, was to allow banking to continue as before until contracts were challenged in court.

The first elaboration of the "interest law" came after one year, in a new supplement to the Civil Law. Several sections dealt with banking matters:

> *Section 82: Obligation to Pay Money*
> If the subject matter of the obligation is payment of money the debtor shall pay that amount of money as it is specified in the contract despite the increase or decrease in the value of money at the time when payment is due.
>
> *Section 281: Stipulation of Excess Benefit*
> If a contract of loan is made subject to any benefit payable to the lender in excess of the principal amount of the loan, except for authentication of the right of the lender, such benefit shall be void; however, the contract shall be valid.
>
> *Section 285 (5): The Borrower's Obligation*
> (1) The borrower shall be bound to return at the expiration of the loan period the same property in quantity, kind and quality as he has received at the time and place agreed upon irrespective of what change might have occurred in its value.[12]

[12] Civil Transactions Act [*Qanūn al-Muᶜāmalāt Madaniyya*] 1984, sections 82, 281, 285 (1). Arabic texts:

> *82. al-ʾiltizām bi-dafᶜ al-nuqūd.*
> *ʾidha kān muḥil al-ʾiltizām dafᶜ mablagh min al-nuqūd ʾiltazam al-madīn bi-qadr ᶜadadihā al-madhkūr fī al-ᶜaqd dūn ʾan yakūn li-ʾirtifāᶜ qīmat hādhihi al-nuqūd ʾaw li-ʾinkhifāḍiha waqt al-wafāʾ ʾayyi ʾathar.*
>
> *281. ʾishtirāṭ al-manfaᶜa al-zāʾida.*
> *īdha ʾishturiṭ fī ᶜaqd al-qarḍ manfaᶜa zāᶜida ᶜalā muqtaḍā al-ᶜaqd siwā tawthīq ḥaq al-muqriḍ lighā al-sharṭ wa ṣaḥḥa al-ᶜaqd.*
>
> *285 (1). ʾiltizām al-muqtariḍ.*
> *yaltazim al-muqtariḍ bard mithl mā qabḍ miqdāran wa nawᶜan wa ṣifa ᶜind ʾintihāʾ muddat al-qarḍ wa lā ᶜibrata limā yaṭraʾ ᶜalā qīmatihi min taghyyir wa dhalika fī al-zamān wa al-makān al-muttafaq ᶜalayhimā.*

This act was also issued as a supplement to the Private Law (*Mulḥaq al-Tashrīᶜ al-Khāṣ*).

Again, the language was secular and the flaw already mentioned persisted since interest-based banking could continue as long as both the borrower and lender agreed on the terms of their contract.

The Bank of Sudan and Enforcement[13]

Despite its status as a central bank with regulatory responsibility for the banking sector,[14] the Bank of Sudan had not at any time been consulted in the process that led to promulgation of the 1983 law; in fact the Bank management first learnt about the Islamization through newspaper reports. The news caused great consternation in the banking community, both at home and abroad. In Washington D.C., where he was attending the bi-annual meeting of the IMF and World Bank, the Governor of the Bank scrambled to find out the implications of the new law while being confronted with a barrage of questions from representatives of foreign governments and commercial banks with interests in the Sudan. In Khartoum, senior managers of the Bank immediately began drafting a memorandum to the President that, first, presented the status quo of the Sudanese economy, and, secondly, argued that the government could not take such a radical step as the prohibition of interest without either the advice of the central bank or a proper assessment of the economic impact. In a separate move, the U. S. Assistant Secretary of State for Africa, Dr. Chester Crocker, is said to have relayed the concern of U.S. banks.[15] A major worry of Bank of Sudan officials, as well as representatives of donors and commercial banks, was whether or not the Sudan would make interest payments on the international debt.[16]

At first, the government stood firm stating that there would be no exemptions for the foreign debt, but after intense consultations Bank of Sudan officials were able to convince President Nimayrī that the Sudan would be ostracised from the international financial community if the government refused to honour the terms of existing loan contracts. Subsequently government lawyers decided that because of necessity (*ḍarūra*) the government could

---

[13] This section is largely based on interviews with former senior officials of the Bank of Sudan.

[14] The Bank of Sudan Act (1959).

[15] Mansour Khalid, *Nimeiri and the Revolution of Dis-Day* (London, 1985), 290.

[16] In 1983, repayment of official loans amounted to LS 84 million but the (positive) net capital inflow was still as high as LS 92.6 million. In 1984, official repayments amounted to LS 26.2 million, and the net capital inflow had fallen to LS 2.4 million. See Bank of Sudan, *Twenty Fifth Annual Report* (Khartoum 1984), 49–51. The Annual Report does not break down the repayment figures into principal and interest. In October 1984 the official exchange rate of the Sudanese pound (LS) was changed from LS 1,8 to 2,1 to the US dollar.

continue to pay interest on the foreign debt;[17] international banks operating inside the Sudan were not, however, exempted from the interest ban.

Having resolved the issue of the foreign debt, the Bank of Sudan confronted the bigger problem of making the domestic financial system work without interest. Officials began studying the experience of Islamic banking in Pakistan, and at home it was possible to draw on the financial technology developed by the two banks that already operated according to the principles now enshrined in the law. The commercial banks were not put under any pressure to abolish interest, and banking continued much as before. The lack of change triggered a strong reaction from individuals committed to the literal application of the September laws. For instance, a judge on the criminal court in Omdurman, al-Mikāshfī Ṭāha al-Kabbāshī, in November 1984 wrote a letter to the Governor of the Bank of Sudan,[18] with copies to other senior jurists, admonishing the bank for not enforcing the interest ban. The Governor did not reply to the letter but went to the President demanding to know if a judge on his own initiative had the right to threaten the Bank of Sudan. Immediately Nimayrī called a meeting at the Palace to discuss the introduction of Islamic principles in the financial sector. At the meeting (which was attended among others by the President, the Attorney General, the Minister of Justice, the Governor and Deputy Governor of the Bank of Sudan, legal advisers, and leading proponents of the Islamization campaign), the representatives of the Bank of Sudan argued for a gradual Islamization of the banking system, and suggested that banks as a first step should be encouraged to open "Islamic windows" while at the same time continuing to operate according to conventional principles. The Bank of Sudan also used the occasion to explain the economic consequences a total abolition of interest.

A heated debate followed. Some accused the Bank of Sudan of not being cooperative with the Islamization program; the economists of the Bank replied that they were not against Islam but insisted on the necessity of recognizing the difference between the non-inflationary nature of the economy at the time of the Prophet and the present currency regime. In the end, the meeting did not agree on any recommendations but the President appointed a committee of high-ranking officials with the mandate to work out ways and means to

---

[17] Interestingly, Ṣādiq al-Mahdī, prime minister in 1986–1989, in a speech to the United Nations General Assembly in October, stated that his government "would not assume responsibility" for the debt accumulated during the previous regime (Mansour Khalid, *The Government They Deserve: The Role of the Elite in Sudan's Political Evolution*, London, 1990, 379). His motivation was not, however, religious but pragmatic and in tune with contemporary opinions expressed by leaders of other heavily indebted countries. Not even the present Government (1999) has, as a matter of principle, refused to pay interest on the Sudan's foreign debt.

[18] The letter is reprinted in al-Mikāshfī Ṭāha al-Kabbāshī, *Taṭbīq al-sharīʿa al-Islamiyya fi al-Sūdān bayn al-ḥaqīqa wa al-ithāra*, 2nd. ed. (Cairo, 1986), 46–47. The letter was dated 23 Ṣafar 1405 h., or November 17, 1984.

implement the new system. In addition Nimayrī asserted that nobody but himself had the right to write to and criticise the Bank of Sudan. Owing to changes in the structure of economic policy making, the new committee failed to become an important forum for policy discussion, and it did not make any recommendations.

The lack of direction in the forced transformation of the financial sector came out very clearly in the Bank of Sudan's Annual Reports; in the report of 1983, there was no mention whatsoever of the prohibition of interest, and the 1984 report simply stated:

> The most notable development in the banking community in 1984 was the abolition of interest rates and that commercial banks will conduct their banking according to Sharia Islamic laws.[19]

Clearly the Bank was at loss as to how to deal with the legal changes of 1983 and 1984, and in circulars to the commercial banks, issued only when all efforts at convincing Nimayrī to be more pragmatic had stranded, it merely repeated instructions received from the judiciary. In December 1984, for instance, the Bank of Sudan instructed the banks to follow Islamic law and therefore use Islamic forms, but it did not provide clarifications or guidelines that could have assisted bankers in working out legal techniques. Having reined in the authority of zealous judges such as al-Mikāshfī', neither the Ministry of Justice nor the Bank of Sudan made any determined efforts to enforce the new laws, and no banks were taken to court for merely making cosmetic changes to their credit and debt instruments in order to continue to do business according to conventional principles.

Return to the Status Quo Ante: The Compensatory Rates

Nimayrī's program of Islamization proved to be the regime's swan song. In 1985, the people took to the streets to protest the escalating economic crisis and abuses of power, and the military intervened, installing a transitional government. Composed of both serving soldiers and civilians, the transitional government suspended some Islamic laws, but basically the Islamic nature of the judicial system remained intact when the democratically elected government of Ṣādiq al-Mahdī came to power in 1986. One of the pressing items on the Prime Minister's agenda was a reassessment of the banking laws.

The problem was acute: the supplements to the Civil Law and the Bank of Sudan's circulars did not provide a framework for a new financial system and almost all bankers claimed interest-free banking could not work. The issue was addressed at a cabinet meeting in late September 1987, and on October 21 the Governor of the Bank of Sudan issued a circular called "The Banking Tariff

---

[19] Bank of Sudan, *25th Annual Report* (1984), 76.

- The Compensatory Rates" (*al-ta*ᶜ*rīfāt al-maṣrafiyya - al-fi*ᵓ*āt al-ta*ᶜ*wīḍiyya*).[20] Described as a means of enriching the Islamic experience and meeting the needs of the contemporary economic situation, the compensatory rates were set at twenty-seven percent per year for all debit accounts (i.e., bank loans) except for loans to the industrial, agricultural and export sectors—here the compensatory rate was set at twenty-four percent per year. For credit accounts (i.e., customers' time deposit accounts), the compensatory rates were fixed along a scale beginning at twenty percent for three-month deposits and ending at twenty-four percent for twelve-month deposits. For savings accounts, the compensatory rate was set at twenty percent, as were the rates for pensions and life insurance premiums. The brief circular contained neither a technical definition of compensatory rates nor an explanation of how such rates were different from interest rates.

In the banking community, the circular met with a mixed response. On the one hand, "commercial bankers" welcomed the government's decision as the triumph of reason over dogmatism and looked forward to the return of business as usual. On the other, "Islamic bankers" viewed the circular as the new regime's capitulation to the secular business community and other forces hostile to Islam.[21] The introduction of compensatory rates did not, however, lead to the phasing out of *murābaḥa* contracts. The reason was quite simple: while the compensatory rates effectively capped the banks' return on loans (at rates that were below inflation), there was no upper limit on the mark-up (*hāmish murābaḥa*) implied in *murābaha* sales. Consequently continued use of the most adaptable Islamic financial technique enabled bankers to increase their profits (and beat inflation).

The Islamic Reaction to Ṣādiq's Compromise

In a memorandum to the Prime Minister, the heads of the Islamic banks' Sharia boards formulated the "Islamic" position against the circular that allowed banks to pay and charge compensatory rates.[22] The ten-page memorandum opens with an exposition of the Koranic prohibition of *ribā* and leaves no doubt as to the seriousness of the issue: *ribā* is viewed as second only to atheism among the moral wrongs condemned in the Sharia, and offenders will burn in hell. Support for this view, not surprisingly, is given by quoting sura

---

[20] Bank of Sudan, 8 *Rabī*ᶜ *al-*ᵓ*Awwal* 1408/ 21 October 1987, circular signed by the Governor, Ismāᶜīl al-Miṣbāh Makkī.

[21] This is not to suggest that "commercial bankers" are not good Muslims or in any way less committed to their religion than "Islamic bankers"; the distinction is intended to bring out differences determined by background and ideology.

[22] Memorandum on "Legal Decision on Bank Tariff—Compensatory Rate issued by the Bank of Sudan ... 31 October 1987," Khartoum n.d. Among the signatories were a former Mufti of the Sudan and judges serving on Sharia courts.

al-Baqara 275-281 and several *hadīths* (traditions of the Prophet), including one where the taking of *ribā* is listed as one of the seven deadly sins.

Next follows a detailed discussion of the background for the Koranic prohibition and definitions of *ribā*. According to the experts, there are two categories of *ribā*. The first is known from the pre-Islamic period and therfore called *ribā al-jāhiliyya*. This type of *ribā* was in two forms: *ribā* of debt (*ribā al-dīwan*) and *ribā* of loans (*ribā al-qarḍ*). Of these, the first referred to situations where a lender gave a loan to a borrower against a promise that he would repay, at an agreed time, the premium with a mark-up that could be in the form of cash or kind. The second form occurred when borrowers avoided loan default by borrowing more money and thereby increased their debt. According to the experts, the difference between the two forms of *ribā al-jāhiliyya* was that in the first form the *ribā* was known to the parties when they agreed on their contract, while in the case of the second it appeared only when borrowers defaulted. In a remarkable digression, the experts put forward the idea that the Arabs learnt to make loans at interest through their association with Jews who, they wrote, have been the custodians of the *ribā*-based banking system. Numerous authorities are quoted in support of the experts' interpretation, and the memorandum confidently states that all authorities agree on the prohibition of (both forms of) *ribā al-jāhiliyya*.

The experts do not discuss the second category of *ribā*, called *ribā al buyūᶜ*, because it falls outside the concern of the *fatwā* (see below).

Having established the historical background and their understanding of *ribā*, the experts address the circular on bank tariffs and the compensatory rates issued by the Bank of Sudan on October 31, 1987. After a brief, but still exhaustive, summary of the main points of the circular, the memorandum unequivocally states that under the system proposed by the Bank of Sudan the relations between banks and their clients will be the same as those between creditors and debtors. Moreover, since the Bank determines compensation on the basis of the length of time money has been deposited, and banks "lend" money at higher interest rates than they "borrow," the rates are nothing but interest rates (*siᶜr al-fāʾida*) and therefore prohibited. To strengthen their case, the experts contrast *ribā* banking with the Islamic system: while the organizing principle of the former is to invest by lending at interest, the latter bans the use of such loans and instead employs Islamic techniques such as buying, partnerships, and investments—all of which are based on the idea that an investor must accept both profit and loss.

This part of the memorandum leads to a *fatwā* (legal opinion) which repeats that the compensatory rates are not Islamic but a form of interest (here they use the term *fāʾida*) and therefore prohibited. Finally the experts conclude—under the heading *al-dīn al-naṣīḥa* ("religion is the best advice")—by calling on the government and the Bank of Sudan to repeal the circular and do as God pleases.

Ṣādiq's Defense

The memorandum represented a direct challenge to Ṣādiq's political and religious authority. He answered it in a letter dated November 23, 1987.[23] The reply is interesting on several counts. The Prime Minister, writing on paper bearing the seal of his office, introduced his defense by assuring the experts that, as legal authorities, they had the right to express their views and give advice to the government, and that, since the political system of the country was based on the principle of consultation (*shūra*), they as citizens were free to express their frank opinion. Having made these points, the Prime Minister turned to the critique expressed in the memorandum and claimed there was no real disagreement on the prohibition of all forms of *ribā* in the monetary and banking systems; but all pretense of being on the same side immediately disappeared because the very next sentence reads: "the issue of the compensatory rates has nothing to do with the concept of compensation for the time-value of money." According to the Prime Minister, what they regarded as interest rates were in fact compensation for a fall in value of the currency.

To support his position, Ṣādiq contrasted the characteristics of currencies in "olden times" and the contemporary world. While silver and gold used to have "fixed" and "objective" values, today the nature of money is quite different because political and administrative decisions influence both the volume of money in circulation and exchange rates, making the value of money neither "objective" nor "fixed". Yet the resulting ups and downs of currency values are not important, as long as there is a balance between purchasing power and prices. Against this background, the compensatory rates should be seen as means to "maintain the [real value of the] currency over a given period and its legitimacy arises from the fact that it makes the money of today equal to the money of yesterday thus preserving both relative value and purchasing power." Therefore, the Prime Minister wrote,

> any compensation or remuneration for time value that falls within the bounds of *ribā* is prohibited. Yet any compensation or remuneration that keeps the value of the original amount by means of an objective measure and does not exceed it falls within the intentions of the Sharia.

The question, thus, is not whether the compensatory rates are legitimate, but if they have been fixed at the right level. On this point (probably to demonstrate both good will and to co-opt the opposition), Ṣādiq offered the heads of the Sharia boards an opportunity to reassess the calculations used to determine the compensatory rates and promised to make corrections if the rates had been set in error.

But the Prime Minister was not going to wait for a second opinion. Two days before his letter was sent, the Bank of Sudan had already issued a new

[23] Letter to Members of the Sharia Boards of the Islamic Banks, 23 November 1987.

circular specifying the government's credit policy and confirming the legality of the compensatory rate.[24]

The 1990s

The military coup of June 1989 led to abolition of compensatory rates, and in the 1990s the government has tried to be more principled in the application of the Islamic laws in the banking sector. In this respect the first effort was to supplement the Company Law of 1925 with the new Banking Regulation Law of 1991 (*Qānūn tanẓīm al-ᶜamal al-maṣrafī li-sanat 1991*) and the Compendium of Administrative and Financial Penalties against Banking Violations of 1992 (*Lāᵓiḥat al-jazāᵓāt al-idāriyya wa al-māliyya li-l-mukhālafāt al-maṣrafiyya li-sanat 1992*).[25] But these laws and regulations did not address the issue of Islamic finance as such, even though several paragraphs established that no banking law or practice could contradict the sharia. The new laws did give, however, the Bank of Sudan the right to fix profit margins, fees and commissions, and to decide procedure for the calculation and distribution of profits.[26]

A more comprehensive attempt by the government to detail proper Islamic financial procedures came in March 1993 when the Bank of Sudan's Supreme Board for Sharia Supervision (*al-hayᵓa al-ᶜuliyā li-l-raqāba al-shariᶜiyya*) issued a circular setting out requirements of legal *murābaḥa* contracts.[27] Specifically, the circular was meant to settle the widespread uncertainty regarding whether the banks could demand downpayments (*hāmish al-jiddiyya*; literally, "margin of seriousness") before they purchased commodities on behalf of clients, and how the mark-up (i.e., profit) should be calculated.

On the first issue, the Bank of Sudan made the legality of *murābaḥa* contracts dependent upon the following requirements:

1. An application submitted to the bank by a client should specify the commodity or describe its characteristics.
2. The client should ask the bank:
   a. to buy the commodity on its own account (i.e. the bank must make the purchase in its own name); and
   b. when the bank buys the commodity for itself, the client should pledge to buy it from the bank at a marked-up price.
3. If the bank accepts the application, it should:

---

[24] "Credit Facilities Policy", 21 November 1987.

[25] Both laws were enacted in early 1993.

[26] Banking Law of 1991, section 20, paragraphs 1 and 2.

[27] *Manshūr al-hīᵓa al-ᶜaliyā li-l-raqāba al-shariᶜiyya raqm 4/1413 h*, dated Khartoum 7 Ramaḍān 1413/28 February 1993; the cover letter was dated Khartoum 15 Ramaḍān 1413/8 March 1993. The five points given here are summaries of those contained in the original. Owing to differences between English and Arabic technical terms, it has been necessary here to employ considerable poetic licence.

a. buy, pay and take possession of the commodity;
b. present the commodity to the client as a new offer.

4. Since this is a re-sale and therefore a separate transaction, the client has the legal right (*al-ḥaq al-sharᶜī*) to renege on his earlier pledge to the bank; this is because if the client were obliged to honour his commitment, the bank would have 'sold something it does not own'.
5. If the client and the bank agree, they should sign a sale contract and the client would receive the commodity from the bank.

Not only because of the prohibition of selling something one does not own, downpayments should also be considered illegal because using the client's money to part-finance the purchase of a requested commodity would transform the *murābaḥa* into a partnership (*mushāraka*) and thereby change the relations between the two parties. In contrast, instalments should be considered legal because they represent set percentages of the price agreed upon between the bank and the client, and they are not part of the capital the bank uses to buy the commodity.

On the second issue, the Bank of Sudan's Sharia Board accepted that the banks' profits from resale had to take these factors into consideration:

1. the bank's need to generate annual profits;
2. the method of payment, since it influences the bank's profit margin; thus clients who make large initial payments and those who pay a small sum, or do not pay at all, should not pay the same amount;
3. whether clients make instalments at regular intervals or pay the whole sum at the end of the agreed period.

The Sharia Board's positions on these issues are remarkable. To begin with the requirements for the *murābaḥa* contract, it is difficult to say which is the more controversial position: to declare illegal all forms of downpayment before the bank makes a purchase on behalf of a client, or to allow the possibility of clients walking away from previous commitments. Clearly both went directly against established banking practice; the legal reasoning, however, was unequivocal: a contract would be invalid if the bank did not take full possession of the commodity requested by the client, and there would be no real risk unless the client had the right to accept or reject the commodity. Here the element of risk is central because without it the bank's mark-up or profit would be equivalent to interest and therefore *ribā*.

Regarding method of payment, the Sharia Board's position is noteworthy not so much because of what it says as what it does not say. By admitting, first, the legality—the term used is "justice demands" (*baida ʾan ᶜadāla*)—of different prices for the same commodity, and, secondly, linking the price scale to the bank's capital costs, the Sharia Board in fact accepted the principle of time-value for money. This can only be seen as contradicting the view of the heads of the Sharia Boards of the Islamic Banks, as expressed in their letter of November 1987, but the circular in important respects agrees with the position expressed by Ṣādiq al-Mahdī as related already. Possibly the intention of the Bank of Sudan's Sharia Board was to meet some of the concerns of the banking community. In the early 1990s, several banks (including at least one claiming the Islamic label) had petitioned the Bank of Sudan for permission to penalize customers by increasing charges when they defaulted or otherwise deferred payment. The Sharia Board's position on profit margins for *murābaḥa* contracts provided an opening for banks to introduce penalties based on the principle of time-value for money and was therefore welcomed by many commerical bankers, even if the circular did not go as far as to sanction interest rates over and above the mark-ups written into contracts between banks and clients.[28]

As mentioned, savings accounts and investment accounts cannot be guaranteed because funds in such accounts are used towards profit-and-loss sharing ventures. This principle notwithstanding, in 1996 the government introduced a compulsory deposit insurance scheme which guarantees accounts up to one million Sudanese pounds per customer.[29] The scheme, called *ṣandūq ḍamān al-wadāʾiʿ al-maṣrafiyya*, is financed jointly by the commercial banks, the Bank of Sudan and the Ministry of Finance. The scheme's motivation was clear enough: only a fraction of available cash—perhaps less than one third of total volume—circulated within the formal financial sector and government guarantees would attract more deposits. Possibly the arrangement would even shift more deposits toward long-term investment accounts. Not surprisingly, the scheme met opposition from the Bank of Sudan's Sharia Board, and the initial proposal was ammended to specify that deposits were only guaranteed against systemic or abnormal losses, and not losses that might occur in the course of normal banking operations. As of March 1999, the guarantee

[28] A related issue is the Bank of Sudan's Sharia Board's controversial approval of the right to impose penalties on banks that over-draw their accounts with the central bank. Also in this case, the Sharia Board comes close to accepting the principle of time value for money and thus by implication interest. Interestingly, an influential scholar opposed to this ruling did not base his argument on whether or not penalties constituted *ribā*, but on the principle of accountability maintaining that such penalties were illegal since they penalised shareholders and not the bank managers responsible for the over-draft. (Personal communication, Khartoum, March 1999.)

[29] See *Qanūn ṣandūq ḍamān al-wadāʾiʿ al-maṣrafiyya li-sana 1996 m*. The Bank of Sudan and the Ministry of Finance contributed 400 and 250 million Sudanese pounds respectively to the fund's initial capital, while upon becoming members of the fund each commercial bank paid 10 million. Compensation to depositors is not, however, meant to come from the core capital but from the accumulated saving of a 2% annual levy on all bank accounts, which is supplemented by annual contributions from the Bank of Sudan and the Ministry of Finance (each is committed to pay to the fund the equivalent of 10% of the total amount collected from bank accounts).

fund had not compensated any depositors for losses; hence the distinction between normal and abnormal losses remained untested and therefore theoretical.

In another unexpected development, the Bank of Sudan's Sharia Board in 1998 issued a *fatwā* that enabled indexation of investment accounts to counter the effects of inflation. Again, the background was the need to find a simple way to increase the level of investments. A remarkable feature of the opinion was the Sharia Board's suggestion that the difference between nominal value of money on account and the indexed value of the same amount after a given period (i.e. compensation for loss of real value) should be paid to depositors by the government. The argument was straightforward: since the government's lax fiscal policy was the primary cause for high inflation rates, it bore primary responsiblity for compensating depositors. The opinion was not implemented. No official explanation has been given for the hiatus but two considerations must have been taken into account by responsible officials. First of all, neither the Bank of Sudan nor the government had the financial resources to compensate depositors, and compensation on the scale necessary to keep up with inflation would in itself considerably add to the inflationary pressures in the economy.[30]

Conclusion

The Sudan represents a unique experiment in Islamic banking. Since 1983, the organizing principle of the financial sector has been the prohibition of all forms of interest. Given the influence of orthodox interpretations of the illegality of *ribā*, this is not surprising, and Sudanese policy-makers have carried out the ambitions of committed Islamists throughout the world. In this respect, the banking laws and regulations of the Sudan represent one of the few comprehensive efforts at creating an Islamic alternative to the conventional (western and secular) institutions that dominate the global economy. But the Sudanese experiment stands out also within the realm of Islamic banking. For instance, while usually it is up to the Sharia Boards of individual Islamic banks to define (and often design) legal financial techniques through the issuing of learned opinions, in the Sudan it is the state through the legal system that defines the system. The difference is striking: while in the Sudan Islamic banking is based on a body of positive law, elsewhere bankers rely on case-by-case *fatwās*.[31] The question can, however, be asked how successful the Sudanese experiment has been. The sudden Islamization caught the commercial community unprepared, and before long the government compromised

---

30 For a commentary, see Aḥmad Hilālī Aḥmad, "Mushrūᶜ al-ḥafāṭ ᶜlī qīma al-wadāʾiᶜ al-Istithmāriyya", *al-Ṣināᶜa wa al-tanmiyya* (Khartoum), Uktūbr-dīsimbir 1998, 15–16.

31 A comprehensive survey is Yusuf Talal DeLorenzo ed. and trans., *A Compendium of Legal Opinions on the Operations of Islamic Banks: Murabahah, Mudarabah, and Musharakah* (London, 1997).

by deciding to honour interest payments on foreign loans. Moreover, the predominance of *murābaha* contracts ensured that the change in the nature of banking was superficial rather than substantial. In the 1990s, stricter supervision by the Bank of Sudan has forced the banks to be more careful to follow the letter of the law, but the new regulations are highly controversial since they go against established business practice. The debate over the compensatory rates and indexation of money on account highlights a lingering paradox: while there is general agreement on the prohibition of *ribā*, there is no agreement on how this principle should be interpreted in practical situations. On the surface the stalemate between the two schools of thought (the historical school and the theoretical school) seems to continue, but recent decisions may indicate that economic pragmatism is winning the day. For instance, the decision to recognize the time value of money (in 1993), the introduction of a compulsory deposit insurance scheme (in 1996), and proposed indexing of investment accounts (in 1998), suggest that the governing authorities in important respects have moved away from earlier orthodoxy. While some may want to argue that these "innovations" demonstrate that Islamic principles are compatible with the demands of the modern world, for those committed to challenging Western concepts and models there is the danger that the Islamic alternative loses its unique qualities and is reduced to nothing but an exercise in semantics.

Bibliography

Note: newspapers and "gray" material are not included but are fully referenced in footnotes.

Abdelwahab El-Affendi. *Turabi's Revolution: Islam and Power in Sudan.* London, 1991.

Aḥmad Hilālī Aḥmad. "Mushrūᶜ al-ḥafᵓāṭ ᶜlī qīma al-wadāᶜiq al-Isthimāriyya", *Majala al-Ṣanāᶜa wa al-tanmiyya* (Khartoum), October–December1998, 15–16.

Ali Rahnema and Farhad Nomani. *The Secular Miracle: Religion, Politics and Economic Policy in Iran.* London, 1990.

—. *Islamic Economic Systems.* London, 1994.

DeLorenzo, Yusuf Talal ed. and trans. *A Compendium of Legal Opinions on the Operations of Islamic Banks: Murabahah, Mudarabah, and Musharakah.* London, 1997.

Fazlur Rahman. "*Riba* and Interest," *Islamic Studies* 3, no. 4 (1964): 1–43.

Izzud-Din Pal. "Pakistan and the Question of Riba," *Middle Eastern Studies* 30, no. 1 (1994), 64–78.

Mansour Khalid. *Nimeiri and the Revolution of Dis-May.* London, 1985.

—. *The Government They Deserve: The Role of the Elite in Sudan's Political Evolution.* London, 1990.

al-Mikāshfī Ṭāha al-Kabbāshī. *Taṭbīq al-sharīᶜa al-Islamiyya fī al-Sūdān bayn al-ḥaqīqa wa al-ithāra.* 2nd. ed. Cairo, 1986.

Udovitch, Abraham L. "Bankers without Banks: Commerce, Banking, and Society in the Islamic World of the Middle Ages," in *The Dawn of Modern Banking*. Center for Medieval and Renaissance Studies, UCLA, 255–73. New Haven, 1979.

Zubair Iqbal and Abbas Mirakhor. *Islamic Banking*. Occasional Papers, no. 48. Washington, DC, 1987.

Imposing a Guide on the *Indigène*: The Fifty Year Experience of the *Sociètès de Prèvoyance* in French West and Equatorial Africa

Gregory Mann and Jane I. Guyer

Introduction

By far the broadest-ranging and longest-lived financial institution that engaged with the ordinary population in the twentieth-century colonial world was the series of *Sociétés Indigènes de Prévoyance* (SIP) instituted by the French, first in Algeria at the turn of the century and gradually throughout the colonies. Premised on services to the population categorized legally as *indigènes,* they were modified when the legal category of the *indigénat* was abolished in 1946; they then became the *Sociétés Africaines de Prévoyance* (SAP). They were completely suspended or transformed into much more modest mutual societies at Independence. In light of the unique longevity and importance of the SIPs, a former colonial administrator understandably takes a classic "plus ça change" ... position with respect to the new initiatives: "The NGOs are reinventing the moon. ... When we see famines following one after the other in the Sahel, we say 'they should have listened to us!'"[1]

None of the older institutions, however, was as consistently successful as this former administrator implies. Rather, they persisted, mediating a changing relationship between policy and local populations, between financial feasibility and local conditions. The history of the SIPs extends over sixty years of changing colonial financial policy, economic transformation, and shifting leadership at all levels, and therefore offers the opportunity to trace out the long-term dynamics of financial engagement between powerful metropolitan finance and poor populations.

This essay reviews the history of SIP/SAPs in French colonial Africa and their structure and operation with respect to social and economic goals. It focuses particularly on their range of functions and the changing emphasis amongst those functions in relation to shifting exigencies and interests. Our examples come from French West Africa for the period from the turn of the century to 1945, and then include Cameroon for the period from World War II to 1960. The SIPs were founded under the League of Nations mandate of Cameroon in 1937, but only fully empowered after the war. Thus their history there represents not only a new locus of operation but a new era of colonial policy.

---

[1] Olivier Colombani, *Mémoires coloniales: La fin de l'empire français d'Afrique vue par les administrateurs coloniaux* (Paris, 1991), 144.

Historical Overview

In formerly French Africa, local credit and cooperative associations, the *sociétés de prévoyance,* were central to colonial development projects. In their original incarnations, these *sociétés* had two primary functions: to encourage cash savings amongst subject populations, offering an alternative to loans from the local informal sector which were seen as usurious; and to operate communal granaries in the context of unpredictable harvests and a sometimes rough transition to cash-cropping. In addition, administrators were quite conscious of the *sociétés* as institutions of social discipline that would educate colonial subjects in credit and savings and in interactions with the state.

The idea of the *société de prévoyance* in Senegal and then elsewhere in sub-Saharan Africa was adapted from the colonial administration of North Africa, particularly that of Algeria. There the *sociétés* were formally instituted in 1894 to operate communal granaries and to encourage cash-cropping.[2] Because the institution had had moderate successes in North Africa, in 1910 administrators in Senegal "borrowed directly" the initial legislation creating *sociétés* in Algeria.[3] However, as West Africans were considered less able than North Africans to benefit from such an institution, two modifications were made. In 1915 new legislation made membership compulsory in *cercles* where a *société* existed; in 1923 local administrators took over the institution's day-to-day management.[4] Gradually the institution became common throughout French West and Equatorial Africa, making loans in cash and kind, and maintaining granaries. Although its functions became increasingly diverse, it continued to provide food in times of shortage, as the *société* in San (Soudan) did in 1938.[5]

Depending on their economic focus, different colonies emphasized one or the other of the institution's two main functions: to provide loans of seeds and capital to farmers at reduced rates; and to ensure a reliable store of staple foods in case of crop failure. In Senegal the *sociétés* provided seed to peanut producers and freed them from the high interest rates of commercial lenders.[6] In areas where cash-cropping was not dominant, such as in the French Soudan and Haute Volta, *société* administrators focused on the creation of food reserves, both in times of crisis or famine and in "average" years. Administrators were concerned about food production and storage because they considered colonies such as the Soudan to be reserves of labor and

---

[2] Marcel Boyer, *Les sociétés de prévoyance, de secours, et de prêts mutuels agricoles en Afrique Occidentale Française* (thèse pour le doctorat, Université de Paris, 1935), 16; Jean Suret-Canale, *Afrique noire occidentale et centrale: L'ère coloniale, 1900–1945* (Paris, 1964), 301ff.

[3] Boyer, *Les sociétés de prévoyance,* 49.

[4] Ibid., 54, 61.

[5] *Journal Officiel du Soudan Français* (1938):354.

[6] Abdoul Sow, *Les sociétés de prévoyance du Sénégal des origines à 1947* (thèse pour le doctorat de troisième cycle, Université de Dakar, 1985).

military manpower. They wanted healthy recruits, but believed that many of the young men in the AOF were underfed.[7] The key to development, wrote one colonial theorist, lay in realizing that "... for many long years, negroes have not eaten enough ... the great secret of African development is essentially to make the Africans eat regularly and sufficiently."[8] On a more fundamental level, the French were well aware that "a people who suffers from hunger is a people ready to rebel."[9] In such colonies, the *sociétés* were geared more towards *"prévoyance"* and the reproduction of a labor supply than towards encouraging cash-crop production.

The 1930s can be considered the *sociétés*' heyday. In that decade they became increasingly active, and they were established across West Africa, partly because they fit the economic tenor of the times. Paradoxically, this period coincides with the Great Depression, and the interwar period as a whole was known for its prevailing *immobilisme* and neglect.[10] Little public capital was invested in the empire during this period, aside from a few large-scale development projects.[11] Furthermore, metropolitan parliamentary coalitions rose and fell rapidly throughout the 1930s. However, being locally operated and largely self-funded, the *sociétés* were well-suited to survive and adapt without direction and funding from above.[12] Gradually they became a fundamental component of the French administrative apparatus. In the 1950s a British colonial officer wrote that the *sociétés* were as paradigmatic of French colonial rule as Native Councils were of British colonialism.[13]

As we describe below, the functions assumed by the *sociétés* became more complex over time, but not until after World War II did they take on finance of processing machines, transport, construction, trade, and the full gamut of sectors in an increasingly commercialized indigenous economy. At that time they became the management institution for funds from the new *Fonds*

---

[7] François Sorel, "L'alimentation des indigènes en AOF," in *L'alimentation indigène dans les colonies françaises*, ed. Georges Hardy and Charles Richet (Paris, 1933), 166.

[8] Lucien Hubert, "L'ascension de l'Afrique occidentale française," *Académie des Sciences Coloniales, Comptes Rendus des Séances, Communications* 9 (1927):45.

[9] Georges Hardy and Charles Richet, "Introduction," in *L'alimentation indigène dans les colonies françaises*, ed. Hardy and Richet, 10.

[10] Robert Delavignette, *L'Afrique noire française et son destin* (Paris, 1962), 20–3; Robert Delavignette, *Robert Delavignette on the French Empire: Selected Writings*, ed. William B. Cohen (Chicago, 1977), 63.

[11] Jacques Marseille, *Empire colonial et capitalisme français: histoire d'un divorce* (Paris, 1984).

[12] In 1933, *sociétés* in the AOF held assets equaling 14,404,580 francs. More than half this amount—8,506,168 francs—came from members' dues, and the remainder came from various, unspecified sources, including interest on loans to members (Boyer, *Les sociétés de prévoyance*, 70–71). Even after becoming eligible for loans from the Crédit Agricole in 1926, the *sociétés*' primary sources of funding remained members' dues (56, 69–72).

[13] Kenneth Robinson, "The *Sociétés de Prévoyance* in French West Africa," *Journal of African Administration* 4, no. 2 (1955):29.

d'Investissement pour le Développement Economique et Sociale (FIDES), and enormous sums of money from metropolitan sources were channelled through the loan mechanisms already in place. Some funds went into infrastructural development such as transport. Others went into an ambitious and imaginative project entitled *Petit Équipement Rural* to increase the primary processing capacities of the commercial rural economy; during the 1950s innovations were made in cocoa drying, palm pressing for oil production, rice milling and so on.

Throughout the fifty years of SIP / SAP operation, within the general mandate of each era and each major region, many key decisions could be made at the local level. Hence there was considerable room for shifting from one agenda to another as seemed to meet the needs and interests of the times. The relative flexibility in the mandate from the top was a persistent characteristic of the SIPs, and partially accounts for their capacity to persevere through periods of neglect and to respond in periods of high demand from government to implement new policies.

Structure and Finance

This combination of colonial discipline and relative regional autonomy was guaranteed by the SIP / SAP constitution, which applied to all colonies. The *sociétés* operated through an institutional structure mandated by the governor-general of the French colonial federation of West Africa (the AOF). Although multiple rounds of AOF legislation tinkered with this structure, its essence remained the same.

Before describing the structure of the *sociétés*, it may be useful to explain the administrative apparatus in which they functioned. French West Africa, one of the two large federations into which France's sub-Saharan colonies were divided, was administered by a governor-general, based in Dakar. He implemented policies of the Colonial Ministry in Paris and supervised the governors of the individual colonies, including Senegal and the Soudan. The governors directed the *commandants* of individual *cercles*, administrative units similar to counties. *Cercles* were broken into subdivisions and into *cantons*; the latter were directed by Africans. Cameroon was not part of the AOF; its governor answered to Paris and was supervised by international organizations, since the area was a mandate. Otherwise its structure was the same.

At the level of the colony government, the key institution of the SIPs was the Common Fund. Local *sociétés* contributed a fixed portion of their proceeds, generally between five and ten percent, to the Common Fund annually.[14] The Common Fund could make or guarantee loans to local *sociétés* for development projects. It drew its capital from multiple sources. In addition to contributions of local chapters, the Fund could receive and

[14] E.g., *Journal Officiel du Soudan Français* (1936):598.

disperse money from the government of the colony and it could contract loans with semi-private entities, such as the Bank of West Africa (*Banque de l'Afrique Occidentale*, BAO).[15] In dispensing capital, the Common Fund could give loans and grants (*secours*) to both local *sociétés* and to individuals for such purposes as the purchase of seeds, "rural improvement," and even, in at least one case, for food.[16] In addition, rather than loaning its own money, it could guarantee loans to its member *sociétés* from banks or other institutions, such as the *Caisse de Crédit Agricole*. Members could then obtain individual loans from their *sociétés*. Thus the Common Fund had a hand in making policy; its director, an administrator appointed by the colony's lieutenant-governor, responded to policy directives from above whenever there was a clear mandate for specific action, which was not necessarily on a continuous basis.

Two examples can illustrate the financial power of the Common Fund and its practical uses, which were in keeping with the *sociétés'* original missions. Both examples are drawn from the colony of the Soudan in 1938. First, when the cercle of San faced food shortages, the Common Fund advanced 750,000 francs to the *société* to help it purchase provisions.[17] Ideally, of course, the local communal granaries the *société* ran could have sustained the cercle. For unknown reasons, it did not. Second, the Fund took two large loans—664,000 francs and 300,000 francs—from the *Crédit agricole mutuel du Soudan Français* (CAMSF) in order to finance a series of rural development projects sponsored by *sociétés* in Kayes, Koutiala, Tougan, and Timbuktu. One of these loans was long-term, and the rate of interest the Common Fund received was only half of the four percent the lending institution would have demanded from an individual.[18] Both decisions were approved by the lieutenant-governor of the colony and promulgated in its official journal, as the Common Fund could not contract loans with individual *sociétés* without government oversight.[19] Even special expenditures, which the *sociétés* paid for themselves, were approved by a higher level of administration, as when the association in Kayes wanted to buy more seeds for its stock.[20]

The local organization of SIPs was determined by the colonial administrative structure, since the manager was always a French official. Each *cercle* (a fairly large territorial administrative unit) had a *société*, which might be broken up into sections either by region or by ethnicity. Whereas an individual *société* as a whole may have had over 100,000 members, a regional section could be much more easily administered. Furthermore, dividing the

[15] Ibid. (1935):360–361.
[16] Ibid. (1938):370, 562, 354.
[17] Ibid., 354.
[18] Ibid., 352, 562.
[19] Ibid. (1935):360.
[20] Ibid. (1938):370.

société into ethnic sub-units recognized in a practical way the varying modes of production different groups pursued.

The local colonial administrator and a small number of administrative assistants and hand-picked local notables directed the operations of the *sociétés*. For two brief periods, between 1910 and 1915, and again from 1919 to 1923, local African notables served as presidents of the *sociétés*, as had been the case in Algeria. Although these notables were hand-picked by French administrators, putting them in charge was later considered "a huge error," and administrators resumed control of their areas' *sociétés*. The African presidents were removed because few could read and write and many lacked sufficient authority to manage the members. Furthermore, the notables were considered even more irresponsible than administrators, who had a marked tendency "to confuse *cercle* finances with the *société* finances."[21] Moreover, although Africans were in charge, French administrators often ran the show behind the scenes while bearing little responsibility for their actions.[22] Nevertheless, when reformed legislation returned leadership to the local *commandants-de-cercle*, critics within the government protested that local administrators would be likely to abuse their power.

For most of the history of the SIPs African participation in the direction of the *sociétés* was limited to a few seats on an advisory council, whose members were nominated by the *société* as a whole, chosen by the *commandant* and approved by the lieutenant-governor.[23] This council had no real power, since the president was only required to inform it of his actions after the fact.[24] African members also sat on the supervisory council of each AOF colony, but as the *sociétés* became involved in selling their members' produce, African membership diminished. Under a 1933 decree, a French commercial agent took the place of one of the supervisory council's three African members.[25]

Membership in the SIP was obligatory for adult men and their dues were paid as if they were a tax. The North African model had been based on voluntary participation, which the administrators had concluded would not work in the "less assimilated" West African context: "There was a risk of reducing the *Sociétés de Prévoyance* to skeletal number and obliging them to mark time ... One had to *impose* a guide on the *indigène* and this guide could only be the *Société de Prévoyance*."[26] Mandatory participation increased both the operating capital the *sociétés* could generate and the resentment of their members. That resentment would later become a severe problem for the institution.[27]

[21] Boyer, *Les sociétés de prévoyance*, 60.
[22] Ibid., 61.
[23] Ibid., 60–1; see example below concerning Koutiala.
[24] Ibid., 59, 67–8.
[25] Ibid., 64.
[26] Ibid., 54. Original emphasis.
[27] Membership was for *indigènes* only; French and African citizens were excluded from the *sociétés* . Women did participate in some *sociétés*; however, this contradicted the in-

The *sociétés* drew their funding principally from members' annual dues. The group of directors set the amount of dues required for membership in the *société*, within a range prescribed by a colony-wide supervisory committee. This amount was then published as a decree from the lieutenant-governor. Dues were occasionally paid in kind, but cash became the dominant mode of payment. For most of the 1930s, these yearly dues were kept at one franc per member.[28] While dues were the principal source of capital for the *sociétés*, they also took in rare subventions from the colony's government, gifts from individuals, and loans from the *Fonds Commun*, or Common Fund, which the administrator could request.[29] Because commandants transferred from one *cercle* to another quite frequently, the *sociétés* and their debts were continually being inherited by new directors, who may have been reluctant to pay the debts and carry on the projects bequeathed to them.

Structure and Flexibility

Extreme flexibility was the most striking institutional trait of the *sociétés*. The funds the *sociétés* generated were meant to be used to benefit the agricultural production of the *indigènes*. In practice, this meant that they could legitimately be spent on a vast range of different projects, as long as the ultimate producers or users could be identified as *indigènes*. European planters and traders were excluded, and the relationship between French traders and the *sociétés* was occasionally antagonistic.[30] Nevertheless, French business indirectly benefited greatly from increased production for sale, an expanded market for seed, and eventually from orders for *petit équipement rural* of all kinds. Illegitimately, the range was even greater, as institutional oversight was limited. Nevertheless, by the 1950s administrators were criticizing the *sociétés* as lacking in flexibility.[31] They argued that the institutional structure was far too rigid to serve the changing needs and programs of the colonial state. The following paragraphs examine the structural nature of the institution's flexibility and how that characteristic was lost.

Throughout most of the period before World War II, the *sociétés* were funded almost entirely by local capital, and they were subject to only moderate control from above. Their functions were ill-defined. The central government mandated that each *cercle* should have at least one *société*, but it gave lo-

stitutions' charters and was considered contrary to the "organisation of the African family." Boyer, *Les sociétés de prévoyance*, 65.

28 Boyer, *Les sociétés de prévoyance*, 70; *Journal Officiel du Soudan Français* (1933):574; (1935):496.

29 Boyer, *Les sociétés de prévoyance*, 72.

30 Cf. Richard L. Roberts, *Two Worlds of Cotton: Colonialism and the Regional Economy in the French Soudan, 1800–1946* (Stanford, 1996), 257.

31 M. David, *La coopération, la mutualité et le crédit agricoles en AOF: La modernisation du paysannat au Cameroun et en AEF* (Paris, 1956), 5.

cal administrators a very broad mandate for the *société* and its funds. The Common Fund monitored its own mandated contributions but beyond that, oversight was sparse. Each *cercle*'s *société* had an advisory council, headed by the *commandant*, who was of course the president. In each colony, supervisory committees were charged with ensuring that administrators did not simply pocket the funds, but they seem to have intervened very little in local expenditures.[32] Local administrators therefore had a degree of autonomy in finding purposes for their extra funds, and the similar uses to which they put them could owe as much to comparable conditions as to grand designs.

Although they may have served vastly different purposes, all *sociétés* in Senegal and the French Soudan shared an institutional history, and with it, two basic functions. They extended credit, in cash or in kind, to farmers, and they created and maintained communal granaries. One or the other of these functions tended to dominate according to an area's economic needs. In addition to these core functions, the *sociétés* tackled a vast array of economic and social projects.

As a central aspect of their mission, the *sociétés* operated communal granaries of seeds and cereals in order to prevent or forestall famine. In terms of ideology and rhetoric, the granaries were a success, as they demonstrated foresight and they addressed some administrators' concerns about nutrition. In practical terms, however, their record was mixed. Some farmers were opposed to contributing to the granaries, and they resented mixing their seeds with other varieties. In one village in the Soudan, farmers re-"appropriated" grain they had contributed, intending to sell it and use the cash to pay their taxes.[33] Although the *commandant* of the *cercle* advocated a severe punishment for the perpetrators' entire village, he had himself argued in an administrative report that the granaries were useless: "The grains spoil very quickly ... for the most part, the stocks are not able to be used, and in the end are no more than a useless and expensive burden on the budget of the *société*."[34] Not everyone agreed with his argument, and later administrators from the same region described the granaries as effective.[35]

Administrators quickly found innovative uses for the *sociétés* and the funds they generated. From the first years of their existence in Senegal, the *sociétés* introduced new varieties of seeds and other technological inputs to farmers.[36] Because they lent seeds to farmers at the beginning of planting seasons, the *sociétés* could easily lend the varieties of seeds the administration's agronomists wished to promote. French commercial agents had long practiced this technique. For example, in Segu before the First World War, a

---

32 Boyer, *Les sociétés de prévoyance*, 75–6.

33 J.Y. Marchal, *Chroniques d'un cercle de l'AOF* (Paris, 1980), 175–6.

34 Ibid., 178.

35 Ibid., 194–5.

36 Sow, *Les sociétés des prévoyance du Senegal*, 114–6.

commerçant had offered African villages cash advances on cotton grown from seeds he provided. Controlling the seeds allowed him to control the quality of the harvest, and guaranteed him a crop to market. The success of this system lay in the farmers' eagerness to accept a cash advance just before the rainy season, when they were poorest.[37] Although this system had been operated as a private enterprise, it was seen as a model of how institutions such as the *sociétés* could spur the use of particular seeds while freeing producers from what were seen as usurious practices.[38]

In Senegal, the *sociétés* gradually began to intervene in the marketing of cash crops, and they did so over protest from private enterprises in the region. In 1933, in the midst of the Depression, the *sociétés* began formally to take responsibility for selling the crops of their members.[39] They would purchase agricultural products and regulate their entry into the market, allowing producers to withhold them from the commercial market until they were offered a favorable price.[40] Thus the markets were no longer flooded with crops at harvest time, depressing prices. This interfered with the practices of private buyers, who had swooped up crops at low prices during the harvest, and sold seeds at high rates when the sowing period arrived. Many *sociétés* in the Soudan also intervened in marketing in order to maintain a cotton price high enough to act as an incentive for further production for export.[41] In both Senegal and the Soudan, the government was placing what it saw as its own economic interests above those of the European commercial agents; those interests sometimes favored farmers as well.

The resources of the *société* were also used to make crops more marketable. While a crop was stored in the communal granaries, it could be sorted into varying qualities, or it could be "finished"—hulled, carded, or shelled, depending on the plant in question.[42] Taking control of another stage in the production of their crops for sale, African producers could exercise more control over the marketing of their goods and could demand consistently higher prices than had been possible previously.

Another benefit of communal marketing could be derived from government subsidies of certain crops. The administration offered bonuses for certain products by the kilogram, but awarded them for other crops only by the ton. For example, sisal earned 800 francs in government bonuses when sold by the ton, but individual farmers might not be able or willing to

---

37 M. Vuillet, "Persévérer," *Académie des Sciénces Coloniales: Annales* 2 (1925):62–3.

38 Ibid., 65.

39 Boyer, *Les sociétés de prévoyance*, 57; Sow, *Les sociétés des p´revoyance du Senegal*, 211.

40 Of course this assumed that the prices the *sociétés* offered were fair.

41 Roberts, *Two Worlds*, 257.

42 P. Gillin, "Pourquoi les silos coopératifs sont-ils nécessaires dans les colonies et pays de protectorat nord-Africains?" *L'agriculture pratique des pays chauds*, 16 (October, 1931):775–7; and *Agronomie Coloniale* 20, no. 157 (1931):159.

produce such large quantities of a non-food crop.[43] In theory, collective marketing made it possible to sell in bulk and receive extra funds.

The move into marketing was only one aspect of the rapid proliferation of the *sociétés'* functions. Although the primary purposes of the *sociétés* were to store grain and loan seeds, local administrators adapted the institution to fit their needs. Because the *sociétés* were seen as "the primordial base of development,"[44] they became the structure through which agricultural improvements and marketing initiatives were undertaken. The lack of alternate structures represents only one reason for this expansion of their functions. The other is quite pragmatic: *sociétés* were largely self-funding, membership was obligatory, and the *commandant de cercle* was almost invariably the president of the governing board of the local *société*. Funds were readily available and oversight was limited, so an administrator's initiative could quickly manifest itself in the form of a new investment.

The *sociétés* became vehicles for a dizzying array of local initiatives. They became involved in the purchase and maintenance of machinery, the digging of wells, the extermination of pests, and the construction of irrigation systems. In one *cercle* of Burkina Faso, the *société* offered bounties for killing predators, and thirty-seven lions were killed in one year.[45] Although conceived originally for farmers, *sociétés* could benefit pastoral communities as well; they could be used to instruct herders in the care of cattle and sheep.[46] They also facilitated the curing of leather.[47] In North Africa, *sociétés* designated specifically for artisans were established in 1938;[48] similar West African institutions expanded marketing possibilities for artisans by encouraging weaving and the production of rugs.[49] An enthusiastic governor of the Cote d'Ivoire even created medical *sociétés* to pay for medicine and for the salaries of some health providers.[50]

Direct involvement in, and management of, processing and even production itself was added in the era of FIDES funding. For a few brief years in

---

43 *Agronomie Coloniale* 21, no. 172 (1932):140–1.

44 M. Frot, "Les sociétés de prévoyance au Soudan français," in *Premier congrès soudanais de technique et colonisation agricole,* vol. 2:69.

45 Marchal, *Chroniques,* 177. Apparently the role of the *société* was to fund the rewards paid to hunters. In 1937, the *prime* paid for a lion rose from fifty to 100 francs. Bounties were paid on twenty-three lions, thirty-two hyenas, and two "panthers." (185).

46 Michel Lallour, "L'élevage du mouton au Soudan," in *Congrès,* 65.

47 1946 document, Archives du Mali (Koutiala).

48 Robert Coetz-Girey, "Le crédit," in *Éléments d'économie coloniale* (Paris, 1943), 379.

49 Jean Clauzel, *Administrateur de la France d'outre-mer* (Avignon, 1989), 50–1; cf. Richard L. Roberts, "The Coercion of Free Markets: Cotton, Peasants, and the Colonial State in the French Sudan, 1924–1932", in *Cotton, Colonialism, and Social History in Sub-Saharan Africa,* ed. Richard L. Roberts and Allen Isaacman (Portsmouth, New Hampshire, 1995), 221–43; and Roberts, *Two Worlds of Cotton.*

50 Danielle Domergue-Cloarec, *Politique coloniale française et réalités coloniales: La santé en Côte d'Ivoire, 1905–1958* (Toulouse, 1986), 537–41.

Cameroon, between 1954 and 1960 when FIDES funds were channelled through them, the SAPs ran veritable commercial and industrial enterprises. Their total expenditure went from twenty-five million francs in 1946 to 2,000 million francs a decade later: a sixty-fold increase.[51] The several major efforts included a dairy industry at Meiganga that serviced the southern cities, contracted food supply for the workers at the SEITA tobacco plantation near Saa, initiatives in growing European vegetables in the highlands at Dschang, an experimental farm for the urban food supply of the capital, and the rice mill at Nanga Eboko. The latter was among the most ambitious; like numerous subsequent schemes in various places, it was intended to compete with cheap imported rice from Asia. Using a technology imported from Indo-China, the mill was provisioned from nineteen satellite paddy storehouses, linked in turn to a local peasant production effort that employed eleven extension workers.[52] Even as late as 1965, when it was just hanging on under an extension rubric of some sort following the suspension of the Common Fund at Independence in 1960, the Nanga Eboko SAP was reported as employing seventy-three people.[53]

The expansion into production schemes that required foreign expertise, and therefore salaries for foreigners, was technically in breach of the spirit of the SIP mandate, which was to support indigenous enterprise. It was justified in the founding charter for the Cameroon SIP "to take all measures which contribute to the development of agriculture, animal husbandry, fishing and gathering," which was interpreted in the expanding commercial economy of 1956 to mean "to alleviate the effects of neglect by the private sector."[54] One cannot read the list of activities mediated by the SAPs in the 1950s without being struck by the enormous opportunity they offered for French business and trade, besides their possible effects in stimulating local production. The U. N. report for 1956 adds project upon project to the list, of which the following is only a partial excerpt: "They ... facilitate the provisioning of their members in construction materials, wood, roofing material, cement, or food items at better prices, and, for their own account, they run quarries, carpentry workshops, and timber-works; they provide seed, fertilizer, and all kinds of goods and merchandise ..."[55] From the mandate of provision in the home and export sectors, the SAP took on the fostering of commercialism in the regional mar-

---

[51] "Report of the French Government to the Permanent Mandate Commission of the United Nations," (1956), 352.

[52] Philippe Antoine, *Les sociétés africaines de prévoyance en Cameroun* (thèse pour le doctorat, Université de Paris, 1954), 36, 120.

[53] Cameroun, Bureau de Documentation, B118.

[54] Antoine, *Les sociétés africaines de prévoyance au Cameroun*, 130.

[55] "Report of the French Government to the UN," 101.

ket, and thereby assumed the formidable task of mediating regional networks.[56]

Undoubtedly French national agendas in commercial and political life influenced the way in which this was done. This would be a new phase but not a new departure in attempts to create the social structure of the market. The *sociétés* and their funds had often been used as leverage in both the formal and informal processes of social engineering and creation of commercial and patronage networks. Like any other government, the colonial government depended on the favor and loyalty of certain individuals and social groups. For example, the administration bid intensely to win the loyalty of ex-soldiers, and the use of local *société* funds was one aspect of this larger project. Thus, veterans of the colonial military were granted lower interest rates on individual loans from the *sociétés,* helping them to establish themselves economically.[57] Veterans were also trained in modern intensive agriculture and encouraged to take up commercial gardening to supply urban markets and even to export to Nigeria.[58] In these examples, the *sociétés* were used both to monetize and catalyze the economy and to re-integrate former soldiers into civilian life.

Another means of extending patronage networks was the granting of loans to individuals. This must have been a highly selective process; it is altogether unclear that these loans were repaid, or that anyone expected they would be.[59] Any attempts to collect repayment can only have been exacerbated by the high rate of turnover among administrators, which left newly arrived administrators the burden of collecting on loans extended by their predecessors. Evidence of loans to individual Africans is extremely scarce in the available records, but there is evidence that some loans were written off altogether. For example, the government of the Soudan colony negated a loan of 16,604.25 francs to a man named Baba Kéita in 1938. The debtor died and the debt was annulled.[60] Although such large loans were probably rare, questions remain—how did Kéita manage to contract such a large debt, and did he or the *commandant* ever expect it to be paid off? Where did the money go? Whatever the answers, it is fair to assume that Kéita was a well-connected man. It is also clear that, if forgiving debt became common practice, the administration was flatly contradicting its own intended lesson of *prévoyance.*

---

56 Roberts (*Two Worlds of Cotton*) notes the marked lack of success the French had in redirecting these networks in the Soudan/Mali.

57 Sow, *Les sociétés des prévoyance du Senegal,*158; *Journal Officiel du Soudan Français* (1938):352.

58 Governor General to AOF Governors, 2 June 1947. Archives Nationales du Mali (Kuluba), 3N41(FR).

59 To address this issue fully would require more extensive archival research.

60 *Journal Officiel du Soudan Français* (1938):441.

Others who received "loans" were in no way eligible for them. When a reform-minded *commandant* took over the direction of the *société* in one Malian town, his first task was to purge the institution of the many loans it had extended to "people with no right to solicit financial assistance from the Mutual fund to which they paid no dues, [people such as] functionaries and merchants."[61]

As tools for local policies, the *sociétés* could also be tools of local politics. The independence of local administrators, combined with mandatory membership, meant that they could use the *sociétés* coercively. Disputes over the rules of the institution made ready proxies for other disagreements among French officials and African intermediaries and producers. One former administrator, Jacques Dequecker, remarked that government control of the *sociétés* and of communal granaries "had become abusive, because it was a means of pressuring a village chief who was inconveniencing us. We decreed that the stocks did not meet regulations and the fellow was punished. We slapped on a fine or whatever."[62] The "average" farmer could also be coerced with the leverage of debt. For instance, when an administrator sought settlers for the Office du Niger project in the 1930s, he threatened to repossess cattle and plows on loan from a *société* if members would not volunteer to relocate.[63] Farmers had no formal means of protesting such strong-arm tactics since the head of the local *société* was almost invariably the local European administrator, who was also the judge who would hear a legal complaint. The coincidence of financial and administrative authority fostered decisive local policy but it greatly hindered the development of any institutions of accountability, as Antoine pointed out in his generally favorable review of the *sociétés* in 1954.

African chiefs and functionaries were also part of the system of the *sociétés*, and they manipulated its impositions to their benefit. Chiefs who might have profited from charging high interests on seed loans before the era of the *sociétés* could easily turn the new regulations to their advantage, earning a *"boni important"* by collecting more grain than was mandated, and skimming off the excess.[64] As with the taxes to which they were linked, paying incentives to chiefs for SIP dues collection ensured enthusiastic collection but also created opportunities for abuses, some of which were ignored by colonial administration as a long as some efficiency was maintained.[65]

---

61 Maurice Méker, *Le temps colonial: Itinéraire africain d'un naïf du colonialisme à la coopération, 1931–1969* (Dakar, 1980), 158.

62 Colombani, *Mémoires coloniales*, 145.

63 Monica van Beusekom, "Colonial Rural Development: French Policy and African response at the Office du Niger, Soudan Français (Mali), 1920–1960" (Ph.D., Johns Hopkins University, 1990), 114.

64 Suret-Canale, *Afrique noire occidentale et centrale*, 304.

65 See Jane I. Guyer, "The Depression and the Administration in South-Central Cameroun," *African Economic History* 10 (1981).

At the outside limit there was blatant illegality. Because *sociétés* were controlled locally and oversight was limited they could quite easily be used as a simple slush fund for administrators, who could divert the *société's* capital to their own purposes. *Commandants* used farmers' contributions to purchase vehicles, refrigerators for administrators' homes, and in one Cameroonian case, furniture for the mayor's house.[66] As a former commandant wrote, "the members of the *société* ... couldn't imagine such a situation. And when they knew about it, they didn't dare say anything."[67] One suspects, however, that African members knew very well where their dues were going, and that this knowledge shaped their conceptions of saving and credit in this institutional form.

A final function for which the SIP/SAP structure was used, at least in Cameroon in the 1950s, was as a monitoring device for other kinds of rural organization, and most importantly for the growing nationalist movement. Kom argues persuasively that control of political activity was one of the purposes of the *petit équipment rural* policy.[68] The French administration's report to the Permanent Mandate Commission of the United Nations was explicit on this point, that the new rural credit program, run through the SAP structure, offered "the promise of stability at the same time as a means of raising the standard of living of the rural population."[69] All cooperatives had to be affiliated with their local SAP—and hence to the colonial administration—to be eligible for loans, and their financial processes were subject to SAP oversight. This effectively put all local groups under SAP—and thereby administrative—surveillance.

Credit, Providence and Civic Education

Through all of these economic and social initiatives ran one common rhetorical thread: French writers lamented that Africans lacked foresight, or *"prévoyance ... et tout l'effort de l'administration n'a pu jusqu'à présent leur inculquer cette vertu."*[70] Such sentiments emerged again and again in colonial writing on food, nutrition, credit, and agriculture. Indeed, both in the colonies and in the metropole, the concept of *prévoyance* was an integral part of what Cooper and Stoler have called "cultures of rule."[71] Nineteenth-cen-

---

66 Méker, *Le temps colonial,* 158; Jane I. Guyer, "The Provident Societies in the Rural Economy of Yaoundé, 1945–1960 (Boston University African Studies Center, Working Paper Series, No. 37, 1980), 3.

67 Méker, *Le temps colonial,* 158.

68 David Kom, *Le Cameroun: Essai d'analyse économique et politique* (Paris, 1971) 281–4.

69 "Report of the French Government to the UN" (1955), 80.

70 Sorel, *L'Alimentation des indigènes en AOF,* 157.

71 Ann Laura Stoler and Fredrick Cooper, "Between Metropole and Colony: Rethinking a Research Agenda," in *Tensions of Empire: Colonial Cultures in a Bourgeois World,* ed. Frederick Cooper and Anne Stoler (Berkeley, 1997), 36.

tury French social reformers in France thought that it was the absence of *prévoyance* that allowed poverty and misery to flourish.[72] Teaching workers "scientific" means of self-management would serve the over-arching goal of defusing class tensions at the end of Europe's volatile nineteenth-century. To figures such as the Catholic reformer Frédéric LePlay (1806–1882), *prévoyance*, banking, and credit acted as social disciplines which allowed exceptional members of the working class to exercise their virtues and improve their living standards.[73] Having been formulated in an effort to reshape France's lower classes into productive laborers and rational economic actors, the ideas of LePlay, Laurent, and other social reformers emerged in the colonies to be reworked by administrators and subjects alike. When the metropolitan idea of *prévoyance* was adopted in colonial contexts, African subjects stood in for European workers, demonstrating how Europe's internal social struggles had been projected outwards into the empire.[74]

In the colonial context, French essayists, agronomists, and administrators believed that the consequences of *imprévoyance* were severe: the inability to plan ahead led to malnutrition, weaker laborers, inadequate military recruits, and could ultimately lead to "the sterilisation of [the African] race."[75] The *sociétés* would prevent these problems by inculcating *prévoyance* among Africans, fulfilling what Governor-General Carde regarded as the state's obligation, to "protect the native against his own nature" by "interven[ing] in Soudanese peasants' cotton production and marketing decision."[76] Through educating farmers in the uses of debt and loans and by encouraging them to adopt new technologies, the government sought to remold local farmers into profitable and productive subjects. In the 1950s, this project remained incomplete; an analyst wrote that in terms of credit and exploitation of African farmers, "nothing has changed since the 18th century ... the method is always the same ... the farmer remains *imprévoyant*."[77]

Behind this rhetoric lay a set of assumptions: that Africans lacked initiative, and that they lacked the foresight to lay aside enough seed and grain to

---

72 See, e. g., Emile Laurent, *Le pauperisme et les associations de prévoyance*, 2 vols. (Paris, 1865).

73 Frederick LePlay, *On Family, Work, and Social Change*, ed. and trans. Catherine Bodard Silver (Chicago, 1982); Paul Rabinow, *French Modern: Norms and Forms of the Social Environment* (Chicago, 1989), 86–91.

74 Frederick Cooper, *Decolonization and African Society: The Labor Question in French and British Africa* (Cambridge, 1996).

75 A. Calmette, "Au sujet de l'alimentation des indigènes," *Academie des Sciences Coloniales: Comptes Rendus des Séances* 1 (1923):113–4. Cf. Henri Labouret, *Paysans d'Afrique occidentale* (Paris, 1941), 152; Sorel, *L'alimentation des indigènes en AOF*,166–8; regarding military recruitment, see Echenberg, *Colonial Conscripts: The Tirailleurs Sénégalais in French West Africa, 1857–1960* (Portsmouth, New Hampshire, 1991).

76 Roberts, *Two Worlds of Cotton*, 163–4.

77 Fernand Wibaux, "L'organisation des coopératives en Afrique occidentale française," *Revue des Études Cooperatives* 25, no. 94 (1953):214.

endure a failed harvest. However, judging from present historical understandings of African production, it was probably not *prévoyance* itself that was deficient, but means of institutionalizing the particular temporalities and social relationships of the colonial cash economy, such as credit in anticipation of crop sales (rather than in response to crisis), credit on longer time-frames for larger amounts of money, the imposition of new qualifications and incentives for loans, and so on.

The original time-frame to which African "providence" was tied was the annual cycle of seasonal income in kind, with extension to managing inter-annual fluctuations in rainfall. It is a very complex question to address, how ill-equipped savannah Africa was to deal with these fluctuations by drawing on its own resources of knowledge and capital. The challenges were amplified by dry periods and droughts, such as the one experienced in the Sahel in 1913–1914. Of course, many societies were re-establishing peaceful production conditions in the wake of warfare, and many of the less obvious methods of inter-seasonal insurance had been disrupted by taxation and other colonial policies. With the *pax française* and the abolition of slavery, various groups began to diversify their productive strategies by adopting pastoralism or agriculture and by appropriating pasture-land for crops.[78] Wherever they changed their modes of production, people altered their economic time-frames to match.

Difficulties in adjusting to a new credit economy can only have been exacerbated by the suppression of a primary means of pre-colonial credit and patronage—the exchange of individuals and their labor through debt bondage, pawning, and slavery. Although slavery was legally abolished in 1905, in practice, all three institutions declined slowly.[79] Indeed, debt bondage and pawning underwent a revival in the 1930s in the Soudan.[80] In sum, the illegality of using human beings as assets in loans and debts would have made credit markets particularly unstable in the first decades of the century. In the context of such high instability, cautious investment of resources would have been only prudent. Perhaps characteristically, the colonial government observed a period of extreme flux yet identified it as stable, interpreting prudence as passivity. Administrators do not seem to have recognized that, to some degree and in some places, colonial government itself created the conditions it sought to ameliorate.

---

78 Mirjam de Bruijn and Han van Dijk, *Arid Ways: Cultural Understandings of Insecurity in Fulbe Society, Central Mali* (Amsterdam, 1995) 81–3. Cf. Richard L. Roberts, "The End of Slavery in the French Soudan, 1905–1914," in *The End of Slavery in Africa*, ed. Miers and Roberts, 282–307.

79 See Toyin Falola and Paul E. Lovejoy, eds., *Pawnship in Africa: Debt Bondage in Historical Perspective* (Boulder, Colorado, 1994).

80 Martin Klein and Richard L. Roberts, "The Resurgence of Pawning in French West Africa during the Depression of the 1930s," in *Pawnship in Africa*, ed. Falola and Lovejoy.

French development planners tended to regard Africans in one of two ways, argues Richard Roberts. They were either rational market producers or ill-disciplined farmers naive and timid in their reactions to market incentives.[81] The *sociétés* were clearly based on the belief that Africans needed some assistance with market behavior, and that they needed lessons in saving, borrowing, and lending. The *sociétés* were to be just such a lesson. They made an impression which contemporary development efforts might do well to address, since we may view them as one of the main tutorials of rural populations in dealing with formal financial institutions and the state.

Some of the critical aspects of that tutorial, and of the SIP system itself, remain unclear to us: the actual incidence of longer-term loans, the system of collateral or guarantee, the heritability of cash debts in case of the death of the debtor, and the sanctions against default.[82] Our impression is that these were very sketchily developed, and may well have depended ultimately on the sanction underlying all infractions under the *indigénat,* namely prison and forced labor, both of which were imposed at administrative discretion.

It is clear, however, that the SIPs directors occasionally behaved in a contradictory fashion. This inconsistent behavior is a commentary both on the flexibility of the institution and on the mixed messages the *sociétés* sent. In contrast to the rhetoric of *prévoyance,* the directors of the *société* may actually have encouraged a play-it-by-ear attitude among members of the *sociétés.* Although membership dues were said to be mandatory, *cercles* who paid no dues occasionally had their debts excused.[83] On other occasions, loans were forgiven rather than collected. For example, in Segu in 1934, 600 plows which had been lent to members two years earlier were simply given to them outright.[84] The sheer paucity of sources on repayment suggests that this was a less carefully monitored process than the payment of dues.[85]

Taken together, such situations—when loans became grants and debts became assets— surely encouraged farmers to extend rather than to re-pay their debts, if at all possible. Insofar as repayment was variably enforced, the *sociétés* violated a fundamental principle of liberal banking, namely, the idea that repayment is obligatory. Foresight in dealing with cash is quite different from and far more complex than dealing with intra- and inter-annual management of grain stores, and here one suspects that the SIPs themselves acted in variable ways.

African farmers could not readily evade the financial impositions of the *sociétés,* but they could evade, oppose, or interfere with the mandated struc-

---

81 Roberts, *Two Worlds of Cotton,* 287–8.

82 Some of these functions were assumed by other equally obscure credit institutions, such as the *Caisse de Crédit Agricole.*

83 *Journal Officiel du Soudan Français* (1934):80.

84 Ibid.

85 See Boyer, *Les sociétés de prévoyance,* 71.

tures in other ways that served their own view of insurance. As the *sociétés* became increasingly involved in farmers' lives, more and more acts of initiative became acts of resistance. For instance, Senegalese farmers who exercised *prévoyance* and established their own individual granaries were considered threatening to the *sociétés'* existence. Rather than paying back seed loans, these farmers used them to create their own reserves. In response to this usurpation of the *sociétés* primary task, the government ordered communal granaries to increase their efforts to recover what they had loaned, discouraging further independent initiatives.[86] Furthermore, many of the limitations on production which colonial authors recognized can be seen as acts of opposition to the invasive nature of the *sociétés*. For instance, Henri Labouret pointed out the general insecurity of African production and "administrative errors"—such as requisitions and forced production of industrial crops—that had made the situation even worse, to the point of famine.[87] Both of these examples suggest that the farmers so often characterized as *"imprévoyant"* were making independent decisions affecting their livelihoods regardless of the government's interference, and that it was not "foresight" *per se* that the *sociétés* were cultivating, but incorporation into the predictable routines of the state, and thereby, dependence.[88]

When security of livelihood was envisaged in ways other than their own, the SIPs showed how deeply indebted they were to a management mission. Rather than being hidden or denied, this mission was proclaimed with increasing enthusiasm. In fact, one might see a developing confidence and breadth of ambition for the *sociétés*, well beyond the specifically *prévoyant* vision on which they were founded. By the 1950s, only a few years before their abolition, the colonial government of Cameroon reported, "The Provident Society is truly a training ground for citizenship,"[89] and an analyst wrote, "This institution can be considered as a masterpiece of paternalist administration."[90]

The Decline of the SIP/SAP Structure

The enthusiasm expressed for SAPs in 1956 preceded by only a few years their total collapse, after decades of flexible adjustment. Originating at all levels of the system, several conditions contributed to their demise.

---

[86] Suret-Canale, *Afrique Noire*, 304–5.

[87] Labouret, *Paysans d'Afrique occidentale*, 200. Labouret wrote several policy-oriented books on West African farmers. (See Roberts, *Two Worlds of Cotton*, 17)

[88] For an analysis of small-scale producers' struggles against industrial dependence, see Tessie Liu, *The Weaver's Knot: The Contradictions of Class Struggle and Family Solidarity in Western France, 1750–1914* (Ithaca, New York, 1994). Unlike West African producers, Liu's weavers lost control over their raw materials and the finished product and "adopt(ed) self-exploitation as a strategy." (10, 94).

[89] "Report of the French Government to the UN," 1954:84.

[90] David, *La coopération*, 5.

First, after 1946, the colonies experienced an influx of public capital from the metropole. Most of these funds were directed through FIDES, essentially an account managed by another newly created institution, the *Caisse Centrale de la France d'Outre-Mer*. Through FIDES, millions of francs were pumped into development and infrastructure projects in the French African colonies. The money came both from metropolitan contributions and from increased taxes for African subjects. Thus FIDES undercut one of the *sociétés'* raisons d'être: the doctrine that the colonies would finance their own development. Furthermore, FIDES generally paid for large-scale projects carried out by French firms. Legally, the *sociétés'* Common Fund could not directly finance French enterprise, even if it had had the capital to do so. With hindsight, it is clear that "the money arrived fifty years too late," [91] but once the metropolitan government began to invest heavily in the colonies and their infrastructure, the need for local, self-financed development declined. Although the organizational capacities and the funds of the *sociétés* facilitated some of the smaller scale projects, such as the building of a reservoir in Sangha, Soudan,[92] the era of the *sociétés* seemed to be over. Despite the institution's flexibility at the local level, the structure of the *sociétés* responded to the post-war financing of large-scale investment only by distorting its original mandate and including large numbers of non-*indigènes* in its enterprises.

Second, new sources of funds called for new accounting. When the capital for the *sociétés* had been generated locally, governors were generally content to allow funds to be managed locally. Once larger sums were at stake, contributed by the metropolitan government, the upper levels of bureaucracy had a greater interest in observing and manipulating that money. Although many *commandants* had used the *sociétés* as their private monetary reserves, the colonies' governments began to intervene more directly in the management of local affairs when the sums became so much larger.

The *sociétés* were vestiges of a pre-war bureaucratic culture which condoned local pockets of power; a new generation of colonial administrators sought to reform that culture. In the late 1940s, the governor-general of the French West Africa federation and the governor of the French Soudan decided to regulate the functions of the *sociétés* more closely. They explicitly targeted operations outside the direct purview of the institution, which they argued should be limited to "those touching on the economic and commercial protection of the members, and should even be suspended where these activities became too limited."[93]

However, they met with opposition from local administrators who fought the devolution of their authority and from notables seeking to hold on to local

---

[91] Colombani, *Mémoires coloniales*, 19.

[92] "Le Génie Rural en AOF", *Bulletin d'Information de l'AOF (Service de l'Information)*, no. 106 (1951).

[93] Document dated 5 May 1949, Archives du Mali (Koutiala).

autonomy. For example, in 1949 in Koutiala, Soudan, the *commandant* called a meeting to address new initiatives from above. He wished to be proactive by redefining the institution and its functions locally. Backed by the local *notables,* he clearly intended to keep the funds for the *société* within the *cercle,* rather than to allow them to be taken over by the higher administration. For their part, the African council member—notables, *chefs de canton,* and a representative of the local veterans—wanted to maintain some voice in local development and in the disposition of the funds. Before agreeing with the *commandant,* however, the African members of the council emphasized the benefits the community had found in the *société* and enumerated the useful projects it had financed among them. In the end, they shuffled the sums by changing the name under which they were collected: *cotisations* became *centimes additionels.* At the same time, they more than doubled the amount due, from twenty-five to fifty-five francs, by mandating an "exceptional contribution."[94] Both the funds of the *société* and the additional tax would go towards building and repairing roads; this was the kind of project the administration would undertake on a larger scale with FIDES. Thus in one maneuver, a local administrator and African leaders attempted to dodge reform from above and preempted the development schemes and rhetoric of a new era. The *roi de la brousse* or the "decentralized despot" may have been a relic of an earlier period, but certainly in this colonial fiefdom, the commandant, local chiefs, and notables felt powerful enough to attempt to create their own substantial budget, protected from the central administration.[95]

Third, a new approach to development arose which relied more on agricultural science and technical interventions than had past approaches. Although the development programs of the interwar period had been based partly on the advice of agronomists and engineers, capital had been scarce and large-scale projects were few.[96] As public replaced private capital after 1945, the nature and scale of development efforts changed. A new staff accompanied the new attitude. These were the "technocrats," whose visions of government and development clashed with those of administrators from an earlier era. Their approaches to agricultural development led to friction with local administrators of the old school.

Such tensions begin to appear in a series of messages written in 1940 between the governor of French Soudan and the local *commandant* and head of the *société* in Gao, Lt.-Col. DuBoin. After the enthusiastic director of the Soudan's zootechnical service had passed through the *cercle,* he urged the

---

94 A note of comparison: the *cercle* tax was 200 francs per year.

95 See Mahmood Mamdani, *Citizen and Subject: Contemporary Africa and the Legacy of Late Colonialism,* (Princeton, New Jersey, 1996).

96 See Monica Maria Van Bueskom, *Colonial Rural Development;* Roberts, *Two Worlds of Cotton.*

governor to mandate a creamery and a vaccination program for the *cercle*. For this program, the director asked for 50,000 francs. Furthermore, he requested that the government forgive loans of 7,200 francs to the *société* for building the creamery, and he cited examples of similar programs in other *cercles* where *sociétés* cooperated to fund epizootic programs. He argued that in Gao, the *société* spent very little on programs for livestock, in spite of the importance of herding for the local economy. For that reason, the director suggested it should fund this project.[97]

When the governor agreed to the plan, he seemed to catch DuBoin off-guard. He ordered the *commandant* to draw up a budget for the *société* that included the project; DuBoin reluctantly gave in to the governor's wishes.[98] Informing DuBoin that the zootechnical director would be passing through his *cercle* within a month, the governor ordered him to train people to vaccinate cattle, to buy serum-producing steer, and to organize a center for "sero-therapy."[99] Thus the entire project was thrown into the *commandant*'s lap, in stark contrast to the years when the *société* and its funds were the *caisses noires* of local administrators. Administration and development from above became an increasingly common phenomenon, in spite of the fact that it was resisted by some.

Finally, African farmers increasingly opposed forced participation in an association which they could not control and which did not always meet their needs. The political climate had changed: a new French constitution made room for nominally greater African participation in government; and forced labor had been abolished in 1946.[100] Forced participation in credit organizations no longer fit the political tenor of the times. In Cameroon, however, as armed resistance to the state waxed and waned, the government regarded the *sociétés* as necessary competition for other associations and independent cooperatives; the latter flourished in the 1940s and 1950s as Cameroonians sought some of the advantages the *colons* had from their *syndicats* but which the *sociétés* did not offer.[101]

African participants had long referred to the *société* as a "little tax," a *petit impôt*. For many years, the administration collected the dues at the same time as the annual taxes. In the 1910s, the same type of administrative ticket or chit

---

97 'Observations du Chef du Service Zootechnique', 11 January 1940. Archives Nationales du Mali (Kuluba), 3N18(FR).

98 DuBoin to Governor of Soudan français, ibid., 5 April 1940 . Perhaps DuBoin was left out of the loop because, like most *cercle* administrators, he was stationed there only temporarily. Colombani, *Mémoires coloniales,* 13.

99 Governor to DuBoin, 23 February 1940. Archives Nationales du Mali (Kuluba), 3N18(FR).

100 See Sow, *Les sociétes de prévoyance du Senegal*, 4.

101 Richard A. Joseph, *Radical Nationalism in Cameroun: Social Origins of the UPC Rebellion* (Oxford, 1977), 53; see David, *La coopération.*

was issued when dues and taxes were paid.[102] The similar practices of collecting taxes and membership dues only underscored the fact that both were government impositions and can only have increased the resentment of members. Administrators had long been aware of this problem. However, most considered it a minor issue when key legislation was drafted in 1915.[103] In the 1940s, the problem merited only a footnote from Delavignette, who wrote that "Africans call this (*société*) subscription 'the little tax,' and there may be a danger here."[104] In the dramatically different political climate of the 1950s, the fact that *société* dues were considered taxes handicapped the institutions' utility and limited its flexibility. As semi-administrative structures based on mandatory participation, they were out of sync with the political orientation of the 1950s colonial world. The lack of local enthusiasm for the *sociétés'* fundraising technique led one administrator to write that the institutions had become outdated and needed to be replaced by cooperatives if the administration were to develop (and in Cameroon, control) "spontaneous" participation in the cooperative movement.[105]

Although the situation was extremely delicate in Cameroon, administrators in other French African territories continued to wield their power through the *sociétés* with a heavy hand. The increasingly explicit links between credit and coercion did not overly trouble an administrator in the French Soudan. At Koutiala in 1956, the *commandant* used the *société's* warehouse as a holding cell for three tons of millet he had confiscated from an African trader intending to transport and sell it illegally in Bobo-Dioulasso.[106] Although the *commandant* wrote to the governor asking for approval for this impoundment, it appears to have been a *fait accompli*. A hearing on the matter had already been held in local court, most likely with the same administrator presiding. Because the *commandant* feared a shortage of millet in his *cercle*, he sought to fine the trader 3,000 francs, or one-tenth the value of the grain. Showing restraint from above, the governor reduced the amount to 2,000 francs.

This case reveals a great deal about the evolution of the *société* as an institution. It was being used in its original capacity, to store grain in case of shortage, and also to control its marketing. One of the goals of the institution had been to persuade producers to participate in the market, but the administrator had a particular market in mind—the local one. Transporting grain to another colony might cause shortages locally, and it also frustrated administrative attempts to reshape regional economies. Thus the local administrator used the *société* as an instrument of control. In this case it served to hinder rather than

---

102 Boyer, *Les sociétes de prévoyance*, 55.
103 Ibid., 56.
104 1950: 126, n. 3.
105 David, *La coopération*, 5, 7, 9; cf. Joseph, *A Radical Nationalism in Cameroun*, 53, 143–4.
106 Document dated 15 December 1956, Archives du Mali (Koutiala).

to promote trade.[107] The *commandant* even suggested to the governor that trade between *cercles* be forbidden altogether, or at least strictly controlled, in order to avoid shortages in his *cercle*. This case underscores the adaptability of the institution, and its use in the struggle for power between varying levels of the administration. In these struggles, local people, low-level administrators, and colonial governors were allied on some occasions and opposed on others.

Continuity and Change: An Assessment

A final assessment of the effectiveness of the *sociétés* cannot safely be made without many local studies, because the policies were so varied, by definition for an institution as decentralized as the SIPs. However, one can infer that by "loaning investment capital in rural areas, [they achieved] some major innovations, albeit largely through the actions of the French administration," and at the cost of hindering development of alternate structures.[108] In addition, the "very success" of the *sociétés* may have been a constraint on the development of indigenous credit institutions, as Gareth Austin has suggested regarding West African credit structures in general. During the *sociétés* tenure, the media through which credit flowed changed greatly, as transactions in human labor and in kind gave way to those in cash. Nevertheless, the "pooling of liquidity" in governmental credit associations could have parched other pools of credit, especially in areas of generally low formal economic activity.[109]

The gradual demise of the SIP/SAP structure left a gap in local economies which new cooperatives could not always fill. This was particularly true in Cameroun where, as we noted above, the state had kept independent cooperatives on a rather short leash. For instance, in the early 1960s when the SAP of Nanga Eboko ceased facilitating the harvesting and marketing of rice, production plummeted. Due to the poor financial situation of the local SAP, it could not purchase the rice crop of 1963 until six months after the harvest, by which time much of the poorly stored rice had been lost. Having learnt not to rely on the SAP to buy their crops, the vast majority of farmers planted no rice at all the following year .[110] Ten years earlier, rice production had been a booming

[107] This had long been a complaint of French *commerçants*. Also, the transportation of grain across *cercle* boundaries was not infrequently forbidden, although the periods of restraint were usually short.

[108] Jane I. Guyer, "Introduction: The Currency Interface and Its Dynamics," in *Money Matters: Instability, Values, and Social Payments in the Modern History of West African Communities*, ed. Jane I. Guyer (Portsmouth, New Hampshire, 1995), 13; Guyer, *The Provident Societies*, 16.

[109] Gareth Austin, "Indigenous Credit Institutions in West Africa, c. 1750–c. 1960," in *Local Suppliers of Credit in the Third World, 1750–1960*, ed. Gareth Austin and Kaoru Sugihara (New York, 1993), 139.

[110] Jean Tissandier, *Zengoaga: étude d'un village camerounais et de son terroir au contact forêt-savane* (Mouton, 1969), 35–6.

regional enterprise, but it was a highly subsidized affair, relying on the *société's* operation of a rice mill run by metropolitan technicians.[111] It is unlikely that a newly created co-operative could have had the capital, the facilities, or the organizational capabilities to step into such a situation and fill the void left by the declining SAP. Whatever their drawbacks, the SAPs were a hard act to follow.

In the years immediately before Independence (ca. 1960), few alternative structures appeared ready to inherit the functions of the *sociétés*. The official structure of the *fonds commun des sociétés* was transformed into a *Fonds de Génié Rural,* which would make capital available to local cooperatives, villages and other *collectivités* which qualified.[112] The SIP/SAP as an institution itself gradually gave way to two new structures with their own acronyms. In an effort to allow more popular participation in the *sociétés,* the administration created the *Sociétés Mutuelles de Production Rurale* (SMPR) in 1953. Very few were actually organized on the ground, however.[113] The SMPR proved to be no more than a stop-gap measure and they were soon outdated as the move towards Independence accelerated. The advent of the *Loi Cadre* (1956), allowing greater administrative autonomy to the colonies, signaled their demise.[114] The institution which replaced them was designed to address the weaknesses of the original SIP structure more fully. The *Sociétés Mutuelles de Développement Rural* (SMDR) were intended to foster local cooperatives, to break the monopoly on co-operative production which the SIPs were thought to have attained, and eventually to become a kind of "union of cooperatives."[115]

Independently, African *mutuelles,* or cooperatives, began to appear in the AOF once metropolitan legislation governing the cooperative movement was extended to the colonies in 1947. The presence of these parallel agricultural cooperatives testifies to the adaptability of farmers to constraints on access to resources. Unable to work through colonial structures, they worked around them, while still maintaining some access to credit from lending institutions.[116] Coupled with evidence from the 1930s, the growth of these cooperatives suggests that African producers were not refusing French technologies

---

111 Guyer, *The Provident Societies,* 11–2.

112 (Lord) Halley, *An African Survey, Revised 1956: A Study of Problems Arising in Africa South of the Sahara* (Oxford, 1957), 1478–9.

113 Joseph Roger de Benoist, *l'Afrique occidentale française de 1944 à 1960* (Dakar, 1982), 246.

114 Abdoulaye Sall, *L'organisation du monde rural au Mali, 1910–1986* (Bamako, 1986), 16–8.

115 A. Hirschfeld, "L'état et la coopération agricole dans les pays francophones d'Afrique noire," *Revue des études coopératives,* no. 177, 33; cf. Sall, *L'organisation du monde rural.*

116 Wibaux, "L'organisation des coopératives."

and financial tactics altogether, but that they were exploiting them in keeping with their own economic strategies.[117]

Perhaps this is why, despite complaints about their shortcomings, the *sociétés* and their institutional heirs continued to operate well into the post-colonial era. Cooperatives based on them became a key element of the economic plans of some of the Independent governments, including that of Algeria, where the *sociétés* had originated.[118] In Mali (the former Soudan), co-operatives began to flourish at the village level. Like the *sociétés*, they sought to help peasants obtain equipment and loans from credit institutions. However, they differed from the *sociétés* in two crucial respects. First, these cooperatives were purchasing as well as marketing groups, and they bought household items like sugar and salt in bulk. Second, they had far fewer members, and the villagers themselves directed their affairs. The post-independence institution most comparable to the *société* was its administrative descendant from the late 1950s, the supervisory SMDR, which "managed primary funds which had to be set up in each administrative area for agricultural credit." Also like the *société*, the SMDR and other state-run co-operatives were resented by farmers who felt they had little say in how "their" organization was run.[119] In each incarnation of these institutions, the lack of local participation was a recurring complaint.

Conclusion

This paper has regarded the *sociétés* in two ways. First, as an institution whose history might deeply affect how people interact with contemporary development and micro-credit projects. We have focused on the *sociétés'* structural flexibility, arguing that this characteristic enabled them to adapt to local needs (whether or not they always did so is a separate issue). This adaptability was the key to their successes, both from administrative and local perspectives. However, such flexibility had a downside, in that the inconsistent policies and behavior of the institution cost it the rigidity and formality credit institutions require in order to maintain trust and effectiveness. Standing always in the shadow of the state, the *sociétés* never won trust. Although they could and sometimes did act effectively, their seemingly arbitrary behavior severely curtailed their ability to achieve much beyond their most basic goals. In the end, the *sociétés de prévoyance* demonstrated their "elastic limit": having flexed too often, they lost their ability to snap back to some kind of standard, in which, at a bare minimum, debts were serviced and dues were paid.

---

117 See Roberts, *Two Worlds of Cotton.*

118 Rachid Tlemcani, *State and Revolution in Algeria* (Boulder, Colorado, 1986), 101.

119 Kary Dembele, "State Policies on Agriculture and Food Production in Mali," in *The State and Agriculture in Africa*, ed. Naceur Bourenane and Thandika Mkandawire (London, 1987), 225–7.

Secondly, we analyzed the *sociétés* as the enunciation of a particular vision of social reform which laid the blame for poverty at the feet of the poor, insisting that it was they who were in need of reform, rather than the system of inequality of which they were a part. Nineteenth-century social reformers and twentieth-century administrators regarded credit, banking, and co-operation as forms of social discipline, as different means of molding improvident subjects into orderly producers and consumers.

From above, the *sociétés de prévoyance* were rational structures operating in a regularized fashion to bring the vision of *prévoyance* and its accompanying social disciplines to the colonies. On the ground, however, their administrators' actions were arbitrary and their message was confused. Other than the use of coercion, which became politically unacceptable, the only way the *sociétés'* administrators could cultivate the discipline they desired was by practicing what they preached. This they did not do. Ultimately, for African participants in the *sociétés*, "foresight" meant holding on to the ability to improvise.

Bibliography

Agronomie Coloniale 20, nos. 157, 159 (1931).

Agronomie Coloniale 21, no. 172 (1932).

Antoine, Philippe. "Les Sociétés africaines de prévoyance au Cameroun." Thèse pour le doctorat, Université de Paris, 1954.

Austin, Gareth. "Indigenous Credit Institutions in West Africa, c.1750–c.1960," in *Local Suppliers of Credit in the Third World, 1750–1960,* ed. Gareth Austin and Kaoru Sugihara, 93–159. New York, 1993.

Boyer, Marcel. *Les sociétés de prévoyance, de secours, et de prêts mutuels agricoles en Afrique occidentale française.* Thèse pour le doctorat, Université de Paris, Faculté de Droit, 1935.

Buell, Raymond Leslie. *The Native Problem in Africa.* Vol. 2. New York, 1928.

Calmette, A. "Au sujet de l'alimentation des indigènes", *Academie des Sciences Coloniales, Comptes Rendus des Séances, Communications* 1 (1923):113–4.

Clauzel, Jean. *Administrateur de la France d'outre-mer*. Avignon, 1989.

Coetz-Girey, Robert. "Le Crédit," in *Éléments d'économie coloniale,* ed. René Maunier, 353–383. Paris, 1943.

Colombani, Olivier. *Mémoires coloniales: la fin de l'empire français d'Afrique vue par les administrateurs coloniaux.* Paris, 1991.

Cooper, Frederick. *Decolonization and African Society: The Labor Question in French and British Africa.* Cambridge, 1996.

David, M. *La coopération, la mutualité et le crédit agricoles en AOF: La modernisation du paysannât au Cameroun et en AEF.* Paris.1956.

de Benoist, Joseph Roger. *L'Afrique occidentale française de 1944 à 1960*. Dakar, 1982.

de Bruijn, Mirjam and Han van Dijk. *Arid Ways: Cultural Understandings of Insecurity in Fulbe Society, Central Mali.* Amsterdam, 1995.

Delavignette, Robert. *L'Afrique noire française et son destin.* Paris, 1962.

—. *Freedom and Authority in French West Africa.* Oxford, 1950.

—. *Robert Delavignette on the French Empire: Selected Writings,* ed. William B. Cohen (with the assistance of Adelle Rosenzweig), trans. Camille Garnier. Chicago, 1977.

Dembele, Kary. "State Policies on Agriculture and Food Production in Mali", in *The State and Agriculture in Africa,* ed. Naceur Bourenane and Thandika Mkandawire, 222–42. London, 1987.

Domergue-Cloarec, Danielle. *Politique coloniale française et réalitiés coloniales: La santé en Côte d'Ivoire, 1905–1958*. Toulouse, 1986.

Echenberg, Myron. *Colonial Conscripts: The Tirailleurs Sénégalais in French West Africa, 1857–1960.* Portsmouth, New Hampshire, 1991.

Escobar, Arturo. *Encountering Development: The Making and Unmaking of the Third World.* Princeton, 1995.

Falola, Toyin and Paul E. Lovejoy, eds. *Pawnship in Africa: Debt Bondage in Historical Perspective.* Boulder, 1994.

Frot M. "Les sociétés de prévoyance au Soudan français", in *Premier congrès soudanais de technique et colonisation agricole.* Vol. II, 133–7. Bamako, 1936.

"Le génie rural en AOF", *Bulletin d'Information de l'AOF (Service de l'Information),* no. 106 (1951).

Gillin, P. "Pourquoi les silos coopératifs sont-ils nécessaires dans les colonies et pays de protectorat nord-Africains?" *L'agriculture pratique des pays chauds.* No. 16 (1931): 775–7.

Guyer, Jane I. "The Provident Societies in the Rural Economy of Yaoundé, 1945–1960." Boston University African Studies Center, Working Papers Series, no. 37. Boston, 1980.

—. "The Depression and the Administration in South-Central Cameroun", *African Economic History* 10 (1981):67–79.

—. "Introduction: The Currency Interface and Its Dynamics," in *Money Matters: Instability, Values, and Social Payments in the Modern History of West African Communities,* ed. Jane I. Guyer, 1–33. Portsmouth, New Hampshire, 1995.

Hailey, Willliam (Baron). *An African Survey: A Study of Problems Arising in Africa South of the Sahara.* Rev. ed. Oxford, 1957.

Hardy, Georges and Charles Richet, eds., *L'alimentation indigène dans les colonies françaises.* Paris, 1933.

Hirschfeld, A. "L'état et la coopération agricole dans les pays francophones d'Afrique noire." *Revue des Études Coopératives,* no.177 (1974):25–46.

Hubert, Lucien. "L'ascension de l'Afrique occidentale française." *Académie des Sciences Coloniales, Comptes Rendus des Séances, Communications* 9 (1927):43–7.

Joseph, Richard A. *Radical Nationalism in Cameroun: Social Origins of the UPC Rebellion.* Oxford, 1977.

Klein, Martin and Richard L. Roberts. "The Resurgence of Pawning in French West Africa during the Depression of the 1930s," in *Pawnship in Africa: Debt Bondage in Historical Perspective,* ed. Toyin Falola and Paul E. Lovejoy, 303–320. Boulder, Colorado, 1994.

Kom, David. *Le Cameroun: Essai d'analyse économique et politique*. Paris, 1971.

Labouret, Henri. *Paysans d'Afrique occidentale*. Paris, 1941.

Lallour, Michel. *"L'elevage du mouton au Soudan"*, in *Premier congrès soudanais de technique et colonisation agricole.* Vol. II, 127–133. Bamako, 1936.

Laurent, Emile. *Le pauperism et les associations de prévoyance.* 2 vols. Paris, 1865.

LePlay, Frédéric. *On Family, Work, and Social Change*, ed. and trans. Catherine Bodard Silver. Chicago, 1982.

Mamdani, Mahmood. *Citizen and Subject: Contemporary Africa and the Legacy of Late Colonialism*. Princeton, 1996.

Marchal, J. Y. *Chroniques d'un cercle de l'AOF*. Paris, 1980

Marseille, Jacques. *Empire colonial et capitalisme français: Histoire d'un divorce*. Paris, 1984

Méker, Maurice. *Le temps colonial: Itinéraire africain d'un naïf du colonialisme à la coopération, 1931–1960*. Dakar, 1980.

Rabinow, Paul. *French Modern: Norms and Forms of the Social Environment*, Chicago, 1989.

Roberts, Richard L. *Two Worlds of Cotton: Colonialism and the Regional Economy in the French Soudan, 1800–1946.* Stanford, 1996.

—. "The Coercion of Free Markets: Cotton, Peasants, and the Colonial State in the French Soudan, 1924–1932," in *Cotton, Colonialism, and Social History in Sub-Saharan Africa*, ed. Richard L. Roberts and Allen Isaacman, 221–43. Portsmouth, New Hampshire, 1995.

—. "The End of Slavery in the French Soudan, 1905–1914," in *The End of Slavery in Africa*, ed. Suzanne Miers and Richard Roberts, 282–307. Madison, 1988.

Robinson, Kenneth. "The *Sociétés de Prévoyance* in French West Africa," *Journal of African Administration* 4, no. 2 (1950):29–34.

Sall, Abdoulaye. *L'organisation du monde rural au Mali, 1910–1986*. Bamako, 1986.

Sorel, François. "L'alimentation des indigènes en AOF," in *L'alimentation indigène dans les colonies françaises*, ed. Georges Hardy and Charles Richet *fils*, 155–76. Paris, 1933.

Sow, Abdoul. *Les sociétés de prévoyance du Senegal des origines à 1947*. Thèse pour le doctorat de troisième cycle. Faculté des Lettres et Sciences Humaines. Université de Dakar, 1984.

Stoler, Ann Laura and Fredrick Cooper. "Between Metropole and Colony: Rethinking a Research Agenda," in *Tensions of Empire: Colonial Cultures in a Bourgeois World*, ed. Frederick Cooper and Anne Stoler, 1–56. Berkeley, 1997.

Suret-Canale, Jean. *Afrique noire occidentale et centrale: L'ère coloniale, 1900–1945*. Paris, 1964.

Tissandier, Jean. *Zengoaga: Étude d'un village camerounais et de son terroir au contact forêt-savane*. Mouton, 1969.

Tlemcani, Rachid. *State and Revolution in Algeria*. Boulder, Colorado, 1986.

Van Bueskom, Monica Maria. "Colonial Rural Development: French policy and African response at the Office du Niger, Soudan Français (Mali), 1920–1960." Ph.D. diss., Johns Hopkins University, Baltimore, 1990.

Vuillet M. "Persévérer," *Académie des Sciènces Coloniales: Annales* 2 (1925):13–66.

Wibaux, Fernand. "L'organisation des coopératives en Afrique occidentale française," *Revue des Études Coopératives* 25, no. 94 (1953):209–26.

Kòse-é-mánì: Idealism and Contradiction in the Yorùbá View of Money

Akanmu G. Adebayo

The literature on the development of African financial systems is growing. In the context of triumphant capitalism in the West and much of Asia, and the economic collapse of several African countries, economic historians are paying more attention to issues of monetization, capitalization, credit, and finance. The coexistence, interaction, and transformation of informal and formal (or traditional and modern) financial institutions are being carefully analyzed. Fiscal management, as Jane I. Guyer has shown, is of paramount importance in the transformation of African economies.[1] Development obviously calls for the refashioning of African financial systems, and the first step in this process is to gain an understanding of them in all their complexity.

This paper focuses on the Yorùbá view of money, and proceeds from the premise that to understand a phenomenon, it is essential to grasp the *idea* on which it is based. An idea takes specific form as an invention, an institutional development, or simply as an historical event. That form is then reshaped as it is affected by subsequent developments. In the case of the Yorùbá, the monetization of theYorùbá economy in pre-colonial times expressed the development of the Yorùbá *idea* of money. As monetization spread, new ideas evolved which in turn influenced the further development of financial institutions. These evolving institutions transformed the idea once again, and so on ad infinitum. Therefore, it should be recognized from the outset that the Yorùbá view of money is dynamic.

The Yorùbá see money in many different ways. According to Toyin Falola, money is perceived as *ẹ̀mí* (spirit) *òsùpá* (moon), *àlejò* (visitor/stranger), or *àjẹ́* (witch).[2] Karin Barber also argues that money in Yorùbá culture is a vehicle for individual self-realization. "It is the medium in which human potential becomes fulfilled," she explains.[3] I suggest in this essay that nothing sums up

---

[1] Jane I. Guyer, ed., *Money Matters: Instability, Values and Social Payments in the Modern History of West African Communities* (Portsmouth, New Hampshire, 1995), 24–6; see also Jane I. Guyer, "Wealth in People, Wealth in Things—Introduction," *Journal of African History*, 36 (1995), 83–90.

[2] Toyin Falola, "Money and Informal Credit Institutions in Colonial Western Nigeria," in Guyer, *Money Matters*, 163.

[3] Karin Barber, "Money, Self-Realization, and the Person in Yorùbá Texts," in Guyer, *Money Matters*, 207.

the Yorùbá view of money better than *kòse-é-mánì*, the idea that money is the Indispensable One.

My exploration of this view has three main parts. The first discusses the advent of money in Yorùbá economy and society. The second explores the Yorùbá *ideal* of money. The third examines the numerous ways in which the Yorùbá contradict this ideal. The conclusion offers an explanation for the contradiction.

I. From Cowries to Coins and Notes: The Currency Revolution in Yorùbáland

Scholars have extensively studied the pre-colonial currencies of Africa.[4] The discussion here is offered as a summary of the relevant literature, and relies heavily on my earlier writings on the advent of money among the Yorùbá.[5] Unlike many West African peoples, the Yorùbá did not use metallic currencies such as gold and silver coins before colonial rule.[6] The main trade currency was cowrie shells, *Cypraea moneta*, imported from the Indian Ocean. The available evidence indicates that cowries came via two major routes: a northern route connectingYorùbáland with the caravan trade, and a southern route by way of the Atlantic coast. It is not clear by which of these routes cowries first came to Yorùbá country. The Portuguese were said to have found cowries in extensive use in Benin at the beginning of the sixteenth century.[7] Given the

---

[4] See Marion Johnson, "The Cowry Currencies of West Africa—I," *Journal of African History* 11, no.1 (1970): 17–49; "The Cowry Currencies of West Africa—II," *Journal of African History* 11, no.3 (1970): 331–53; Marion Johnson, "The Nineteenth-Century Gold 'Mithqal' in West and North Africa," *Journal of African History* 9, no.4 (1968): 547–69; Jan Hogendorn and Marion Johnson, *The Shell Money of the Slave Trade* (Cambridge, 1986). See also Jan Hogendorn, "Slaves as a Medium of Exchange in the Sokoto Caliphat" in this volume; Paul Lovejoy, "Interregional Monetary Flows in the Precolonial Trade of Nigeria," *Journal of African History* 15, no. 4 (1974): 563–85; J. H. Latham, "Currency, Credit and Capitalism on the Cross River in the Pre-colonial Era," *Journal of African History* 12, no.4 (1971): 599–605; A.G. Hopkins, "The Currency Revolution in South-West Nigeria in the Late Nineteenth Century," *Journal of the Historical Society of Nigeria* 3, no.3 (1966): 471–83; M. Hiskett, "Materials Relating to the Cowry Currency of the Western Sudan," *Bulletin of the School of Oriental and African Studies* 29, no. 1 (1966): 122–42, and vol. 30, no. 3 (1967): 340–66; G.I. Jones, "Native and Trade Currencies in Southern Nigeria During the Nineteenth Century," *Africa* 28, no. 1 (1958), 43–54; Stephen Baier, *An Economic History of Central Niger* (London, 1980) 25–35, 105–115; Eugenia W. Herbert, "Aspects of the Use of Copper in Pre-Colonial West Africa," *Journal of African History* 14 (1973): 179–94.

[5] A.G. Adebayo, "Money, Credit, and Banking in Precolonial Africa: The Yoruba Experience," *Anthropos* 89 (1994): 379–400.

[6] In the case of southwestern Nigeria, colonial rule came early with the conquest of Lagos in 1851, and British coins were in use along the coastal cities particularly by the returnees, traders and missionaries. Despite this, coins were not in wide circulation. In the hinterland, according to Johnson, they were "regarded more or less as a curiosity."

[7] Johnson, "Cowry Currencies I," 18.

close historical, political, and commercial relations between Benin on the one hand, and Ile-Ife and other parts of eastern Yorùbáland on the other, the diffusion of cowries from Benin to Yorùbáland can reasonably be assumed. This suggestion is further supported by the similarity in the cowrie numismatics of the Edo and Yorùbá.[8] According to S.A. Akintoye:

> The earliest contacts between Ekiti, Ijesa and Akoko with Benin were commercial. It is generally believed that these earliest contacts dated to the fifteenth century. Benin traders brought corals, European cloth, cowry shells and European iron implements and, at a later date, guns and gunpowder, and took away home-spun cloth and camwood as well as beads and potash ... Akure was the *entrepot* of this trade and a considerable number of Edo people soon settled permanently at Akure.[9]

The above clearly indicates that certain eastern routes were as important to the spread of cowries to Yorùbáland as the southern route through Ijebu country. On the other hand, cowries were known to have been imported into the Western Sudan centuries before the Portuguese set out on their voyages and before Europeans traders began importing cowries along the Atlantic coast of West Africa. They were known to be the currency in the Niger Bend countries, having come there through the trans-Saharan caravan trade of which the Oyo Empire was a southern terminus. Thus, a northern route for the diffusion of cowries into Yorùbáland is also suggested. Earlier efforts to date the origin of cowrie shells as a currency among the Yorùbá have led to the claim that they were probably introduced sometime during and no later than the fifteenth century.[10] The fact that Yorùbáland combined the practices of stringing cowries—as was done in the Bights of Benin and Biafra—and of counting them individually (more prevalent in the Western Sudan) shows that monetary policies as well as cowrie sources were diverse.

The participation of Yorùbá traders in the Atlantic trade probably reduced the volume of cowrie importation by way of the northern (i. e., trans-Saharan) route from the seventeenth century onwards. It has been demonstrated that the slave trade increased the extent of cowrie importation into West Africa. It has also been shown that several Yorùbá states, including Ijebu, Egba, Egbado, and Old Oyo, took part in the slave trade (although the degree to which the political economy depended on this trade is still debated[11]). Commercial relations between the Ijebu and the Portuguese were established as soon as the

[8] Idem, 41; also Claudia Zaslavsky, "The Yoruba Number System," in *Blacks in Science: Ancient and Mo dern*, ed. Ivan Van Sertima (New Brunswick, 1983), 125–6.

[9] S.A. Akintoye, *Revolution and Power Politics in Yorubaland, 1840–1893* (London, 1971), 25–6.

[10] E. Adeniyi Oroge, "Iwofa: An Historical Survey of the Yoruba Institution of Indenture," *African Economic History* 14 (1985):75.

[11] Robin Law, *The Oyo Empire, c. 1600–1836: A West African Imperialism in the Era of the Atlantic Slave Trade* (Oxford, 1977); see also his more recent study, *The Slave Coast of West Africa, 1550–1750: The Impact of the Atlantic Slave Trade on an African Society* (Oxford, 1991).

latter reached the Bight of Benin.[12] Although they dealt initially in in other commodities, slaves subsequently predominated. The exchange of cowries for slaves and the popularity of the shells as currency were soon to pit the Ijebu in commercial competition with their neighbors in the hinterland. Thus, Oyo expansion in the seventeenth and eighteenth centuries toward the Atlantic coast was due partly to the business elite's quest for control over the sources of money (cowries). This also was the main source of the rivalry—often seen in larger, sub-ethnic terms—between Oyo and Ijebu traders. As could be expected, the Ijebu, being closer to the Atlantic, dominated the trade in cowries until the Oyo opened their own port of trade in the central part of the Bight of Benin.

Before the introduction of modern (European) currency, the Yorùbá referred to cowries simply as money: *owó*. However, with the spread of British metallic currency in the nineteenth and twentieth centuries, a distinction between cowries and the new currencies emerged. Cowries were called *owó ẹyọ,* meaning literally, "loose" or "numerated money," and the metallic currency was simply called *owó,* or by the Africanized names of the denominations such as *kọ́bọ̀* for copper coins, *sílè* for shillings, and so forth. Not surprisingly, the sources of cowries were shrouded in myth, mystery, and ritual. The central myth and its variants claim that Olodumare, the Yorùbá supreme God, reveals the secret of cowries to only a select few:

> They are living things with shells, small in size like snails. To obtain them, a hole was dug in the ground. When the hole has reached a certain depth, a sheep (with a rope tied around its neck) was thrown into it and buried alive. These living things would then crawl up the carcass of the sheep and stick to it. When there were many of them, the sheep would be brought out (with the help of the rope tied to its neck) and the living things sticking to its body would be removed, put into a pot which would be covered to make them die within a few days. After this, they would be taken to a river and would be washed very thoroughly to remove the decay of the cowries. The shells were then put into circulation as money.[13]

This account can be seen as functioning in two major ways: by promoting the belief that the Yorùbá "manufactured" their own cowries, and by providing the business elite with a useful ploy for monopolizing information about the true sources of their wealth. My own view is a combination of the two interpretations, and is supported by the fact that, although there is only one dominant species of cowrie currency in Yorùbáland (the *C. moneta*)—suggesting importation from the Maldive Islands rather than production in the Bight of Benin—there are certain other species of cowrie in limited circulation which resemble the type the Benin were using before the Atlantic trade. This would also suggest internal production along the Atlantic coast of Yorùbáland.

[12] R.C.C. Law, "Contemporary Written Sources," in *Sources of Yoruba History,* ed. S.O. Biobaku (Oxford, 1973), 9–11.

[13] Mrs. Misitura Yusuf, interview by author, Iwo, 16 December, 1991.

Moreover, the lower class was discouraged from "looking for money" (*wá owó*) because of the huge expense involved in the above ritual, and this worked to limit access to wealth.

Although counterfeit cowries did not exist, as is a hazard of coins or paper money, at least two types of shells were in circulation. This may in fact explain the confusion reported by Ekpo Eyo (via G. Basden) that "west of the Niger River the larger cowries (i.e., *C. annulus*) were preferred, whereas east of the Niger the smaller type from Maldives, *C. moneta*, was in vogue."[14] It can be assumed that both the larger and the smaller types were in circulation in Yorùbáland. Both appear in current research, but the testimonies of many informants suggest that the smaller variety was more acceptable and had greater value than the bigger type. According to Falola and Lawuyi:

> *Cypraea annulus* [imported from Zanzibar] were generally recognized as of less value than *Cypraea moneta*. This was not a consequence of an esthetic judgment or issue of identity, but probably related to the problems associated with transporting heavy materials, since more money and more labor are involved in moving heavier materials across the country by land.[15]

Like any form of money, cowrie shells were unstable in value. Aside from the late nineteenth-century inflation, discussed by A.G. Hopkins and Marion Johnson, the value of the currency increased in direct proportion to its scarcity; thus, it had a higher value in the hinterland than along the coast. Hopkins has summarized in these terms how the value fluctuated widely in the period:

> The steepest fall was during the first stage, from 1851 to 1865, when the value of one head of cowries (2000 K) dropped from 4s. 9d. to 1s. 3d., as a result of the increased shipment made by the competing German and French firms. During the second stage, from 1865 to 1879 (and to 1883, in the case of Badagri), the value of the cowrie fell from 1s. 3d. to 1s. per head. This period of relative stability may be explained by the tendency for net imports of cowrie to fall; by an upward movement in demand for cowries following the general expansion of trade in the period after the creation of the Colony of Lagos in 1861; and ... as a side effect of speculation in the dollar. The third stage, from about 1880 (or 1884 in the case of Badagri) to about 1895, was a period of renewed upheaval and fluctuating exchange rates, during which the value of one head of cowries dropped from 1s. 0d. to 6d ... The changes in this period were not caused by over-issue, for the import of cowries continued to decrease, but were primarily the result of other monetary innovations, namely the demonetization of the dollar and the introduction of British silver coin, both of which had adverse effects on the value of the already depreciated cowrie currency.[16]

---

[14] Ekpo Eyo, *Nigeria and the Evolution of Money* (Lagos, 1979), 58.

[15] Toyin Falola and O.B. Lawuyi, "Not Just a Currency: The Cowrie in Nigerian Culture," in *West African Economic and Social History: Studies in Memory of Marion Johnson*, ed. D. Henige and T.C. McCaskie (Madison, 1990), 30.

[16] A.G. Hopkins, "The Currency Revolution," 474–5, 477.

Ekpo Eyo also reports the impact of inflation on the value of cowrie shells.[17] He provides the table (Table 1), drawn from M. D. W. Jeffreys's study. Moreover, cowrie currency played a role in the settlement of international disputes. King Dosumu in 1861 transferred sovereignty over Lagos to the British for an annual payment of 1,200 bags of cowries valued by Ekpo Eyo in 1979 as 2,000 Naira.[18]

Table 1. *Instability of the Cowrie Currency*

Date	Number of cowries per oz of gold
11th century	1,150
16th century	3,000
1816	2,000
1853	3,000
1880	6,000
1912	12,000

Source: Ekpo Eyo, *Nigeria and the Evolution of Money*, 60.

By the end of the ninteenth century, the value of cowrie shells in Yorùbáland had adjusted according to what became known as the "standard" of calculation in relation to British currency then being gradually introduced into the hinterland. According to Samuel Johnson, "... the rate of exchange became practically fixed at 6d. for a 'head' ... i.e., 2,000 cowries; hence 3d.=1,000 cowries."[19] However, because copper money was regarded as inferior in value, one penny (minted in copper and called *kọ́bọ̀* in Yorùbá) was worth 300 cowries. Thus, 3d. in copper money would be 900 cowries rather than 1,000. Bigger figures were based on the 2,000 cowries (*ẹgbẹ̀wá*) to 6d. rate; thus, 5s. was 20,000 cowries (*ọ̀kẹ́ kan*) and one British pound was 80,000 cowries (*ọ̀kẹ́ mẹ́rin*).

Cowrie shells were in wide use in the internal and international commerce of Yorùbáland. Nevertheless, not all transactions occurred in the market. Non-monetary exchanges were as valid as buying and selling with cowrie shells as the unit of account. It would seem that one "bag" of cowries was a lot of

17 Ekpo Eyo, *Nigeria and the Evolution of Money*, 60.

18 Ibid.

19 Samuel Johnson, *The History of the Yorubas* (1921; reprint, London, 1976), 119. Other Nigerian communities counted their cowries differently. A good summary of this from Ekpo Eyo goes thus: "The Ibos, according to Jeffries, counted their cowries in units of six; a unit was called *ekpeti* and ten *ekpeti* made up one string or *ukwu*, twenty *ukwu* were equal to one *awka* and twenty *awka* made up one bag (*akpa*) ... The value of the larger cowries was one third that of the smaller ones. Among the Fulani, the cowrie was known as *sedere* and twenty of these made up one *jalo*, five *jalo* were worth one *hemre* and ten *hemre* made one *zambarre* and one hundred *zambarre* (100,000 cowries) bought a slave ..." See Ekpo Eyo, *Nigeria and the Evolution of Money*, 59.

money. According to oral information, a farmer in the nineteenth century had to be really affluent to earn as much as one "bag" of cowries (approximately 5s.) in a single harvest season. Also, a trader could begin a successful venture and participate in long distance (caravan) trade with one "bag" of cowries.[20] Because of the bulk and weight of the shells[21] and because animal diseases such as trypanosomiasis (spread by the tsetse fly) prevented the use of donkeys, camels, and other beasts of burden, long distance traders engaged head porters whose sole function was to carry money from one market to another. Because of the threat of attack by highwaymen, traders did not transport the money conspicuously. According to oral information from those who were still engaged in the caravan trade early in this century, the cowries were usually put in a sack, which was then placed in a wide-brimmed calabash for easy carrying on the head. In this way, too, no one could distinguish a load of cowries from a load of goods. In any case, protection was offered, even in periods of interethnic warfare, because most traders were also warriors and many trading caravans had armed guards.[22]

The transition from cowries to Western-type currencies coincided with the advent of British colonial rule in Lagos in the middle of the nineteenth century. The history of modern currency in Yorùbáland is intertwined with that of banking and finance and, like the history of cowrie currency, is closely linked to the experiences of other West African societies. The role of money in Yorùbáland in the immediate colonial era was inseparable from that in the rest of the region.

As early as 1825, the British had introduced the gold sovereign, silver, bronze, and nickel-bronze coins.[23] For approximately the next fifty years, European and African merchants conducted business using both cowries and British coins; however, as the century wore on, and especially after Lagos became a colony, several problems arose. First, there were inconsistencies in the demands and practices of the British. The evolving British administration began to insist on the coins as the medium of exchange, and it seems that cowries were being phased out. At the same time, many British companies, especially the Royal Niger Company, insisted on trade by barter, in order, according to Ekpo Eyo, "to make double profit."[24] The problem persisted into

[20] Oral interviews at Iwo and Ilesa. Persons interviewed had been, in their prime, traders and farmers.

[21] See Marion Johnson, "Cowrie Currencies I," 24–32, for a discussion of the relative weight of "big" and "small" cowries.

[22] See Toyin Falola and Akanmu Adebayo, "Owoseni: The Politics and Culture of Money among the Yoruba," MS, chapter 5.

[23] Ekpo Eyo, *Nigeria and the Evolution of Money*, 91. At the same time the French introduced the five franc pieces and the Napoleon and, according to Eyo, "even the American gold double-eagle, the eagle, and the half-eagle " could be seen in circulation along the West African coast.

[24] Ibid.

the twentieth century when, in 1903, Lord Lugard complained that the Royal Niger Company's barter trade was hindering the adoption of coins in Northern Nigeria. Another problem was the growing dichotomy between the coastal markets in Lagos and Badagry and the hinterland markets. While coins and cowries were used along the coast, only cowries were accepted in the markets of the Yorùbá hinterland. Other problems were caused by instability in the rates of conversion from cowries to coins, the difficulties faced by an illiterate population in recognizing different coin denominations, and the fear in Britain that the coins issued for West Africa might be rejected.

There were still other difficulties during the latter part of the nineteenth century. British trading and shipping companies had problems handling large sums of money, and the British administration in West Africa had problems finding enough coins to pay the troops. Even when the government had enough coins, there was the challenge of transporting them, for the new currency was, like cowries, unwieldy. When the government had a sufficient number of porters for the money, it still had to provide armed escorts, especially during the period of Egba-Ijebu and Ekitiparapo-Ibadan wars. The need for a modern financial institution was apparant. In response to the exigencies of expatriate business, modern banking was initiated in Nigeria in 1872 when the African Banking Corporation (ABC) was established in Lagos.[25]

In addition to performing normal commercial bank functions, the ABC was charged with the distribution of Bank of England coins and notes in the Colony of Lagos. In 1893, however, the ABC left Lagos to concentrate its efforts in South Africa. In the same year, the Elder Dempster & Co., a Liverpool shipping company, established the Bank of British West Africa. Bank of British West Africa (BBWA) soon severed its links with the shipping company after it was registered in London as a limited liability company under the name of First Bank. It was an instant success. It was also charged with the importation of British currency into the colony. First Bank maintained a monopoly on banking in Lagos Colony and in Nigeria throughout the nineteenth century. Early in this century, however, the Barclays Bank (now called Union Bank) and the United Bank for Africa were established, primarily to provide banking services to British companies and other arms of the colonial enterprise in Nigeria. By extension, therefore, the banks provided credit facilities to favored expatriate businesses in Nigeria.

The focus had thus far been on importing British currency to Nigeria. Toward the end of the nineteenth century, opinion in Britain favored issuing a special silver currency for West Africa. The plan materialized in 1912 when the West African Currency Board was established under the auspices of the BBWA. Its first silver coins were issued in 1913. According to Ekpo Eyo:

[25] The discussion on modern banking in Nigeria is based on S.I. Ajayi and O.O. Ojo, *Money and Banking Analysis and Policy in the Nigerian Context* (London, 1981).

> The Bank notes were in units of £1 (one pound), 10/- (ten shilling), 2/- (two shillings) and in 1918/19 1/- (one shilling). In 1919, £5 (five pounds) notes were issued but withdrawn in 1923 as being too large a denomination. It was however reintroduced in 1954, justified by the growth in the economy. Coin denominations were florins (two shillings), shilling (1/-), sixpence (6*d*), three pence (3*d*), one penny (1*d*), half penny (½*d*), quarter penny (¼*d*) and in 1918–19 one-tenth penny (1/10 *d*) or *àníní*... Originally, the silver coins issued by the Board were 0.925 fine, comparable to what obtained in the UK at the time. However, with the UK Coinage Act of 1920, the fineness was reduced to 0.500, at which point the Board decided to abandon silver coinage and introduce nickel-brass coins in 2/- (two shillings), 1/- (one shilling), 6*d* (six pence) and 3*d* (three pence) denominations.[26]

At the demise of the West African Currency Board, as colonial rule was ending, the Central Bank of Nigeria was established in 1959. One of its responsibilities was to issue and regulate currency in the country. The Bank has pursued this role very actively, and reached a major landmark when it issued a truly national currency, the *Naira* and *kobo,* in decimal form, in 1973.

The discussion in this section can now be summarized. The initial form of money in circulation was the cowrie shell introduced in pre-colonial times. Inflation, fluctuation in the value of the shells, commercial expansion, slave trade, state formation, and political instability all produced refinements in the view of money at various times and among different Yorùbá groups before the nineteenth century. The revolutionary events of the nineteenth century—including the fall of the Oyo empire, intra-ethnic warfare, the growth of new urbanized communities, renewed attempts at state formation, economic competition among new states, and such external forces as the abolition of the slave trade and the expansion of British interests—further contributed to the reconsideration of certain ideals about money. The next form of currency came in the wake of the "currency revolution," promoted under colonial rule by the introduction of British currency.

Having monetized their economies before colonialism, large sections of Yorùbáland were at an advantage when the British introduced the new currency. In most cases they simply vested the new money with the ideals they had developed before colonialism. When these failed to match new realities, they either invented other ideals or adapted European ones that came with the British currency. These ideals will now be examined.

II. Yorùbá View of Money: The Ideal

Money can be viewed as an objective reality and as a subjective ideal. An object takes on meaning only when it is defined or conceptualized. In this section I explore the Yorùbá conception—or *ideals*—of money. The Yorùbá have defined and redefined money several times; I will discuss what can be considered the prevalent paradigm of money among the Yorùbá.

---

[26] Ekpo Eyo, *Nigeria and the Evolution of Money*, 95–6.

A few words on the sources of these ideals are appropriate. Yorùbá society is complex. It is home to several ethnic groups speaking dialects of the Yorùbá language.[27] The culture and world-view of these groups is not homogeneous, but an aggregation of various values arising in different circumstances. What I intend here is to examine the shared logic in their view of money, with attention to the most widely used and accepted proverbs (*òwé*), wise sayings, idiomatic expressions (*àsàyàn ọ̀rọ̀*), myths (*àlọ́*)[28], and Ifa verses (*ẹsẹ Ifá*).[29] My sources for these, apart from several published works, are informal discussions and formal interviews conducted over many years in Iwo, Ile-Ife, Ado-Ekiti, Ondo, and Oyo.[30]

There can be no question about the validity of these texts as sources of deep philosophical and cognitive ideals. The texts—proverbs, myths, family histories, and idiomatic expressions—are all taught to the Yorùbá from childhood. They are considered important enough to constitute an integral part of the informal educational system. They are employed in settling minor and major disputes within or between families, and are the sources of Yorùbá legal institutions, which constituted the basis of the colonial customary court system.[31] Kings, chiefs, and other people directly involved in the judicial system use these ideals to determine who and what is right. The position of Ifa verse is slightly different. Ifa is the embodiment of collective wisdom and collective memory. For the most part, the corpus is sacred and the verses are not openly recited. Nevertheless, Yorùbá culture makes available to everyone several stories from Ifa verse, primarily to teach the young. In other words, Ifa and its priests do not monopolize the philosophy; rather, it is allowed wide circulation. Whereas Ifa priests may not tell tall tales, storytellers (*pàlọ́-pàlọ́* or *àwọn apàlọ́*) may adapt Ifa verses for their use.

My point, therefore, is that it is possible to identify Yorùbá ideals and to differentiate them from religious beliefs. Ideals are ethics, principles, or stan-

---

[27] The classic text on this matter is Samuel Johnson, *History of the Yoruba*.

[28] Among others, see Bakare Gbadamosi and Ulli Beier, *Not Even God Is Ripe Enough: Yoruba Stories* (London, 1968); Ulli Beier, *Yoruba Myths* (Cambridge, 1980); M.I. Ogumefu, *Yoruba Legends* (London, 1929); Abayomi Fuja, *Fourteen Hundred Cowries: Traditional Stories of the Yoruba* (London, 1962).

[29] On *Ifa*, see William Bascom, *Ifa Divination: Communication between Gods and Men in West Africa* (Bloomington, Indiana, 1969); Wande Abimbola, *Ifa: An Exposition of Ifa Literary Corpus* (Ibadan, 1976); idem, *Ifa Divination Poetry* (New York, 1977); Afolabi A. Epega, *The Sacred Ifa Oracle* (San Francisco, 1995).

[30] I do not use *oríkì* in this essay, partly because it is not very clear at what point an individual's praise name can be generalized for the community. However, for more information on *oríkì*, see Ademola M. Adegbite, *Oriki: A Study in Yoruba Musical and Social Perception* (Ph.D. thesis, University of Pittsburgh, 1978); also Karin Barber, *I Could Speak until Tomorrow: Oriki, Women and the Past in a Yoruba Town* (Edinburgh, 1991).

[31] See G. B. A. Coker, *Family Property among the Yorubas* (London, 1966), especially part I, "The Impact of English Law on Native Law and Custom."

dards which aim for perfection: they are goals which society aspires to realize. In this section, I will discuss nine major ideals of money.

1. Kòse-é-mání ni owó. The first ideal is that money is the Indispensable One.[32] This is one of several ways money has been personified by the Yorùbá. It is this personification, this *idea,* that I will explore in depth in this paper. Conceived as such, Money warrants being spelled with a capital M.

Money is important. The sign on the side panel of lorries, owned by a rich Idofian transportation entrepreneur, that carried passengers between Ilorin and Lagos and passed through my city in the 1970s, read *Owó ni kókó,* "Money is important." Money is truly indispensable in any market economy as a medium of exchange and as a measure of value, transaction, and relationship. This indispensability is recognized in all societies, but not every society views money as a *being*. Jane Guyer's discussion implies that money is only an object. "Money is mundane," she says. It is a "mundane mystery" to most people. The material of money—shell, paper, iron, cloth, plastic—in many cultures is certainly mundane. Even where gold and silver and other precious metals are used, money is still an inanimate object. With the high level of inflation and the unequal exchange rates of many African "soft" currencies vis-à-vis the "hard" currencies of capitalist Europe and the United States, money may indeed be seen as mundane.

The Yorùbá personify money, and see it as the Indispensable One, that is, *Kòse-é-mání.* They conceive of money as a life form in itself, and epitomize it in the figure of Aje, on whom they bestow certain abilities and powers. They think of Money as an active participant in human relationships. She is considered as a guest or visitor, and she decides for herself "whose house to visit." The statement *àlejò l'owó* ("Money is a guest") itself encourages the host to treat her well. According to Karin Barber, "Only a fortunate person can expect [money] to settle down permanently with him or her."[33] In other words, the result of the visit could be to establish friendship with a good host or to leave a bad host unceremoniously. Thus, the Yorùbá fervently pray that God will make Money their friend. In another sense Money is viewed as a grandmother, and the very rich are said to have *iyalaya owó,* "the grandmother of money."

In addition, the Yorùbá confer many human attributes on money. Money is capable of smiling. This is why they often say of the rich, "Money favored [or smiled on] so-and-so." She is capable of sitting. Thus, when the Yorùbá see the wonders a wealthy person has done with money, they exclaim, *"Ajé o kú ìjokò!"* This is a form of greeting to someone comfortably seated. Money can

[32] I am grateful to Mr. A.A. Adediran, Vice-Principal of Iwo Grammar School, for the notion of money as *Kòse-é-mání,* that money is the Indispensable One. He expressed this idea in a letter written to me five years ago.

[33] Barber, "Money, Self-Realization and the Person in Yorùbá Texts," 216.

also spend the night, as expressed in the statement, "*Owó ya ilé sùn,*" meaning "Money sleeps over in her friend's house." In addition, Money can bear witness for and strongly support her favorites. They say, "*Owó jẹ́rì fún un* ," or "*Owó sisẹ́ fún un,*" meaning "Money is his/her witness." This is especially the case when a rich person buys his or her way out of a bad situation. Money is likewise capable of reproducing or hatching, so they say "*Owó rẹ̀ pa' mo,*" with regard to someone whose investment is successful and whose wealth seems to be multiplying. Money is capable of going and coming; so when one becomes rich, it is said that one's Money has arrived *(Owó rẹ̀ ti dé)*. Money is swift but it bodes well if she is crippled *(Owó y'arọ)* or even dies *(Owó kú)* in one's house, for then she will not fly away. A more recent formulation acknowledges that Money is capable of making a mistake, or of associating with the bad crowd. When, for example, an upstart becomes wealthy, or when a rich person shows no creativity in his spending, Money is said to "miss road" (pidgin or colloquial for "being lost," or "being wasted").

Many more expressions could be cited, but the important thing to note is that the Yorùbá imbue money with several personalities and a great deal of power that make it quite indispensable. To have power in Yorùbá society, one must first have money, or be close to someone who does.

2. Sŭrù l'érè. The second ideal is that one must have patience to acquire money. Patience is profitable, *sŭrù l'érè,* say the Yorùbá. Patience as a moral ideal is taught from childhood. The following *àlọ́* (myth or creative oral literature) bears this out:

He Who Has Patience Has Everything

In the olden days there lived a man who was so poor that he had only one cloth and that was in rags. He had only a single wife, and she was childless. They had no other work to do except collecting firewood in the bush and had no reasonable hope of ever improving their condition. Nevertheless, they were content and believed that the future might bring them a better lot.

The poor man also had a friend called Abinuku—he is angry to death—who hated everybody in his heart, but did not show it in his face. The poor man thought he had a friend—but in reality he had nobody to love him, but himself.

The poor man prayed to God for many years, asking him to better his life; when at last the time came that the almighty God was ready to help him, He sent three heavenly creatures to visit the poor man, and they were called Money, Child, and Patience. He told the poor man that he would be allowed to keep one of these wonderful creatures, while the others must be allowed to return to their maker.

The three wonderful creatures accordingly set out on their long and troublesome road from Heaven to Earth. One day they arrived at a large river. The water was cold and deep, but Patience quietly walked through the flood. Then Child said to Money: "I am too weak to cross this river. You are big and strong. Please carry me across." But Money said angrily: "You impudent Child! Would you make your senior work for you? It is you who must carry me through the river—or there will be trouble." They were fighting for a long time, but in the end Patience returned and carried them both across.

The three wonderful creatures finally arrived at the poor man's house. They were well received by the poor man, who gave them all the food he could find in his home. The poor man felt pleased and honoured by the visit, but when he heard what they were coming about he got worried and confused. He felt quite unable to choose and so he asked the advice of his wife.

"You foolish man," the wife said. "Don't you realise that we need money most of all? If we have a child, what can we feed it on? And if we have patience—what use is that?"

The poor man was still not sure what to do and so he went to his friend Abinuku and asked his advice too. Abinuku was very jealous because the three wonderful creatures had not come to him. He did not want Abinuku to have either money or children and so he advised him to choose Patience. "If you choose Child—you will not have money to feed it. But if you choose Money and you have no child—your property will go to slaves after your death. So you had better have Patience."

The poor man did not know the answer to that and so he went and chose Patience. His wife was very annoyed when she saw Money and Child leaving the house and Patience settling down to live with them. But the poor man was content and Abinuku secretly triumphed.

Now Money and Child went on their way and they came back to the same river and they began to argue again, who should carry the other across. They quarrelled for a long time, and in the end they decided that, as they were unable to cross the river, they might just as well return to the poor man's house.

When they arrived at the poor man's house there was great happiness and the house became a house of song.

Thus Money and Child will in the end settle down where Patience has made its home. Patience is the father of every good thing in life.[34]

There are several versions of this story. The most popular, it seems, is the one that *jùjú* musician Ebenezer Obey made famous in the late 1970s. In this version, the poor man's name is Ogbon (meaning "wisdom") and he has two wives. One wife has children but the other does not. Ogbon, the poor man, was also given a choice among Patience, Money, and Child, and Long-life as well. The childless wife insists on Child, the wife who already has children insists on Money, and his friends advised him to accept Long-life. Ogbon realizes that the wives were advising him out of their own self-interest. Probably to appear partial impartial, and possibly in his wisdom (after all, his name is Ogbon), and most certainly because he still listens to his parents, Ogbon chooses Patience. Money, Child, and Long-life leave together, but they soon begin to miss Patience. At the end of the story, Money, Child, and Long-life finally seek out Ogbon so as to live with Patience.[35]

The lesson of the story is that in the end patience is profitable, that money and all other good things of life will come if only one has patience. The Yorùbá frown upon impatience; indeed, impatience is considered chief among

[34] Gbadamosi and Beier, *Not Even God is Ripe Enough*, 21–3.

[35] Chief Commander Ebenezer Obey & His Inter-Reformers Band, "Adventure of Mr. Wise," OC 138 (1973; re-released by Ebenezer Obey Music Co. Ltd., 1996).

vices.[36] Patience is counselled for all occasions, except when one is in personal danger. *Sùrù* ("patience") has several synonyms in Yorùbá, including calmness *pẹ̀lẹ́ pẹ̀lẹ́* ("calmness"), *ìfaradà* ("endurance"), *ọgbọ́n inú* ("inner strength or reflection"), *ìfọkànbalẹ̀* ("contentment"), and *ìfarabalẹ̀* ("resting easy"). Patience is never considered as total resignation. At the same time, the Yorùbá frown upon opportunism. Ideally, the patient person will not take undue advantage of other people. *Onìsùrù ni yíò j'ogún ayé*: The patient person shall inherit the world. Certainly, the Yorùbá say, every good thing, money included, will come eventually to he who waits.

3. *Ìbànújẹ́ ni ọjọ́ orí, owó l'àgbà.*[37] Thirdly, wealth and age need not correspond; and in any case *ọjọ́ orí* (age, or the state of being older than someone else) only brings sadness if it is not accompanied by *Owó* (money, or being rich). Yorùbá society is gerontocratic, yet it gives positions of seniority (*àjùlọ*) to wealthy people. The new version of this ideal is contained in the expression Karin Barber referred to in her essay in these terms: "*Olówó n sọ̀rọ̀, tálíkà lóùn ní ìdéà* (The rich person speaks [and is obeyed], while the poor person says s/he has an idea)."[38] In other words, no matter how old the poor person is, he/she will be considered poor, and no matter how young the rich person is, he/she will be given the respect due an elder. According to Akinwumi Isola, no matter how old a laborer is (the proverb puts it beautifully as "no matter how long and gray a laborer's beard is"), his employer (i. e., the owner of the farm on which he is working) is his senior.[39]

4. *Owó kò ni'rán*. The fourth ideal is that money does not discriminate against lineages. This is the difference between *orò*, wealth or property, and *owó*, money. Money is acquired but wealth is inherited.[40] It is true that money creates wealth and that money can be used to acquire property; but wealth has typically belonged to a family over several generations. It is also true that the beginning of a lineage's wealth, as I have shown elsewhere, may have nothing to do with money. Before society became monetized, wealth or property existed in several forms, including the size of farmland under cultivation, the number and sometimes the color of one's horses, the number of wives and children, the number of dependent clients and slaves, one's chieftaincy position or status (*ipò*), and certain personal attributes such as knowledge, apti-

---

[36] *Ara ko bale ni oloori arun*: Impatience is the head of all diseases.

[37] The conclusion of this proverb varies. Sometimes it is *ipo lagba*, that is status is more important. However, status can also be based on money.

[38] Karin Barber, "Money, Self-Realization and the Person in Yorùbá Texts," 219.

[39] *Bí irungbọ̀n alágbàro ti gùn tó, ẹnití ó gb'óko fún un ni ọ̀ga rẹ.* This proverb is based on the Yorùbá ideal that grayness of hair and length of beard are marks of distinction and old age. See Akinwumi Isola, *Efunsetan Aniwura, Iyalode Ibadan.* (Ibadan, 1970), 5.

[40] Money can also be inherited. The Yorùbá say *ọmọ olówó j'ogún owó* (A rich person's child inherits money).

tude, skill, experience, character, and wisdom. Social status was not permanently fixed, but mobility was difficult. The problem of social mobility began to ease with monetization, even when money consisted of cowrie shells. Any individual or lineage could make money, acquire property, reinvest profit, be seen as wealthy, make more money, and use the money to buy popularity or acclaim (*f'owó ra'yì*). Money transformed the social structure, and the size of one's accumulation became a factor in the determination of one's position on the social ladder.

Age (*ọjọ́ orí*), wealth (*ọrọ̀*, status (*ipò*), and money (*owó*) are interdependent, with one factor affecting the others. Currently, money is critical among them. Consider age, which used to be very important—these days it is no match for money. A new Yorùbá saying is *àjùlọ kò kan àgbà*, which signifies that seniority is not always measured in terms of age. Rather, it may come with wealth. The rich use money to purchase property and to accumulate wealth. As for status, money can now be used to purchase chieftaincy titles, even honorary doctorates. It is true that certain positions or statuses command respect, but they must be accompanied by money. A king or chief is only as big as the size of his wallet. Moreover, with increased monetization and with the spread of materialism, people accept certain positions only if those positions will guarantee continued access to money. In fact, people in particular lines of work do not look forward to promotions despite the accompanying increase in status. A good example is the Nigerian Customs and Excise Department. Many customs officers make their money at border patrol posts, usually by accepting bribes from smugglers. Once promoted, the officers are expected to return to some office at headquarters where, they say, "there is nothing to eat" (*kò sí ìjẹ*). Promotion (i.e., elevation to a higher status) is dreaded by many police officers and is seen as an act of malevolent superiors to "take food from their mouth" (*gba oúnjẹ l'ẹ́nu wa*). Promotion is viewed, and in some cases used, as a punishment. Money is a powerful instrument in the determination of a person's status.

5. *Owó ni kẹ̀kẹ́ ìhìnrere*. Money has established an important place for itself in Yorùbá religious expressions, be they traditional or foreign. Money is considered in all the local religions as a vehicle (*kẹ̀kẹ́* or, literally, bicycle) for missionary activity and as the surest medium for speeding effective prayers on to God.

In Yorùbá traditional religion, money is offered in sacrifice to the *òrìshà*. Many Ifa priests receive cash payments for consultation, and they often prescribe sacrifices that involve money. It seems to me that these practices began very early, for most Ifa verses mention sacrifices of specific amounts of money. Money is referred to as cowrie shells in these verses, but the Ifa priest could use his discretion to choose the kind of money used. Many of my informants confirmed that cowrie shells are used in sacrifices if cash is required; but priests ask for *real* money as payment. Traditional healers and herbalists also demand money for their services, sometimes charging much more than is actually spent in preparing the medicine. Many of those interviewed explained that this is done so that the charm (*òògùn*) will appear to have value, because *òògùn tí a ò f'owó se, ẹ̀hìn ààrò ní gbeé* ("A charm for which one has not paid good money is not highly valued"). Thus, money plays a major role in the entire process of consultation, evaluation, and treatment.

Money plays a major role in church ministry, too, and Christians receive constant reminders to tithe and get involved in mission work. Indeed, *owó ni kẹ̀kẹ́ ìhìnrere* ("Money is the engine for [spreading] the gospel"). Money is employed in very ingenious ways by the various Africanized churches, such as Cherubim and Seraphim, and Celestial Church of Christ, where prayer sessions for the needy often involve the use of money in ways not unlike those traditional religion employs.

In Islam, especially at naming, wedding, and other ceremonies, money likewise plays a significant role. Here, the ability of money to carry prayers to God is emphasized. The more money one gives, the greater the chances of the prayer being answered. Several Islamic leaders I interviewed assured me that there is no religious sanction for this practice. One of them called it "bold-faced robbery." Most say it is something done by corrupt Muslims for personal profit. Nevertheless, anyone who has attended any of the so-called Muslim naming or wedding ceremonies conducted by members of certain Islamic denominations will come away with the impression that money really intercedes for people before Allah. Consider the following prayer session recorded at a function in Ile-Ife in February 1993:

Baba Tájù mú owó wá	Taju's father offer money
Wọ́n ní kíá fi se àdúrà fún ọmọ wọn	He asks us to offer prayer for his son
Tí ó wà ní òkè òkun Russia	Who is studying abroad in Russia
Pé kí Olúwa sọ́ ọmọ náà	That Allah may protect his son
Pé kí Olúwa bá wọn mú ojú ko ojú	That Allah may bring them together again
L'ólá Fatiha	[Let's pray by reciting the] esteemed Fatiha

Similar prayer sessions or cash-for-prayer transactions can be readily encountered in most Yorùbá towns with a sizeable Muslim population. They can be heard in many mosques belonging to certain denominations during the regularly scheduled prayers, or in private homes during a naming or other ceremony. Whenever this happens, money has become the enforcer, the facilitator, and the carrier of prayers to God. *Owó ni kẹ̀kẹ́ ìhìnrere* has, therefore, acquired a new meaning— money is the fuel running the vehicle that brings good news from God. So the more money one gives, the faster the vehicle travels and the sooner the good news (e.g., a better paying job, a new car, healing, or protection for a loved one) is delivered.

6. *Owó èrú kìí gb'ọ́wọ́.* The sixth ideal is that money should be acquired honestly. Otherwise Money will not last. To the Yorùbá, the end does not always justify the means. Money can attempt to justify itself, but it cannot legitimize itself. Although people may kowtow and show endless respect for the rich, what really matters to them is not how much an individual is worth but how he or she came by the money. The culture stipulates, even urges, that it be acquired cleanly. Wanting *owó tútù* (literally, wet or cold money), people could be seen at major functions putting money—cowries and coins subsequently, but not paper currency—in cold water to cool and wet it for its recipient. Cold water, it is believed, symbolizes purifying and regenerative processes and protects the recipient from harm.

Owó èrú (money acquired by mischief, treachery, or deceit), *owó gbígbóná* (literally, hot money acquired through satanic activities), *owó òjijì* (sudden money), *owó ìdọ̀tí* (dirty money), and *owó ẹ̀jẹ̀* (blood money) are just a few examples of the types of money the Yorùbá frown upon. Lotteries and betting on football are also discouraged. Any money made at the expense of another person is considered dishonest. Curiously, money acquired through the slave trade was not frowned upon. This is probably because it was the major, and for some time the most lucrative, economic activity among the Oyo ruling class. The slave trade was "clean", which made kidnapping at the time also clean.

Another clean way of accumulating money is hard work. *Iṣẹ́ l'òògùn iṣẹ́*, say the Yorùbá (Hard work is the antidote for poverty). They differentiate between hard work (*iṣẹ́*) and useless, aimless labor (*agbára*). The path to riches is through hard work, not purposeless labor (*owó níní o kan agbára*), and one who labors thoughtlessly and without focus is considered the biggest of fools and the laziest of people.[41]

The ideal of earning money the clean way does not imply that a person must perform only white-collar jobs. Indeed, one must get one's hands dirty. *Ìsàlẹ̀ ọrọ̀ l'ẹ́gbin* ("At the bottom of most prosperity is some dirt"). Moreover, *ẹni tí ò lè se bí aláàrù l'Óyìngbò, ò lè se bí Ajíjọrọ̀ l'Ọ́jà'ba* ("One who cannot do the lowliest job at Oyingbo [a market in Lagos] cannot expect to wear the best attire like Ajojiro at Oja'ba [another Lagos market]").

The ideal of making money cleanly also allows the entrepreneur to keep the secret of his/her success from all. He is advised to *bá'nú sọ, má b'énìyàn sọ*, to tell no one but himself the secret of his prosperity. This capitalistic way of proceeding denies others the opportunity to compete, and the secret may be lost in the process.Those not privy to the secret would be at an unfair disadvantage, perhaps compelling them to expend time on inexpedient short cuts.

7. *Ẹni yá ẹgbàá tí kò san o bẹ́gi dínà egbèje.* The seventh ideal is to avoid debt in general and bad debt (*gbèsè*) in particular. Because of its history, especially in

[41] The Yorùbá say: *Alágbára má m'èrò ni baba ọ̀lẹ.* ("Brawn without brain is laziness.")

the age of the slave trade when it was often abused, debt has acquired a bad name among the Yorùbá. During the years of the slave trade, in extreme circumstances (then not all that rare) a creditor could sell the debtor into slavery; and until the first half of this century, a debtor could pawn himself or his child to the creditor. To have good credit among the Yorùbá is, therefore, to have money in your hand (*l'ówó l'ọ́wọ́*) and not to have debt like a noose around your neck ready to choke you (*ní gbèsè l'ọ́rùn*). Good credit is secured in a transaction by cash payment (*san'wó*) and not by effecting it on credit (*gbà'wìn*).

This ideal does allow the individual to borrow money for a pressing need or emergency. But it discourages defaulting on a loan (*àyá-à-san*). Ideally, one promptly settles his debts so that his credibility is maintained. The Yorùbá say *ẹni yá ẹgbàá 'tí kò san o bẹ́gi dínà egbèje*, admonishing that one should pay off big debts in order to qualify for small loans. To allow debt to accumulate and have no apparent means of paying it off is to invite the wrath of the creditor. Another thing to avoid is leaving a large debt for one's offspring to repay following one's death. It is always desirable that one manage to pay one's debts in his lifetime (*ẹmí tí o jẹ gbèsè ni yìô san-án*) so that his children are spared any such burden. Along with their disadvantages for the individual debtor, bad debts can drag his entire kin-group into disrepute.[42]

8. Owó fún ni kò tó ènìyàn. The eighth ideal stipulates that having money is not everything—being a person of good character is of greater value. The rich are cautioned against boastfulness, and reminded that probity counts for more than ill-gotten gains. Since power corrupts, and money is power, money too is subversive of ethical conduct. This ideal restrains reckless behavior by the rich, especially behavior that might oppress the poor.[43]

9. Àyànmó ko gb'óògùn. The ninth ideal affirms that being rich (i.e., having money) is an act of fate or destiny. Perhaps it is important to state at the outset that most Yorùbá strongly believe in destiny. Destiny is that which is chosen for someone in the mythical world inhabited by spirits before his birth; it also dictates the course of his life, predetermining who will succeed and who will not. Certain people are fated to be rich or poor, to have or come by money, regardless of how they conduct themselves. Like money, destiny is personified as that all-powerful if invisible being who smiles on some and torments others. The following story from *ẹsẹ Ifá* (Ifa verse) explains the process by which individuals choose their destiny or fate in the spirit world:

---

[42] For further information on this, see my "Money, Credit, and Banking in Precolonial Africa: The Yoruba Experience," *Anthropos* 89 (1994): 379–400.

[43] For more information on this ideal, see Emmanuel D. Babatunde, *A Critical Study of Bini and Yoruba Value Systems of Nigeria in Change: Culture, Religion, and the Self* (Lewiston, 1992), 87–119.

Choosing a Fate

Mokewure, the priest of goats, and Mojewara, the priest of sheep, cast the Ifa oracle for three children:

> Orisanku the son of Ogun
> Oritemere the son of Ija
> and for Afuwape the son of Orunmila.

It happened that these three children wanted to come into the world, and they must choose their own fate. None of them knew how to go about this and what to choose and what to avoid. But Afuwape's father, Orunmila, consulted the oracle. The priest told him that his son would be successful in the world. But before his son left heaven, Orunmila must make sacrifice for him.

Orunmila followed the instruction for sacrifice and gave his son a thousand cowries, as advised by the *babaláwo*. He told him that he must spend this money in the house of Ajalamo, "the one who moulds new children."

When Orisanku and Oritemere had been waiting for Afuwape for some time and did not see him, they left for Ajalamo's house. When they arrived, they could not see Ajalamo. They saw many beautiful "heads" (*orí*), which they thought will be good for them, and they picked the ones they liked. Then they left for the world.

Later Afuwape arrived. He saw an old woman sitting on the floor, who seemed to be waiting for something. Afuwape asked her what was the matter? She replied that Ajalamo had bought some maize beer from her, but he had not paid her. Afuwape asked how much he owed her. She said, "One thousand cowries." Then Afuwape gave her the money.

The old woman asked him what he had come to do. He said he had come to pick his own "head" (*orí*). She told him that two other children had been there before him and they had chosen the heads they liked. Then she left, thanking him for the money.

Then Ajalamo came down from the rafters where he had been hiding. He thanked Afuwape for what he had done. Then he led him to the garden, where he kept all the heads. He showed him the beautiful heads that everyone liked to pick, but which might not let a man survive. He told him that some who picked beautiful heads do not succeed in the world and others will be surrounded by enemies. He warned him not to touch those beautiful heads.

Then Ajalamo showed him the right head to pick, and he told him that human beings bring trouble upon themselves, because they do not know what a good head is. Then he prayed for Afuwape and sent him to the world with his blessing.

Then Afuwape left for the world to become a successful and wealthy man. Orisanku the son of Ogun and Oritemere the son of Ija were surprised. They said, "Was it not the same place in which we picked our own heads?" That is why they sing:

> I don't know where my friend picked his head
> I would go and pick my own
> It was the same place where we picked our own heads
> But fate is different
> If I knew where Afuwape chose his head
> I would go and choose my own again.[44]

It is significant that the Yorùbá see destiny or fate as *orí* (head). To them, the head is the most important part of the body. To the Yorùbá, the head is the

[44] Ulli Beier, *Yoruba Myths*, 4–6

house of wisdom (*ilé ọgbọ́n*). It has two manifestations: the metaphysical or inner (or hidden) head (*orí inú*) and the physical or outer head (*orí òde*). The physical head protects the metaphysical head, and the metaphysical head projects an individual's total personality and identity. Thus, one of the most powerful prayers offered by the Yorùbá is *kí orí inú mi má se ba t'òdé jẹ́*, which asks God to protect one's metaphysical head so that others will respect him.

Destiny always prevails, but witches can change a person's good fortune to bad. Witches, it is believed, can make the rich poor by causing *àgbànà* to strike. According to Falola, "the problems attributed to *àgbànà* were probably no more than the inability of an individual to manage his resources, the failure to sustain an avenue for regular income, or ruination brought by a succession of misfortunes."[45] So strong is the myth of *àgbànà* that a rich person would offer sacrifices recommended by an Ifa priest (*babaláwo*) to avoid it.

Destiny, therefore, determines where and to whom money goes. This notion is beautifully put in a song by Orlando Owoh in which one is urged to inquire after one's destiny before entering any relationship, starting a business venture, or doing virtually anything. Unfortunately, as the above *Ifá* verse indicates, one's destiny is the unknowable element in the calculation. The rich and the poor choose their destiny in the same place. The poor are advised either to accept their fate or to seek help from the *babaláwo* in order to have their destiny changed.

The foregoing discussion of the nine ideals paints a picture of the way a perfect society would conduct itself. But there is no such society, certainly not Yorùbá society. The discussion in this section shows how it idealized money, placed its ruling class upon a pedestal, and demanded high moral conduct from its members. Several mechanisms and institutions were developed to induce or coerce its members to comply and conform, with appropriate rewards for compliance and punishment for waywardness. Despite such mechanisms, Yorùbá ideals are not free of contradictions, many of them as old as history, others just emerging. I turn now to these contradictions.

III. The Yorùbá View of Money: The Contradiction

The Yorùbá view of money has not been altogether consistent. Many of the ideals examined above are fraught with contradictions. Clearly, the Yorùbá maintain a double standard. There were, and still are, different sets of rules for the young and the old, the rich and the poor, and for men and for women. For example, take the ideal that money matters less than good character. The Yorùbá also posit that good character is itself a function of one's station on the cash scale. *Owó kò sí, ènìyàn kò sunwọ̀n* (Without money there can be no good

[45] Falola, "Money and Informal Credit Institutions," 166.

character).[46] Money, therefore, determines how people evaluate character—the standard for measuring character fluctuates according to the wallet of the person in question. To put it mathematically, a poor person has to be twice or thrice as good as a rich person for his/her character to be duly recognized. Clearly, there is a deliberate perversion of the standard that privileges money (*owó*) over good conduct (*ènìyàn*).

Another contradiction can be seen in the ideal of patience. Patience is not always a virtue because often to wait patiently can be to wait forever. The following sarcastic saying, intended to deride the opportunistic attitude of Lagos businessmen and the street smarts of Lagos women, proves the point: *Àwọn ọmọge ìwòyí kò gbé Sŭrùlérè mọ́, Olórunsògo ni wọ́n n´gbé* (Ladies nowadays do not live in Surulere but take up residence in Olorunsogo). Surulere and Olorunsogo are both suburbs of Lagos, and Surulere means "patience is profitable."[47] Well, people have moved away from patience and have now embraced (literally, taken up residence at) Olorunsogo, which itself means "God has provided," or "God has given the opportunity." They have rejected the ideal of patience and embraced the gratification of opportunism. This contradiction has spread from Lagos to other urban centers and is filtering gradually into rural areas.

Another contradiction pertains to the development of the credit system. The ideal used to be to *have* (not to *owe*) money. The boundaries used to be clear: The *olówó* (rich person) owns money, the *òtòsì* (poor person) wants money, and the *onígbèsè* (debtor) owes money. As Western ideas of credit spread and became firmly rooted during colonialism and beyond, these boundaries became blurred. In today's Yorùbáland, both rich and poor alike are in debt, and chances are that the rich person's debt is proportionately higher than the poor person's. Yusuf Olatunji, the *sakara* musician, once put this in perspective in a song: *Ohun tó se olówó tó fi n´ rojú, tó bá se tálíkà wọ́n à ti gbàgbé ẹ̀* (Whatever would make a rich person sad [or complain] has the capacity to kill a poor person).

This point about money and debt does not need further elaboration, but it requires a little illustration. In the course of my research in Iwo, my informants constantly referred to *owó àtijọ́* (old-style money) and *owó ìgbàlódé* (new-style money). I always thought they meant cowrie shells and Naira, respectively, until one informant clarified the situation with an illustration using two chiefs, whom I will refer to as Chief P and Chief Q:

---

[46] Note that the Yoruba call good conduct *ènìyàn*, i.e., person or human being. This implies that a person of bad or questionable character is not a human being but an animal (*ẹranko*), or baboon (*ọ̀bọ*).

[47] Surulere is a better place than Olorunsogo, which is a slum. But life in Olorunsogo is fast paced. It is possible for street-smart people to make money very faster in Olorunsogo than in Surulere.

> Chief P spent old-style money, but Chief Q is spending new-style money. They are both rich, but wait until you see Chief Q's name in the papers for owing National Bank or some other bank. Then you will know who is *really* rich. As for me, I pray to God to give me the Chief P type of money, because it comes with no strings attached, and it will not land me in prison.[48]

By some coincidence, Chief P was for a brief period Chief Q's father-in-law. P was a big-time farmer who had several people working for him. It cannot be ascertained whether or not P borrowed money to start his farming business, but, being illiterate, he probably did not borrow from the bank. People have the impression that he followed the ideal of avoiding debt. He was prosperous, many people were indebted to him, and he had several *ìwọ̀fà* who worked for him. To be rich in the old style is to owe no debt. Rich people in the old days were lenders, not borrowers. They did not build their houses on credit nor did they did purchase their property on credit. Their gross worth was also their net worth. To be rich in the new style is to be in huge debt, and my informant believed Chief Q to be in that category. It is also to have a net worth that is lower than the people's perception of the gross. It is clear why my informant, a farmer himself, would prefer Chief P's type of wealth. It did not matter to him that Chief P would qualify as an exploiter from the old school, with serfs and slaves working for him. However, the Q way is the new way, the capitalist way, and—we've been reminded—the only way.

One more example of contradiction deserves to be considered at some length. The ideal is to make money in a clean, honest way, and its perversion is to make money by any means necessary. People have always found various short cuts to riches. Several methods common in the pre-colonial era continued later, but others spread in the colonial and post-colonial eras, including stealing (*olè jíjà*) and burglary (*ilé kíkó*). Both are old vices that probably began with property ownership and subsequently expanded with the monetization of the economy. Stealing and burglary became so widespread in Ibadan early in its growth in the nineteenth century that the *oríkì* of Ibadan proudly called it the city of the boldest and meanest of thieves, who operated on horseback (*Ìbàdàn ọmọ a g'ẹsin kó'lé*). Stealing, burglary, pickpocketing, and armed robbery are all criminal short cuts to riches in today's modern cities.

At the level of ritual, for which it is very hard to find concrete evidence, there are various acclaimed magical effects used to make money (*òògùn owó*), arising from a conviction that money can in fact be produced or conjured magically, that some people sell their soul to the devil (*gbé lùkúdì mì*) to achieve wealth, and that human sacrifice can be employed in churning out crisp, new currency notes. Furthermore, my informants believed that kidnapping, usually of children and pregnant women, increases in frequency whenever there is a change of currency. The reason, they explained, is that the old ritual becomes invalid once the name, color, or design of the currency is

[48] Adeyemo Ojo, Bale of Obamoro, interview by author, February, 1993.

changed, and a new ritual has to be prepared with the same materials. However, none of this can be proved. There is proof that ritual killing has continued, but no concrete evidence connecting the kidnapping to a supposed ritualistic money-minting venture. Nevertheless, the notion cannot be ignored.

As might be expected, there was and still is counterfeiting, the so-called *owó Ìjèbú*,or Ijebu money.[49] Using government sources and bank reports, Falola reveals the pervasive nature of this short cut to riches in colonial southwestern Nigeria from the 1920s to the 1950s.[50] With several pages of tables on the frequency of counterfeiting cases in Yorùbáland as evidence, he explains that counterfeiting offenses only added to the list of old and new crimes with which the British had to deal. "Colonial rule created counterfeiting in two ways: the currency that it introduced was amenable to forgery; and the monetization of society pressured individuals to seek opportunities to enrich themselves in both legal and non-legal ways."[51] Simply put, the people found an additional means of flouting the ideal of making money in a clean manner.

One must not forget deceit (*èrú*) and cheating (*ìyànjẹ*), which reach their extreme in embezzlement, kickbacks, and other forms of graft. This perversion of the ideal comes from the sophistry that it is acceptible to spend other people's money without asking their permission. *À t'owó olówó, à t'owó ẹni, Ọlọ́run má jẹ́kí ọ̀kankan wọ̀n ni* (Whether it's mine or other people's, God please put money at my disposal). This prayer probably arose in late colonial times among the elite with some access to state funds. The present-day significance of this travesty of the ideal is partially evident in the corruption that pervades local, state, and national politics. Spending "other people's money" is not ethical, but it is not unusual either. It is viewed positively in some quarters as "eating soup" (*ìlábè*) or "eating money" (*ìkówójẹ*).

Finally, on the same theme, there are the dirty tricks. The tricksters exploit the ideal that money is the Indispensable One while playing on people's gullibility. Smartly dressed, sharp-eyed, and sweet-tongued, the tricksters promise their would-be victims that they will double or quadruple their money. Once a person has been sucked in, it is hard to get out. Often there is a perceived regional dimension to the tricks: the tricksters are believed to be from Lagos or some southern part of Yorùbáland, while their victims are hinterland people who may in fact be residing in Lagos.[52]

---

[49] The Ijebu are known for their business skills. It is also probable that, unable to find the secret of Ijebu business success, other Yoruba groups accuse them of counterfeiting. The records, however, show counterfeiting in all Yorùbá provinces under colonial rule. For more information, see Toyin Falola, "'Manufacturing Trouble': Currency Forgery in Colonial Southwestern Nigeria," MS, 1995.

[50] Ibid.

[51] Ibid., 41.

[52] Today, the phenomenon is widespread, but it is more prevalent in Lagos than anywhere else. The "419" con business is not a monopoly of the Yorùbá any more than it is

In addition to sharpening the contradictions of Yorùbá ideals, the monetization of the economy has also challenged some common values. One of these is the proposition that money is more important than children as a measure of individual worth: *Owó l'èŸgbọ́n, ọmọ l'àbúrò*. The Yorùbá actually struggle with the question of ranking money and children. *Owó ju ọmọ lọ tàbí ọmọ ju owó lọ?* (Which is more important: money or child?) There is no doubt that they value both—success is measured by the simple process of ascertaining the amount of money or number of children a person has, or by a somewhat complex process of aggregating both money and children. The ideal picture of a successful person is one who has many children and a lot of money.

However, there is no consensus on the question of ranking Money and children. It can be argued that money is more valuable: you need money to have a wife or wives who will give you children. But a case can also be made for the value of children: not even the rich can purchase their own child. And, until recent medical breakthroughs, it was believed that you cannot *make* a child, you can only *make* money. That is, you can only *have* a child of your own. And once you have children, you can make them earn money for you in a number of ways: by making them work for you, by pawning them (as in bygone days) to raise a loan, or by selling them into slavery. Under present circumstances, most people will agree that money is more valuable than children. It is no longer mandatory for children to work for their parents, and the institutions of slavery and pawnship are dead. On the other hand, one needs money, a huge quantity of it, to bring up children today. And as Yorùbá society becomes increasingly capitalistic, the preoccupation of the people—educated elite and peasantry alike—is more with money than children.

Conclusion

The Yorùbá view of money has been dynamic. The ideals and their contradictions have been shaped and reshaped by the local, national, and international environments of which Yorùbáland is a part. As the economy developed and as the financial system became more complex, changes were introduced in the people's view of money. Nevertheless, the image of money as *Kòse-é-mánì*, the Indispensable One, has been constant.

The contradictions of Yorùbá ideals are manifest, and possibly indefensible. In any case, they can be explained in four different ways. First, Yorùbá culture is not homogeneous, but rather is a complex mixture in which the component parts never fully lose their individuality and uniqueness. What is considered fair game in one part of Yorùbáland can be a crime in another.

Furthermore, Yorùbá philosophy and the Yorùbá world view are not always consistent. (Perhaps we should hasten to state that no human society has

---

local—American media networks have carried stories of the international dimension of the business. One thing still stands out—the gullibility of the victim.

offered a uniform, consistent body of thought.) The Yorùbá recognize and frown upon inconsistencies. Inconsistent people are called double-tongued (*ẹlẹ́nu méjì*), wishy-washy (*sèhín-sọ̀hún*), and bad people (*aráyé!*),[53] and are compared to the devil in their mischief. At the same time, the Yorùbá recognize that people will always creatively find ways out of tight situations. If one idea locks a door, then another idea must be found to open or break it down.[54] A more recent notion of dealing with contradiction is *òyìnbó t' ṣe pencil ló ṣe eraser* (The same white people who make the pencil also make the eraser). The goal is to make money—it does not matter how many ideals are contradicted, transgressed, or erased in the process.

Another explanation of the contradictions is that they are a class affair. That is, the Yorùbá place certain ideals, or their contradictions, at the service of class interests according to the status of the persons concerned. Thus, a poor man is expected to follow the ideal: for him the ideal is law. It used to be the rule that both rich and the poor were bound by the same principles, but that is becoming less and less so. Indeed, in some cases the rich, if they are not clearly above the law, skirt its limits. Bashorun Gaha, for example, lived above the law,[55] and there are several others like him among today's wealthy Yorùbá.

Finally, the contradictions are the products of an evolving historical context. Every perversion of an ideal arose from increased pressure to meet new political and economic challenges. Patterns of livelihood and accumulation have undergone rapid changes. According to Sara Berry, "Commercialization, political centralization, and the resulting patterns of production and investment have created an economy in western Nigeria in which prosperity is possible but uncertain."[56] The result is that this uncertainty has compelled people

---

[53] This is borne out by the saying *ẹnu aráyé l'ẹbọ: ẹnu tí wọ́n fi pe Adégún ni wọ́n fi pe Adéògún* (People who double deal are bad: for they use their mouth to say "Ade is straight" and also say "Ade is crooked").

[54] *Bí igbá kò bá ṣe sí, à fọ* (If a calabash is impossible to open, then break it).

[55] See Johnson, *History of the Yorubas*, 178–87. Gaha was the Bashorun of Oyo Empire in the age of Oyo's imperial expansion between the 16th and 18th centuries. A long squabble arose over, among other issues, the question of who was to control the economic advantages of imperial conquest. There were two sides: the *Aláàfin* (king) and the chiefs headed by Gaha. According to Johnson, "Gaha had a great influence with the people, and a great many followers who considered themselves safe under his protection." It seemed at first that the *Aláàfin* and the princes lacked the power to deal with the conspiracy; for, between 1735 and 1770, Gaha deposed four *Aláàfin* and forced them to commit suicide. In the same period, he sent his own agents to the provinces to collect the annual taxes and tributes. As the years wore on, cracks began to show in the ranks of the chiefs. Possibly because Gaha had become too greedy (he was said to have refused to share the booty and tributes equally among the other chiefs), and partly because the military was tired of arbitrary orders from the *Basorun*, the *Àrẹ-ọ̀nà-Kakañfò* (Field Marshall) Oyabi changed sides and gave *Aláàfin* Abiodun military support to overcome the Gaha conspiracy in 1774.

[56] Sara Berry, *Fathers Work for their sons: Accumulation, Mobility, and Class Formation in an Extended Yoruba Community* (Berkeley, 1985), 82–3.

to intensify competition over "resources, profits and influence." Indeed, the Yorùbá economy, like the economies of several coastal West African societies, has responded to pressure on several previous occasions by reconceptualizing money. A brief examination of economic transition within the last two hundred years will illustrate this.

In the latter part of the eighteenth century, many parts of Yorùbáland participated in the slave trade. The Yorùbá elite who acted as collaborators in the trade determined what qualified as good behavior. However, by the middle of the nineteenth century, this slave trading elite and the trade itself were challenged head-on by the British. Legitimate commerce was introduced, and a new elite arose in response. The change of power in Lagos from Kosoko to Akitoye clearly illustrates the British preference for new collaborators, but from within the same class. A still more significant development was the emergence of the new mission-educated elite. These were the men and women who took Yorùbáland into the mid-twentieth century. Their ideals and values were different. With their mission education, many were opposed to traditional values and ideals, and expressed a preference for Western ideals. A few of them wrote to extol the essence and value of Yorùbá culture, history, and tradition, but most lived Western-style in such cities as Lagos, Badagry, and Abeokuta. For them, it was permissible to charge usurious interest rates and to help draft formal loan agreements that borrowers could not understand.[57] The transition to the educated elite is the subject of an extremely interesting novel, popular among the Yorùbá but not very well known by others. Isaac Delano's *Aiyé Daiyé Òyìnbó* (*It is a White Man's World*)[58] demonstrates vividly the demise of the old warrior aristocracy in Egbaland and the emergence of a new elite of mission-educated clerks and petty traders.

Some members of the old slave-trading elite took advantage of the emerging export trade in legitimate commodities, by adapting the slave-trading networks to the new trade in palm oil, for instance; but a majority did not. One reason for the inability of the old elite to remake itself was their lack of capitalization. Another was the nature of accumulation during the era of slave trade. Earnings from the trade, when that came in the form of money, usually went into supporting relationships or property of dubious economic value in the new environment. Such relationships were a drain on financial resources, and property like clothes and firearms did not reproduce wealth.[59] Assets that participants in the system fondly yet pejoratively called *bẹ̀ṣinkáwọ̀* were not the kinds of wealth that could easily be converted into cash and capital for engaging in the increasingly formal economy developing with legitimate

---

[57] For more information on this, see my "Money, Credit, and Banking in Precolonial Africa."

[58] Delano's *Aiyé Daiyé Òyìnbó* is similar to Achebe's *Things Fall Apart*, but the former is written in Yorùbá and therefore has a smaller audience.

[59] I have found Jane Guyer's synthesis very useful on this theme. See her "Wealth in People, Wealth in Things—Introduction," 83–90.

British trade. Finally, cowries began to lose ground to the new British currency, and the conversion rates fell progressively until the shells became virtually worthless and unacceptable as legal tender.

With this economic transformation and the winding down of colonial rule, another generation of educated elite was emerging. Its members were carefully and deliberately groomed by the departing British administration to become the new capitalist and entrepreneurial class to whom economic power would be entrusted. The British used the colonial administration's funds to foster its emergence, extending credit facilities and grants-in-aid only to individuals and groups who met certain criteria for engaging in small-scale industrial projects in, for example, food processing and minor manufacturing. In the process, new virtues and ideals were spawned. To this class of new men (and a few women), borrowing occured on a relatively grand scale, and defaulting on loans was a mark of political power and business acumen. Government money earmarked for the people was *owó olówó* (other people's money), commandeered by the new elite for its own purposes.

In conclusion, my argument can be summarized as follows: with the disarticulation of the old Yorùbá elite and the rise of the new class came financial change which favored the latter. This in turn led to a transformation of values and attitudes toward money. The current contradictions in Yorùbá notions of money mirror the effort of a dynamic society to come to terms with the changing economic environment. These new values, which often take the form of a blatant sort of materialism, can be understood primarily as symptoms of the strains of post-colonial society, and hence of the continuing legacy of the colonial past. In these conditions, the Yorùbá have come to cherish money. It determines value. It has power. It commands respect. All local religions agree that money ensures favorable and speedy answers to prayers, and so they elevate it. They personify money and worship it as Aje, whom everyone covets. They espouse high ideals in order to ensure fair competition in the race to amass it, and transgress them and forge new ones in order to rationalize and facilitate their access to it. For them, money is truly *Kòse-é-mánì*, the Indispensable One.

Bibliography

Abimbola, Wande. *Ifa: An exposition of Ifa Literary Corpus*. Ibadan, 1976.

—. *Ifa Divination Poetry*. New York, 1977.

Adebayo, A.G. "Money, Credit, and Banking in Precolonial Africa: The Yorùbá Experience." *Anthropos* 89 (1994):379–400.

Adegbite, Ademola M. "Oriki: A Study in Yorùbá Musical and Social Perception." Ph.D. diss., University of Pittsburgh, 1978.

Ajayi, S.I. and O.O. Ojo. *Money and Banking Analysis and Policy in the Nigerian Context.* London, 1981.

Akinytoye, S.A. *Revolution and Power Politics in Yorùbáland, 1840–1893.* London, 1971.

Babatunde, Emmanuel D. *A Critical Study of Bini and Yorùbá Value Systems of Nigeria in Change: Culture, Religion and the Self.* Lewiston, New York, 1992.

Baier, Stephen. *An Economic History of Central Niger.* London, 1980.

Barber, Karin. *I Could Speak Until Tomorrow: Oriki, Women and the Past in Yorùbá Texts.* Edinburgh, 1991.

—. "Money, Self-Realization, and the Person in Yorùbá Texts," in *Money Matters,* ed. Jane I. Guyer, 205–24. Portsmouth, New Hampshire, 1995.

Bascom, William. *Ifa Divination: Communication betweeen Gods and Men in West Africa.* Bloomington, Indiana, 1969.

Beier, Ulli. *Yorùbá Myths.* Cambridge, 1980.

Berry, Sara. *Fathers Work for Their Sons: Accumulation, Mobility, and Class Formation in an Extended Yorùbá Community.* Berkeley, 1985.

Coker, G.B.A. *Family Property among the Yorùbás.* London, 1966.

Epega, Afolabi A. *The Sacred Ifa Oracle.* San Francisco, 1995.

Eyo, Ekpo. *Nigeria and the Evolution of Money.* Lagos, 1979.

Falola, Toyin. "Money and Informal Credit Institutions Colonial Western Nigeria," in *Money Matters,* ed. Jane I. Guyer, 162–87. Portsmouth, New Hampshire, 1995.

Falola, Toyin and O.B. Lawuyi. "Not Just a Currency: The Cowrie in Nigerian Culture," in *West African Economic and Social History: Studies in Memory of Marion Johnson,* eds. D. Henige and T.C. McCaskie, 29–36. Madison, Wisconsin, 1990.

Fuja, Abayomi. *Fourteen Hundred Cowries: Traditional Stories of the Yorùbá.* London, 1962.

Gbadamosi, Bakare and Ulli Beier. *Not Even God Is Ripe Enough: Yorùbá Stories.* London, 1968.

Guyer, Jane I., ed. *Money Matters: Instability, Values and Social Payments in the Modern History of West African Communities.* Portsmouth, New Hampshire, 1995.

—. "Wealth in People, Wealth in Things—Introduction." *Journal of African History* 36, no. 1 (1995):83–90.

Herbert, Eugenia W. "Aspects of the Use of Copper in Pre-Colonial West Africa." *Journal of African History* 14, no. 2 (1973):179–94.

Hiskett, M. "Materials Relating to the Cowry Currency of the Western Sudan." *Bulletin of the School of Oriental and African Studies* 29, no. 1 (1966):122–42 and vol. 30, no. 3 (1966):340–66.

Hogendorn, Jan and Marion Johnson. *The Shell Money of the Slave Trade.* Cambridge, 1986.

Hopkins, A.G. "The Currency Revolution in South-West Nigeria in the Late Nineteenth Century." *Journal of the Historical Society of Nigeria* 3, no. 3 (1966):471–83.

Isola, Akinwumi. *Efunsetan Aniwura: Iyalode Ibadan.* Ibadan, 1970.

Johnson, Marion. "The Nineteenth-Century Gold 'Mithqall' in West and North Africa." *Journal of African History* 9, no. 4 (1968):547–69.

—. "The Cowry Currencies of West Africa I." *Journal of African History* 11, no. 1 (1970):17–49.

—. "The Cowry Currencies of West Africa II." *Journal of African History* 11, no. 3 (1970):331–53.

Johnson, Samuel. *The History of the Yorùbás.* [1921]. Reprint, London, 1976.

Jones, G.I. "Native and Trade Currencies in Southern Nigeria During the Nineteenth Century." *Africa* 28, no. 1 (1958):43–54.

Latham, J.H. "Currency, Credit and Capitalism on the Cross River in the Pre-Colonial Era." *Journal of African History* 12, no. 4 (1971):599–605.

Law, R.C.C. "Contemporary Written Sources," in *Sources of Yorùbá History*, ed. S.O. Biobaku, 9–24. Oxford, 1973.

Law, Robin. *The Oyo Empire, c. 1600–1836: A West African Imperialism in the Era of the Atlantic Slave Trade.* Oxford, 1977.

—. *The Slave Coast of West Africa, 1550–1750: The Impact of the Atlantic slave Trade on an African Society*. Oxford, 1991.

Lovejoy, Paul. "Interregional Monetary Flows in the Precolonial Trade of Nigeria." *Journal of African History* 15, no. 4 (1974):563–85.

Ogumefu, M.I. *Yorùbá Legends.* London, 1929.

Oroge, E. Adeniyi. "Iwofa: An Historical Survey of the Yorùbá Institution of Indenture." *African Economic History* 14, (1985):75–106.

Zaslavsky, Claudia. "The Yorùbá Number System," in *Blacks in Science: Ancient and Modern*, ed. Ivan Van Sertima, 110–26. New Brunswick, New Jersey, 1983.

Contributors

Akanmu G. Adebayo
Department of History and Philosophy,
Kennesaw State University

Jane I. Guyer
Program of African Studies and Department of Anthropology,
Northwestern University

Jan Hogendorn
Department of Economics, Colby College

John Hunwick
Department of History and Department of Religion,
Northwestern University

Robin Law
Department of History, University of Sterling

Gregory Mann
Department of History, Northwestern University

Endre Stiansen
The Nordic Africa Institute

James L.A. Webb, Jr.
Department of History, Colby College